BIRTH BEHIND BARS

Birth Behind Bars

The Carceral Control of Pregnant Women in Prison

Rebecca M. Rodriguez Carey

NEW YORK UNIVERSITY PRESS
New York

NEW YORK UNIVERSITY PRESS
New York
www.nyupress.org

© 2025 by New York University
All rights reserved

Please contact the Library of Congress for Cataloging-in-Publication data.

ISBN: 9781479815791 (hardback)
ISBN: 9781479815814 (paperback)
ISBN: 9781479815845 (library ebook)
ISBN: 9781479815838 (consumer ebook)

This book is printed on acid-free paper, and its binding materials are chosen for strength and durability. We strive to use environmentally responsible suppliers and materials to the greatest extent possible in publishing our books.

The manufacturer's authorized representative in the EU for product safety is Mare Nostrum Group B.V., Mauritskade 21D, 1091 GC Amsterdam, The Netherlands.
Email: gpsr@mare-nostrum.co.uk.

Manufactured in the United States of America

10 9 8 7 6 5 4 3 2 1

Also available as an ebook

To all the little girls with big dreams, especially Cecilia, Julianna, and Leticia.
You can do hard things.

CONTENTS

Preface ix

Introduction: A Pregnancy like No Other 1

1. Welcome to Prison: Two Pink Lines and the Disruption of Plans. 27

2. The Unruly Maternal Body: Struggles to Be Heard 53

3. Pregnancy 101: The (Un)Making of Mothers. 80

4. The Ultimate Cage: Birth as a Site of Surveillance and Control 108

5. Silenced Cries: Punishment in the Postpartum Period 135

6. Coming Home: Mothering on the Margins 161

Conclusion: Beyond the Prison Gates. 191

Afterword. 209

Acknowledgments 213

Notes 217

Bibliography 235

Index 255

About the Author 265

PREFACE

I am not free while any woman is unfree, even when her
shackles are very different from my own.
—Audre Lorde, *Sister Outsider: Essays and Speeches*

My body was a property of the state.
—Melody

Nearly fifty years after the landmark ruling in *Roe v. Wade*, a case that constitutionally protected the right to an abortion, the Supreme Court of the United States overturned its decision in the summer of 2022, stripping millions of women of their reproductive freedom.[1] Following this reversal, nearly half of all states have issued either total bans or restrictions that allow for an abortion only in very limited circumstances, with many legal scholars predicting that birth control restrictions and investigations into menstrual cycles are next.[2] And yet, there is irony in the timing of this ruling, as it came in the wake of a nationwide shortage of baby formula, in a country that offers neither universal paid maternity leave for workers nor healthcare coverage, where firearms are relatively unregulated despite increasing acts of mass violence—leading many Americans to suggest that guns have more rights than women.[3] For many, this dystopian environment is nothing short of a war on women.

Comparisons to author Margaret Atwood's *Handmaid's Tale*, a book and later television series that focuses on the erosion of reproductive freedom, abound, with many taking to TikTok and Instagram to post red cloaks and white bonnets—references to Atwood's work—as a way to signify that this period marks the *beginning* of a destruction of reproductive rights.[4] However, these references to a *fictional* work ignore the lengthy history of *actual* reproductive-justice abuses that have been occurring in the United States for centuries—abuses that have disproportionately affected women of color.[5]

From unlawful sterilizations and gynecological experiments performed on enslaved women to forced pregnancies and gendered violence in chain gangs to the eugenics movement and the astronomical maternal morbidity and mortality rates disproportionately affecting Black women, the carceral regime's control of women's bodies is anything but a *new* war on the bodily autonomy of women but is rather a *continuance* of reproductive injustices.[6] Indeed, the *Roe v. Wade* overruling reaffirms that decisions regarding pregnancy and birth still belong to those in power rather than to women themselves and reveals how pregnancy and birth are not neutral but instead are political and rooted in power dynamics fraught with social inequalities and oppression.[7]

Yet, what is missing from discussions about reproductive rights and bodily autonomy are the reproductive needs of those at the *periphery* of society, i.e., those who are literally locked away in cages, socially isolated and effectively removed from society in a deliberate and methodical practice known as mass incarceration. "Mass incarceration" refers to the increasing number of people behind bars in the United States.[8] This practice, disproportionately affecting people of color, is tied to slavery and hell-bent on subjugation and oppression intertwined with capitalism, as there is a financial incentive to surveil, control, and incarcerate.[9] Accordingly, it comes as no surprise that the United States spends over $80 *billion* annually on corrections.[10] Despite the substantial funding designed to strip the incarcerated of their humanity and their reproductive selves, the reproductive needs of women do not cease during imprisonment.

Nearly 80 percent of incarcerated women report being sexually active with men in the months preceding their incarceration; of these women, less than 30 percent report using contraceptives.[11] To no surprise, some of these women *will* be pregnant when they enter prison, as most incarcerated women are confined during their prime reproductive years. Recent numbers suggest that about 4 percent of women in prison are pregnant, resulting in approximately just over three thousand pregnant women who come through the US prison system each year.[12] Despite these high numbers, little information is known about the pregnancy, childbirth, and postpartum experiences of those in prison—a troubling matter, given that the incarceration of pregnant women provides important insight into the ways in which *all* women, including those outside the prison system, have their pregnancies surveilled, regulated, and controlled.[13]

I have long been interested in pregnancy and motherhood and the ways in which women are stripped of their bodily autonomy during pregnancy. My own pregnancies helped to refine and shape the arguments of this book, which focuses on how the prison system subjugates women and strips them of their bodily autonomy during pregnancy and birth, reducing them to mere vessels.

I grew up in Hutchinson, Kansas, a rural prison town and home to the Hutchinson Correctional Facility (HCF). HCF and the prison system were backdrops in my sleepy home town; although many industries have come and gone from my hometown over the years, the one constant has been HCF standing for over 140 years.[14] To this day, HCF remains one of the largest employers in my hometown, keeping the collapsing economy afloat, yet remains mostly out of sight and out of mind for all who pass by. The widespread hunger, poverty, and addiction in Hutchinson mirror many of the same social disadvantages in the communities my participants called home, leading me to consider how imprisonment and pregnancy converge.

I took to research to understand how pregnancies behind bars are shaped by much larger social forces controlled by powerful carceral regimes. The disregard for women during pregnancy provides insight into the prevalence of "obstetric violence," a term that refers to the medical system's mistreatment of pregnant women, who are devoid of much power and autonomy.[15] Nearly 40 percent of women have experienced obstetric violence during either pregnancy, birth, or the postpartum period.[16] The prevalence of obstetric violence is not surprising, given how pregnancy and birth are talked about in US society, where women are erased from their own birth experiences and forced to take a back seat behind a patriarchal medical system, where doctors are credited for the work of bringing a baby into the world through a method known as "delivery" (as if the baby were a pizza).[17]

To be sure, it is a rarity for women to be credited for the physical, emotional, and mental *work* that goes into *birthing* their baby. And while the differences in these phrasings may seem subtle, this distinction is important because this terminology provides insight into how patriarchy is embedded within conversations around pregnancy and birth both behind bars and within the "free world." The patriarchal system strips women of their power and erases them from the conversation entirely, as if they were nothing more than incubators reduced to a passive state of submission.[18]

In interviewing women who were once pregnant and incarcerated in prisons across the heartland of the United States, I noticed that many of their stories also contained instances of obstetric violence, as well as other forms of regulation and control. This control was not exclusive to the medical system or the prison system. Indeed, much of it operated together and was particular to the state of being pregnant *in* prison. Upon closer analysis, it was clear that my participants were experiencing another form of control entirely. It was one that was tied to the *intersection* of punitive or carceral forces that govern incarcerated pregnant women, including but not limited to the prison system, the medical system, the child welfare system, gendered racism, poverty, and even families. Separately, I argue, each of these carceral forces produces its own form of regulation and control, yet collectively, they converge to create a unique type of control that is even more powerful and one that is specific to incarcerated pregnant women, forever altering their pregnancy, birth, and motherhood through a concept that I call the "maternal web of control."

Throughout this book, I show how the maternal web of control operates and argue that incarcerated pregnant women are regulated in the most extreme of ways through subjugation and oppression and through the near-countless and archaic rules governing pregnancy and motherhood behind bars. Using a reproductive-justice framework, I introduce the maternal web of control and show how the criminal legal system works in conjunction with other social systems to further repress the reproductive rights of women, where reproductive decisions are not left to pregnant women but remain in the hands of powerful carceral systems that collectively disrupt entire families, neighborhoods, and communities.[19]

Although the narratives in this book describe grave injustices and unsettling stories that demonstrate the maternal web of control in action, this book also contains stories of hope, highlighting how pregnant women may not only survive but thrive behind bars and at times resist or even circumvent the maternal web of control. I introduce readers to Angel, a Black, forty-four-year-old mother of three, who found an advocate in a volunteer doula; Bonnie, a White, thirty-six-year-old mother of three who came to prison pregnant and managed to still find joy through a makeshift baby shower held by her peers; and Lacey, a thirty-two-year-old, Black mother of one who shared how her cellmates engaged in advocacy to ensure she did not go hungry.[20] Even more women mentioned that this was the first time they had been clean during pregnancy, while for others, this was the first and only time they had ever had access to prenatal vitamins or healthcare, marking a shift from their previous pregnancies.

These powerful stories of hope show that despite the maternal web of control, women may still be able to find joy and a sense of community in their own unique ways. And while incarceration may be marked as a low point, substantial growth happens during pregnancy no matter where it takes place. Many shared how they were proud of the person they had become since their incarceration and how proud they were of their children, illustrating that regardless of how or where pregnancy unfolds, it remains a transformative period for many and certainly served as a turning point for those profiled in this book.

Birth Behind Bars is ultimately a story about how the US prison system transforms pregnancy, birth, and motherhood in the most powerful and extreme of ways. In doing so, this book offers important insight into the reproductive experiences of not only incarcerated women but women everywhere. I write this book with the hope of generating discussion and *real* change—the kind of change that brings about a reduction in the number of women behind bars *and* a reduction in the number of reproductive injustices happening both behind bars and in communities. It is my hope that this kind of change brings incarcerated women out of the periphery and into the center of conversations around pregnancy, birth, and motherhood and that the narratives contained within are recognized as central to conversations about reform—both behind bars and within birth spaces everywhere, for these narratives are timely and more relevant than ever.

Introduction

A Pregnancy like No Other

As a society, our decision to heap shame and contempt upon those who struggle and fail in a system designed to keep them locked up and locked out says far more about ourselves than it does about them.
—Michelle Alexander, *The New Jim Crow: Mass Incarceration in the Age of Colorblindness*

I never thought that I would end up in prison, let alone have a child in prison.
—Faye

Faye, a White, twenty-nine-year-old mother of three young children, bounces back and forth between her friends' one-bedroom apartments and dreams of one day having a place to call her own. A former certified medical assistant, she now folds laundry and washes linens for a living in the Midwest. As we talked, she shared with me her ongoing struggles to put food on the table and provide for her family. We met at a local Christian social service agency. It is the same social service agency that has been helping her get back on her feet after spending time in prison during her third pregnancy.

During her first two pregnancies, she read about the bodily symptoms of pregnancy and gestational development from the comfort of her upholstered couch. With this third pregnancy, she read on a metal bed inside the concrete walls of her prison cell. All the down time in prison gave her much to think about when it came to her pregnancy and her role as a mother. What would she name her baby? Would she one day tell her baby that she was pregnant with him in prison? And if so, how would she tell him? And how would she even begin to contend with the many ways that incarceration would alter both herself and her baby and, really, her whole family for years to come? Now released, Faye, a self-described recovering methamphetamine addict, told me, "I never thought that I would end up in prison, let alone have a child in prison."

***

Gloria is a twenty-seven-year-old Native American mother of three young children. Originally sentenced to four years in prison for a nonviolent crime, she now lives at home in the Midwest with her children in a small, run-down apartment. As we conversed, I overheard the giggles and cries of her children playing in the background. She apologized for their noises, and I told her that it was not a problem; as a mother myself, I understood. Once she tended to each of her children, she shared her youngest's birth story with me and described how she had to ask a correctional officer to unshackle her so she could use the bathroom during labor. She then explained how correctional officers "sit there, and they watch you."

Being shackled at the wrists and ankles, leaving her unable to change positions during labor, and being deprived of privacy are just a few of her many frustrations related to the healthcare she received behind bars. After undergoing an unplanned cesarean section, she requested medication to numb the pain from her surgery, a request not out of the ordinary for women who have recently had a cesarean section.[1] But her appeal for medication was denied, due to a rule at her state prison that prohibits the incarcerated, including those who have just given birth, from having access to narcotic pain relievers, which made for a "pretty horrible" postpartum experience.

***

Latrice, a Black mother of two, was thirty-nine years old when she went to prison. Now released from prison but forever branded as a felon, she shared with me her ongoing struggles to locate housing and employment in her small town in the Midwest, where resources for the recently released are hard to come by, as well as her failed attempts to reconnect with her sons, who harbor immense resentment and embarrassment about their mother's absence. As Latrice and I talked, there was sadness in her voice, as she told me about her baby who was born stillborn while she was in prison.² For Latrice, "coming home" has meant an opportunity to finally process her grief.³ Through broken words and tears, she told me, "I never dealt with my loss because that's like a sacred thing to me, that's my child, and I didn't feel like being in there [prison] was the appropriate place to grieve the loss of my child, so I always told myself when I get home, I'll deal with it then."

Latrice's ability to cope with the loss of her infant is further complicated by the fact that she cannot help but wonder whether the use of shackles contributed to her baby's untimely birth and subsequent death. Stepping up into a correctional van, on the way to what was supposed to be a routine doctor's appointment, Latrice's legs got caught up in her shackled ankles, leaving her unable to properly catch herself with shackled wrists, and she fell on her large belly. Days later, she gave birth to a stillborn baby.

* * *

For Faye, Gloria, Latrice, and the other women I interviewed, prison was never a place they imagined being pregnant. And while the nature and exact circumstances of their cases vary, their stories all share a similar thread. They all experienced a pregnancy that was devoid of much autonomy and choice behind bars, and each embodies one story within the vast social experiment known as mass incarceration—a practice focused on the targeted removal of millions of people from society and into literal cages.⁴ It is a practice grounded in social inequalities and systemic racism and one that destroys entire families, neighborhoods, and communities.⁵

Pregnancy, at least in the United States, means a destruction of bodily autonomy and choice.⁶ It means the erosion of decision making over one's own body and the imbalance of power, along with the expectation that one will freely accept this loss of power.⁷ To be pregnant means to be viewed not as an individual but as an object, a mere vessel that is public property available for public consumption, scrutiny, and evaluation. It means to be controlled and contained at all costs, often at the hands of doctors, politicians, or even the most mediocre of men.⁸ To be pregnant *behind bars* then is yet a *hyper* form of control and a *complete* erosion of bodily freedom and reproductive justice. It is the expectation of willing submission not only to doctors, politicians, and men but also to other agents of control, be they child welfare workers, correctional officers, family members, or any other members of the carceral regime. Above all, it means being caught in a network or complex web of interlocking systems of control and oppression that are unique to pregnancy behind bars through what I call the "maternal web of control."

My central argument is that reproductive and carceral control collide in the United States to create a *maternal web of control*, where pregnant women in prison have their pregnancy, birth, and motherhood surveilled, policed, and controlled in the most extreme of ways—ways that only the carceral state can do, forever linking children's birth stories to the US prison system and altering the lives of women long after their sentence is served.[9] As Latrice said, "It's hard to tell where the effects of incarceration really end. It's like they go on, and on, and on, affecting each generation in some way, shape, or form."

Locked Out

The scope of pregnant women in US prisons is difficult to calculate. The exact number is not known because national statistics have not been kept.[10] A lack of national data reflects the patriarchy embedded within the criminal legal system, where matters affecting women, like pregnancy, are an afterthought, not deemed worthy of full data collection, despite decades of research and scholarship indicating the need to seriously consider the unique needs of women in prison.[11] In the absence of much data, medical anthropologist and obstetrician-gynecologist Carolyn Suffrin and her research team led a landmark study to capture the extent of pregnant women in prison, revealing that about 4 percent of women in state prison are pregnant (affecting over three thousand women).[12]

Despite the plethora of women whose pregnancies have been altered by incarceration, little information is known about their unique experiences. Aside from the occasional depiction on screen in television shows like *Orange Is the New Black* or through an article in the *New York Times*, most Americans hear very little about the incarceration of women, let alone about the pregnancy experiences of those under correctional control.[13] From a historical perspective, this exclusion can be explained, in part, because female criminality is counter to conventional notions regarding deviance and criminality.[14] The discipline of criminology has long been bathed in patriarchy, where women offenders have been excluded from scientific inquiry, resulting in significant gaps of knowledge and inadequate care.[15]

In response, a new perspective called "feminist criminology" was developed in the 1960s to bring attention and awareness to the unique issues within criminology that affect women, resulting in a number of research studies that have since been conducted to explore the particulars of women in the criminal legal system and those behind bars. Feminist criminology scholars have urged the US criminal legal system to pay attention to women behind bars, but the criminal legal system has generally not kept pace with these calls for action—a fact that also highlights how the incarceration of women is political and grounded in the bottom line, offering little financial incentive for prisons to change to better reflect the gendered needs of women.[16] Among the research studies devoted to the incarceration of pregnant women in *prison*, none has explored this topic using a reproductive-justice framework with specific consideration to the narrative accounts of women, including even *after* they have their babies and are released from prison—an important period, as the maternal web of control continues to shape motherhood even after women give birth and are released from prison.[17]

Punishing Pregnancy

Power, domination, regulation, and control are central themes of this story. Reproduction has long been surveilled, monitored, and regulated by institutions both within and beyond the prison system. Anthropologists Lynn M. Morgan and Elizabeth Roberts coined the term "reproductive governance" to refer to the many entities that regulate and monitor reproduction.[18] According to Morgan and Roberts, "Reproductive governance refers to the mechanisms through which different historical configuration of actors—such as state, religious, and international financial institutions, NGOs, and social movements—use legislative controls, economic inducements, moral injunctions, direct coercion, and ethical incitements to produce, monitor, and control reproductive behaviors and population practices."[19] It comes as no surprise, then, that maternal bodies are framed as threatening and unruly, in need of containment, where the punishment and regulation of women are viewed as essential to the protection and best interests of fetuses, making pregnancy itself a space of public inspection.[20] The prison system, then, is yet another actor that has a vested interest in these controls, and the incarceration of women during pregnancy is the result.

Under these regimes, pregnancy belongs not to a woman but to the public, including but not limited to strangers, family members, healthcare providers, politicians, child welfare workers, and the criminal legal system. Indeed, there are countless examples of how even nonincarcerated pregnant women have their pregnancies policed, regulated, and even criminalized.[21] As sociologist Suzanne Sutherland said, "At no other time in a woman's life is her identity more obviously supervised and regulated socially than during pregnancy."[22] Pregnant women are the targets of unsolicited advice and are subjected to (unwanted) commentary and even unwanted touch from strangers, healthcare providers, and family alike. Not only are unwanted hands placed on bellies, but they are also inserted into the vaginal canals of pregnant women without their consent.

This emphasis on control over the reproductive capacities of women comes as no surprise given that the United States was founded on the controlling of people's bodies through chattel slavery.[23] Pregnancy was no exception, as slave owners had the legal right to forcibly rape enslaved women to maximize profit, making pregnancy and reproduction a matter of state interest.[24] In anthropologist Sarah Haley's book, *No Mercy Here*, Haley provides a historical context for the imprisonment of women and shows how Black women were subjected to punitive sanctions and hard labor through convict leasing and chain gains and, later, domestic servitude, providing linkage between chattel slavery and the modern-day prison system.[25] Black women were subjected to widespread gendered racism and violent rape resulting in forced pregnancy and the denial of medical care, highlighting how the shackling of pregnant women, described later in this book, is not new but rather a continuation of existing practices performed on Black women.[26] Haley's analysis provides context for how gendered racism and oppression are embedded in the prison system and how these same oppressive forces are still at work today.

During pregnancy, the maternal body is on full display, and women are expected to conform to a number of cultural norms and expectations—any deviation is punished. Historically, pregnancy was a source of stigma and shame when it occurred among those outside of narrow cultural norms, including among teenage mothers and unmarried women.[27] Low-income, Black, single mothers in particular have had to contend during pregnancy with the controlling image of the welfare queen, which classifies one too many pregnancies as a strategic decision made by women in order to receive more "handouts."[28] Pregnant women who work in sex work and use drugs during pregnancy have also had to contend with controlling images that paint them as inadequate mothers.[29]

The recent reversal of *Roe v. Wade* illustrates that when it comes to matters of reproduction, governments have long had an interest in regulation and control. The more recent fetal-protection laws that criminalize harm done to a fetus in utero, including in cases where women seek an abortion, result in avoidance of the medical system for fear of criminalization and punishment, leaving women with inadequate care during pregnancy. To be pregnant, then, means navigating a model of medicine that works alongside the criminal legal system to infringe on autonomy and choice, highlighting how *reproduction* itself is an institution of control, and pregnant bodies are subject to this oppressive state.[30]

Still, it is recognized that all women have their bodies and pregnancies policed to some degree. Writer Adrienne Rich compared her postpartum body to being incarcerated, suggesting that to be pregnant means to be held prisoner in the body.[31] I argue that the regulation of pregnancy and the loss of reproductive freedom are amplified in carceral settings like prisons, where women who are actually incarcerated, held captive both behind bars and in their body, experience a *hyper* form of control that emanates from the intersection across multiple forces of control and oppression. Philosopher Michel Foucault has written extensively about how the panopticon design of prisons allows constant surveillance through a central watch tower without the incarcerated knowing whether they are actually being watched, making prisons ideal places of extreme regulation and control.[32] Not only are the incarcerated physically surveilled through a central watch tower, but the many power dynamics within ensure adherence to authority and self-regulation.[33] The nature of prisons as sites of extreme regulation and control carries over to pregnancy, especially for low-income women of color who are at the center of multiple matrices of oppression.[34]

This regulation of pregnancy inside correctional settings is a prime example of "reproductive oppression," a term that refers to "the controlling and exploiting of women and girls through our bodies, sexuality and reproduction (both biological and social) by families, communities, institutions and society."[35] It is a phenomenon that is widespread, given that "mass incarceration, by its very nature, compromises and undermines bodily autonomy and the capacity for incarcerated people to make decisions about their reproductive well-being and bodies; this is done through institutionalized racism and is disproportionately done to the bodies of women of color."[36]

Certainly, reproductive oppression is antithetical to the ideals of "reproductive justice," a term and movement, first coined by the Black Women's Caucus in 1994, that is focused on the preservation of reproductive rights and bodily autonomy and control.[37] At its core, reproductive justice is concerned with matters such as the right to have children, the right not to have children, and the right to parent with dignity in a safe and healthy manner.[38] It is a commitment to dismantling systems of oppression and control with consideration to the ways in which race and class and gender, among other factors, affect reproduction and motherhood.

The Maternal Web of Control

"Carcerality," a term that describes the punitive overemphasis on surveillance, regulation, domination, control, and criminalization, is central to the functioning of reproductive oppression and the maternal web of control. A lengthy history of reproductive injustices that have occurred within the US prison system, including but certainly not limited to the denial of reproductive care and forced medical procedures, all provide insight into how carcerality allows reproductive oppression to flourish behind bars in places that are predicated on punitiveness and control.[39]

The Carceral State Project, a symposium research initiative, brings to light the extent to which elements of carcerality permeate society: "The concept of carcerality captures the many ways in which the carceral state shapes and organizes society and culture through policies and logic of control, surveillance, criminalization and un-freedom."[40] Carcerality is certainly not limited to the prison system and includes nearly everything in society where control permeates. Additionally, "The carceral state includes all aspects of life in which people are subject to surveillance and the threat of punitive policies under the premise of safety."[41]

Carcerality and punishment are by no means exclusive to the prison system, for each of the complexes the women I interviewed came in contact with during their time behind bars as pregnant and birthing women was carceral and had underlying mechanisms of regulation and control made easier through forms of oppression.[42] Indeed, scholars have written about how carcerality operates beyond the prison system and how it infiltrates other sectors of society to exert both punishment and control. In her seminal book, *Shattered Bonds*, and in her most recent book, *Torn Apart*, sociologist Dorothy Roberts shows how the child welfare system is really a "family regulation" or "family policing system," an extension of the criminal legal system that has the power and authority to tear apart families through the removal of children from their homes and through intensive forms of surveillance and control, all under the auspices of protection and care.[43] Sociologist Victor Rios has also written extensively about how the education system acts as a carceral system, particularly for Black and Latino youth, by pushing them out of schools through strict rules and regulations, including zero-tolerance policies that thrust students into the revolving doors of the criminal legal system, where they are punished and criminalized by both the school system and the criminal legal system through a phenomenon that he calls the "youth control complex."[44]

The social institutions or systems that incarcerated pregnant women encounter throughout their pregnancy behind bars work in similar ways, controlling the reproductive and familial experiences of those in prisons. On its own, the medical system produces varying forms of carcerality, subjecting pregnant women to the infantilized status of patient, making it easier to engage in practices without informed consent. The overmedicalization of pregnancy and birth means that women experience considerable limits on choice, while any and all behaviors throughout pregnancy, including their diet and lifestyle choices, are highly regulated.[45] On its own, the child welfare system also acts as a carceral system during pregnancy, policing the behaviors of women deemed threatening to the fetus, and has the power to initiate legal action and punishment, particularly in places that have fetal protection laws.[46] The disadvantaged neighborhoods that incarcerated pregnant women tend to come from are also rife with overpolicing practices and structural discrimination that subjugate pregnant women further.[47] In her book *Arrested Justice*, sociologist Beth Richie illustrates how Black women in particular simultaneously experience multiple forms of violence and oppression under the carceral state, where surveillance, punishment, and criminalization are commonplace and where "helping" systems have the opposite effect, hindering women and their families.[48]

Collectively, these forces collide with and work alongside the prison system to produce an entirely new form of control and one that is *specific* to incarcerated pregnant women in the United States who are caught in the center of these powerful carceral forces through the maternal web of control. The maternal web of control contains a complex web of actors that each produce multiple, interlocking elements of control and surveillance that work to regulate and govern the lives of pregnant, birthing, and postpartum women trapped in the US prison system. The maternal web of control is chiefly concerned with matters of *maternity*, that is, pregnancy, birth, postpartum, and motherhood. I use the term "web" to denote the trappings of multiple carceral layers of control that each converge to create a web or structure that *controls* pregnancy, birth, postpartum, and motherhood through oppression, authority, surveillance, domination, and regulation across various settings, confining women in the ultimate cage. Examples of these carceral entities include but are not limited to the medical system, the child welfare system, poverty, and gendered racism. I argue that incarcerated pregnant women are at the center of these carceral forms, caught inside a web of control that governs their pregnancy, birthing experience, and motherhood.

Feminist theorist Marilyn Frye provides an excellent visual of how the maternal web of control becomes strengthened, with each additional actor or "system involvement" creating a network of domination and surveillance that is nearly impossible to escape. In her work *The Politics of Reality: Essays in Feminist Theory*, Frye explains,[49]

> If you look very closely at just one wire in the cage, you cannot see the other wires. . . . You could look at that one wire . . . and be unable to see why a bird would not just fly around the wire. . . . It is only when you step back . . . and take a macroscopic view of the whole cage, that you can

see why the bird does not go anywhere; and then you will see it in a moment.... It is perfectly *obvious* that the bird is surrounded by a *network* [emphasis added] of systematically related barriers ... which, by their relations to each other, are as confining as the solid walls of a dungeon.

As the excerpt from Frye indicates, each additional wire or system involvement produces its own form of control that becomes strengthened and reinforced through the addition of other carceral forces—collectively, they create a network of carceral control that impinges on the pregnancies and motherhoods of incarcerated women, reaffirming that the most intimate of pregnancy and birth-related decisions are "best" made by those in authority positions rather than by those who are actually pregnant. Whether it is through technocratic forms of surveillance, such as the use of fetal monitoring or urine testing as a component of prenatal healthcare, or even with shackles imposed on women during labor, pregnant women in prison are continuously subjected to hypercarcerality across multiple forms.

It is acknowledged that there are good people working in the medical system, the child welfare system, and even the prison system who may enact moments of care and concern; however, my analysis remains sociological, focused on the systems themselves, as I argue that at its core, all these patriarchal *systems* are predicated on power and control. Any diversion reflects the care and concern of *individuals* working within these systems rather than the systems themselves. Collectively, these systems of control produce a stronger, more powerful hold on women: a maternal web of control that, as the name suggests, controls the lives of pregnant women in prison who are at the center of this web of interlocking carceral systems.

In many ways, this maternal web of control and the denial of reproductive justice are still mostly either overlooked or viewed as *simply* the price one pays for doing crime. That is, the regulation of pregnancy and the removal of autonomy and choice is treated as *just* another consequence of doing crime that becomes punished through incarceration. Still, I argue that the maternal web of control goes beyond criminal punishment and extends past prison walls and enters the most intimate of spaces—the very bodies of pregnant and birthing women—transforming their health and families for generations to come.

Incarcerated pregnant women are punished in ways that incarcerated men are not, for women are held prisoners not just behind barbed-wire fencing but also within their bodies. Fundamentally, the maternal web of control is concerned with power, where pregnancy and birth decisions are laced with paternalism, disguised in rhetoric of safety and care, leaving women without any say in even the most intimate of birth procedures, including cervical checks and cesarean sections. Their status as prisoner only reaffirms that their maternal bodies are out of control and unruly, in need of protection from the state. The subjugated status of both prisoner and patient means that the incarcerated pregnant woman is expected to simply accept her subjugation or risk further punishment.

Behind bars and in birth spaces, the prison system works with other social systems to control and regulate all matters related to pregnancy, resulting in uncertainty, trauma, ongoing power struggles, and at times even maternal, perinatal, and infant mortality. The emphasis on surveillance and control threatens the health and well-being of both women and their children, forever altering families, even after women give birth and are no longer incarcerated.

The degree to which this maternal web of control operates reflects a variety of factors, such as race and ethnicity, socioeconomic status, gender identity, age, geographical location, abilities, and so forth, as well as the particulars of each prison, for each correctional facility has its own institutional rules and culture that govern the lives of those within. Consequently, some of the White women I interviewed shared that their time behind bars was "not that bad," in part because it was the first time they had ever had prenatal care, a contrast to some of the White women I interviewed who were accustomed to more resources and support and said that their pregnancy behind bars was "the worst experience" of their life because the healthcare they had in prison was glaringly inadequate compared to their healthcare on the outside. The women of color I interviewed had another take on their healthcare, for they also had to navigate the racism embedded within both the medical system and the prison system, highlighting the ways in which race, among other identity markers, affects experiences.

These differences in experiences reflect the social positioning of women and exemplify a framework called "intersectionality"—a term coined by legal-rights scholar Kimberlé Crenshaw.[50] The concept of intersectionality is based on the premise that people have multilayered markers of identity and experience different forms of privilege and oppression, with the social markers of people's identities converging to affect their experiences, including those that pertain to pregnancy, birth, and motherhood.[51] As the differences in experiences described above illustrate, although each of the women I interviewed shared the same prism of gender, their experiences were heavily influenced by other markers of their identity, including race and socioeconomic status, to name but a few.

For some, the loss of control that marks pregnancy and incarceration may not be viewed as completely unusual but rather something that is expected and *just* another part of life because of how carcerality is ever present in their disadvantaged neighborhoods. Others shared how their incarceration during pregnancy resulted in *greater* control because incarceration ensured that their basic needs were met, allowing them to focus on "staying clean" without having to simultaneously worry about finding shelter or food for the day—a freedom in its own right.[52]

Though, to be sure, incarceration, particularly while pregnant, was not the life that anyone I met had ever envisioned, some were not all that surprised that their pathways led them to prison *because* the presence of carceral forces had been so engrained and normalized from a young age. Some shared painful yet vivid memories from childhood in which one or both parents were taken away in handcuffs only to be imprisoned for long stretches of time, and it was not uncommon to have drug paraphernalia in the home or to have to rely on the generosity of a teacher or neighbor when there was not enough food for the week. Some acknowledged that they never second guessed the idea of skipping school during their teen years, and that as adults, it was not uncommon to have to spend a night or two in county jail.

Many were well versed in the trappings of poverty, systemic racism, and the all-too-frequent check-ins with intrusive child welfare workers long before they ever came to prison. They were what many sociologists might call "marginalized."[53] And while some of these women were White, most were Black, and a couple were Latina—patterns that illustrate how racial inequalities are embedded in contacts with carceral systems.[54] Perhaps legal scholar Kimberlé Crenshaw best explained the overrepresentation of women of color within these interlocking systems of control when she said, "These intersections are constituted by a variety of social forces that situate women of color within contexts structured by various social hierarchies and that render them disproportionally available to certain punitive policies and discretionary judgments that dynamically reproduce these hierarchies."[55] In other words, these intersections mean that poor women and women of color remain particularly vulnerable to the maternal web of control, including long after their release from prison, when schools, neighborhoods, local economies, and even police all contribute to this web to ensure that surveillance, domination, and control permeate nearly every aspect of life.

Still, there were others I talked with who had grown up never having had much contact with the criminal legal system at all. And while some of these women grew up without a father or came from homes where the occasional joint was smoked, these women were largely able to avoid the long arm of the carceral state. Typically, they were the first in their family to ever spend more than a day or two in jail, and they were also the first in their family to ever go to prison, aside from perhaps a distant relative. Most of these women, though not all, were White. Many had a high school diploma and some had college experience.

For the most part, they had grown up sheltered not only from contact with the criminal legal system but also from other forms of oppression, like gendered racism and systemic poverty, that permeate disadvantaged neighborhoods—forms of oppression that many of their Black counterparts, and even some of their low-income White peers, had already come to know all too well. Consequently, they were more likely to talk about how incarceration entailed a *complete* loss of autonomy and control, leading them to experience an intensity of culture shock upon their arrival. Most already had a healthcare provider before they came to prison and could easily identify a support person or even a collective group of people to rely on if they ever needed to seek counsel and refuge from the hardships of the world.

They were mostly able to avoid what sociologist Patricia Hill Collins refers to as the "matrix of domination," a concept that refers to the collective oppression resulting from the intersection of systemic racism, structural poverty, and sexism.[56] Though, on occasion, they struggled to pay rent or had a check bounce, none of them regarded the prison system as a safety net that offered respite, emotionally, physically, medically, or otherwise, from the chaos of the streets. These were women who came from a more working-class or, in some cases, a middle-class background. For them, incarceration was vastly different from anything they had ever known and was considered by many to be the *last* place they ever pictured being during pregnancy.

Although they were protected to some degree from oppressive systems of control, they were not entirely immune to the maternal web of control, for the expanse of the carceral state is vast, punishing even women in rural places who were once sheltered from these surveilling forces. Their incarceration offers insight into how the policing and surveillance that once predominantly affected Black men in more urban areas have spread to even the most desolate and isolated of places, locking away even White women, like Faye, who commit nonviolent offenses.[57] As mentioned in the preface, when it comes to matters of reproduction, the carceral state has long had an interest in regulating reproduction, and the regulation and control of pregnant women behind bars is a consequence of much larger forces.[58] Throughout the text, I show how the regulation and control of pregnancy, birth, and motherhood are magnified behind bars, where every aspect of life is tightly controlled, leaving in their wake collateral consequences for both the incarcerated and their families.

How Did We Get Here?

As with any story, it is important to start at the beginning, and while the maternal web of control effectively *begins* on the first day of incarceration, the carcerality that lands women in the prison system is at work much sooner—well before women are ever pregnant and well before they are ever arrested and incarcerated. That is, the incarceration of pregnant women is shaped by social, political, and economic forces that collectively create a carceral environment, where even the slightest criminality is punished, especially for those who are already disadvantaged and at the center of surveilling forces of control.[59]

The US penal system has a lengthy history, predating slavery, that still shapes the incarceration of women today.[60] While the earliest forms of prisons are linked to early Mesopotamia, the modern-day US prison system as we know it dramatically shifted in the 1970s, when then president

Richard Nixon declared an all-out "War on Drugs," committing substantial federal funding and resources to eliminate drugs at any cost.[61] Though this was referred to as a war on *drugs*, it was arguably a war on *people* and certainly a war against people of color, as President Ronald Reagan enacted more punitive policies focused on interdiction.[62] Under the Reagan administration, even the most nonviolent and low-level offenders encountered a crackdown of police presence and tougher sentencing, such as three-strike laws and mandatory minimums, marking a shift away from evidence-based approaches.[63]

Although there are more calls for criminal legal reform and "smart on crime" policy approaches today, even calling the incarcerated "residents" in lieu of more degrading terms such as "inmates" across some correctional facilities, the damage left by the War on Drugs is still evident.[64] In 2018, in the United States alone, more than six million people were still under some form of correctional supervision, despite this being a near twenty-year low in the number of people on supervision.[65] Just over two million are incarcerated in state or federal prisons.[66] And while the United States is home to only 5 percent of the world's population, it is home to roughly 25 percent of the world's prison population—startling numbers that illustrate the vast expanse of incarceration and how the widespread punishment and imprisonment of pregnant women is unique to the United States.[67]

Since the War on Drugs was launched and these "tough on crime" approaches were enacted in the 1970s and 1980s, the number of women under correctional control increased considerably—women are now considered the fastest-growing correctional population.[68] Research shows that between 1977 and 2007, the number of women in prison grew by 832 percent, which is twice the rate of growth for men during the *same* period.[69] To put this into perspective, in the 1970s, prior to the prison boom, about eight thousand women were incarcerated in the United States; today, that number is closer to 110,000.[70]

In discussing incarceration further, Crenshaw argues, "The problem of mass incarceration is not simply a problem of criminal justice per se but of the disciplinary practices of the state and private social power writ large."[71] This expansion of the carceral state comes at the same time as support and funding for social service programs have waned, particularly in rural places marked by a dwindling economy, where social disadvantages are widespread, resulting in more punitive encounters.[72] To be sure, the regulation and control of pregnancy, particularly within correctional settings, is an outgrowth of the inequities and disadvantages that occur in the "free world," where reproductive freedom is limited and surveillance and punishment are ubiquitous.[73]

Unsurprisingly, the expanse of the criminal legal system was not lost on the women I interviewed. Latrice reminded me of an important truth: "I'm just one of many, one of many . . . I'm not the only one." That is, the narratives in this book provide only a snapshot of the millions of families whose lives have been forever altered by mass incarceration. Latrice acknowledged that *who* spends time behind bars is not random either—an important observation that sheds light on the racial disparities within the US prison system and how the maternal web of control disproportionately affects women of color.

People of color are more likely to be behind bars than their White counterparts, with recent data revealing that about two thirds of women in prison are of color.[74] Blacks have a rate of imprisonment that is two times higher than that of Whites.[75] Many women in prison have experienced poverty and have a low educational level, placing them at a higher risk for unemployment in the months preceding their imprisonment.[76] Among those who are employed in the formal economy (before coming to prison), they are more likely to be employed in low-wage, entry-level work, earning around 41 percent less than their nonincarcerated counterparts.[77]

It is not uncommon for women to be incarcerated for drug or property crimes and to have extensive histories of abuse and trauma that threaten their health.[78] They are also more likely to have mental health issues, as well as HIV and other sexually transmitted diseases that complicate the ability to have a healthy pregnancy.[79] Further evidence reveals that around 70 percent of incarcerated women struggle with addiction and substance-abuse problems, with the result that many are already under some form of correctional supervision prior to coming to prison.[80]

In addition, many also have children; nearly 60 percent of women in prison are mothers.[81] In comparison to incarcerated fathers, mothers are more likely to be the primary custodial parent prior to their incarceration, and are likely to be the sole economic provider for their children.[82]

These collateral consequences of incarceration extend further in that because there are few women's prisons in any given state, especially in comparison to men's facilities, when women are incarcerated, they are *more* likely to be incarcerated further away from their children, making visitation all the more difficult, especially for families in rural areas with limited public transportation.[83] On average, incarcerated women are housed in facilities over 160 miles away from their home.[84] The magnitude of parental incarceration is perhaps best evidenced through the following statistic: over five million children have experienced parental incarceration, affecting about 7 percent of US children.[85] To be clear, incarcerated women and their children have their lives controlled and disrupted in ways that undoubtedly transform pregnancy, birth, and motherhood, ultimately compromising their health and well-being.

Narrative Criminology and the Power of Stories

As a researcher, I wanted to learn more about *how* exactly the incarceration of pregnant women in US prisons affects not only women but also their children and families. In my quest to know more, I was not able to find much about the narrative *particulars* of these experiences. I was interested in the information that could not necessarily be found in statistics alone. In other words, I was interested in the *stories* of those who had been pregnant in prison—what they said and what they left unsaid.[86]

This inquiry into the particulars of stories and storytelling derives from a theoretical perspective that sociologists Lois Presser and Sveinung Sandberg call "narrative criminology," a unique area within criminology that is centered on the study of stories and storytelling as a means of understanding the trajectories of how crime becomes created or desisted.[87] As Sandberg and criminologist Thomas Ugelvik wrote, "The sharing of stories is an important part of the human condition. . . . We make sense of ourselves and our relationships with others by sharing stories and through our individual on-going inner narrative. Stories are, simply put, at the core of what makes us who and what we are."[88] Thus, it comes as little surprise that when a crime happens, people are interested in the details—what happened and why. They are curious about the information that cannot necessarily be found in numbers or statistical analyses alone but rather can only be contained within stories.

The use of stories is central to the creation and understanding of knowledge, as it allows people a means of holistically describing their experiences and constructed realities and interpretations of those experiences.[89] Individuals interact with others *through* storytelling, for storytelling itself is a significant social process that allows for empowerment, growth, and self-reflection—all matters that became apparent very quickly as I listened to the stories of women who had experienced a pregnancy behind bars. Using narrative criminology, I conducted in-depth interviews with women who were once pregnant and incarcerated in state prisons in the Midwest to better understand how the prison system and reproduction collide, providing a unique insight into the structural forces they encounter during pregnancy that collectively create a maternal web of control that ultimately threatens both women and their families.

The Study

The women profiled herein are just a sampling of the thousands of women who are pregnant in prisons across the United States every year; their stories provide important insight into the reproductive injustices and the collateral consequences caused by maternal incarceration. The data for this book comes from in-depth interviews that I conducted in the late 2010s with thirty-five women who are now released from prison but at one point were pregnant and incarcerated in state prisons in the Midwest in places where there are only one or two women's prisons per state.[90] The changing economic landscape and the rise of carcerality affect even those in rural areas in the Midwest that are devoid of much opportunity, where addiction permeates, stigma is thick, and social resources are hard to come by.[91] These rural pockets and least-populated areas are often ignored in traditional prison research, despite calls for more inquiry into the particulars of rural areas amid high rates of imprisonment in rural places, even surpassing imprisonment in urban settings, making this work an important contribution.[92]

Although each prison has its own classification systems and unique subcultures that affect women in varying ways, none of the women in this study were held in solitary confinement, meaning that they all spent their incarceration surrounded by peers—something that would prove to be important as they created collective systems of support in the absence of much familial support to both navigate and resist the maternal web of control.[93] I acknowledge from the onset that none *reported* becoming pregnant *after* they entered prison, though this has been documented elsewhere.[94]

Interviews allowed participants to discuss and describe their experiences at length, allowing me to capture nonverbal communication and to seek clarification as needed. Finding and recruiting these women was especially difficult. As several participants told me, rarely do women carry a large sign advertising their time behind bars. For in the rural towns where they are from, the stigma attached to incarceration, while pregnant no less, remains deep and difficult to shed, causing many to conceal their past as best they could. Several shared how they worked extremely hard to conceal their incarceration from new friends, from employers, and in a couple of cases from new partners because of the stigma attached to incarceration, especially in their small towns—a finding that illustrates the power of the maternal web of control and its hold over women, even after they are released from prison.

There were others I interviewed who did not make much of an effort at all to conceal their past and were eager to share their story with others. These women shared how they were especially proud of the life they had built after their incarceration and wanted to be a source of inspiration to others in a similar situation. This does not mean that those who made more of an effort to hide their past were not proud of the life they had built after prison; in many cases, they were—a point I discuss in more detail in the afterword.

I found interviewees by working closely with social service agencies like housing shelters, food pantries, thrift stores, church missionaries, reentry support groups, and other organizations devoted to criminal legal reform. I acknowledge that the experiences of women who do *not* seek out these services may not be included in this book. Due to this limitation, I contacted a variety of social service agencies, as a means of increasing the diversity of the sample, and I also relied on the participants themselves to refer me to other women they knew who experienced a pregnancy in prison. Interviews were conducted at various public places, including fast-food joints, coffee houses, and even a couple of workplaces, unless distance prohibited travel.

Interviewing the women after they had their baby and were released from prison was a strategic decision because it allowed me to capture a greater range of topics, such as postpartum life and how incarceration affects family ties and women's relationships with their baby still today—important topics that all produced themes of domination and control, revealing how pregnancy itself is a site of surveillance and punishment that becomes hypercontrolled and contained behind bars. To date, these are topics that have not been explored in depth by many scholars, which is a strength of this work. I acknowledge that time has passed since the interviewees were pregnant and incarcerated, and the construction of the narrative accounts in this book are shaped by time and the various circumstances and experiences that have taken place since their release from prison.[95]

The art of storytelling is influenced by a myriad of social processes, with researchers also bringing their own social positioning into their work, highlighting the ways in which narratives may unfold differently with a different interviewer.[96] I acknowledge my more privileged social positioning as an academic researcher.[97] As a Latina who is told on countless occasions that I look "young" for my age and who is affiliated with a university, I was not viewed by my interviewees as someone associated with the criminal legal system but rather was seen as an eager, perhaps nerdy researcher simply looking to learn more for her "school project," as they called it. I was open about my connection to a university, as I did not want them to view me as a cop or a snitch, which made the establishment of rapport easy—a strength of this study. Many were taken aback and pleasantly surprised that someone from a university wished to talk to them and learn from them—a contrast to many of their experiences in the "free world." I made an intentional decision not to interview correctional officers or obstetricians, as I wanted to center the experiences of the real experts on the incarceration of pregnant women—those with lived experience—and I was extremely grateful that they shared their stories with me. I will be the first to acknowledge that the narratives contained within are not my stories—they belong to those I interviewed.

The way women perceive the maternal web of control and the loss of autonomy is also influenced by their social positioning and lived experiences, including their race and ethnicity, socioeconomic status, and other particulars, such as whether they are first-time mothers or have a partner or support system, and the extent of any previous experiences with the prison system. At points, those I interviewed referenced these factors to account for their time behind bars—though, a more overt discussion of race and even socioeconomic status was noticeably absent among some—a finding that reveals how the "color-blind" ideology permeates the United States, where people are socialized to disengage from conversations about race entirely, particularly in smaller, more conservative towns, as if simply conversing about race and racism perpetuates its existence.[98]

Interviewees all came from various backgrounds. Fifteen were White or Caucasian, while fourteen were Black or African American.[99] One was Asian, one was Native American, and one was Hispanic. Three identified as biracial. At the time of the interview, their ages ranged from twenty-four to fifty-eight, with a mean age of 40.2 years. While some participants had college degrees, others had their GED, with one having just middle school experience.[100] All identified as cisgender.[101] When I asked about their socioeconomic backgrounds, all but one said they were "middle-class," while the remaining one self-identified as "White trash."[102] However, some of the situations they described, like living in between homeless shelters or panhandling to survive, were not exactly middle-class markers but rather experiences that more closely resembled poverty. This finding is not surprising given that most people in the United States self-identify as middle-class.[103] For the purposes of confidentiality, I do not reveal the particulars of my interviewees' criminal charges nor their prisons but instead classify their crimes as either violent or nonviolent. Thirty-one were incarcerated for nonviolent crime(s), while four were incarcerated for violent crime(s).[104] About half of the participants had been pregnant before coming to prison, and most had custodial care of the resulting children prior to their incarceration. The number of children each had varied. Some had one child, while others had seven. The mean number of children was three.

The amount of time each woman spent in prison varied. The mean sentence length was 41.7 months or 3.5 years. However, not all served the entirety of their sentence; some were released early from prison on parole supervision, while others were released early due to overcrowded inmate populations, among other reasons.[105] While some of the women featured in this book had been to prison before, I only focus on the prison stay in which they were pregnant. The names I use in this book and the circumstances of the women's cases, as well as other identifying information, such as the specifics of their crimes and the names of the prisons they were incarcerated in, have been intentionally left out to protect their confidentiality. In a few cases, minor details may have been changed or merged with other participants' stories to provide further protection.

The experiences of those behind bars are also specific to the particulars of the policies and practices of the facility they are incarcerated in, especially as no single policy governs the treatment of incarcerated pregnant women in US state prisons, resulting in a wide variation of treatment and care. Some places have more progressive and humanitarian policies and practices than others, and many of the policies and practices of each correctional facility are heavily influenced by the sentiments of taxpayers and state legislatures, as well as those in the upper administration of correctional facilities.[106] Each facility is different, and there is much variation within and across facilities. As noted earlier, most of the women described in this book were incarcerated in the Midwest, where conservative correctional approaches are the norm and calls for reform are slow—a stark contrast to some European countries, where incarceration is reserved for the most violent of offenders and even then, the incarcerated are not routinely separated from their children.[107] These political climates shape both criminal legal policies and other areas of society, including the control and containment of women and all things pregnancy, birth, and motherhood. That is, the criminal legal system and its respective policies and practices do not occur in a vacuum but rather reflect the political and economic climate of communities that work in conjunction with the prison system to produce carcerality and the maternal web of control. As with any qualitative study, the findings from this book are not meant to be generalizable but rather provide an intimate portrait into the larger issue of how the prison system controls and surveils pregnancy, birth, and motherhood.

An Overview of the Book

What became of Faye, Gloria, and Latrice? In the chapters that follow, I continue their stories, as well as introduce other women who were pregnant and incarcerated, providing a chronological portrait of the way pregnant women account for their experiences behind bars. A central theme is that pregnancy itself remains subject to domination and control, especially in the prison setting, a total environment, in which every aspect of life is tightly controlled; pregnancy, then, is hypercontrolled across multiple entities that collaborate with the prison system to control women.[108] Ultimately, this book shows how reproductive oppression proliferates behind bars and how incarceration and the maternal web of control transform not just pregnancy but also motherhood and family dynamics for years to come.

In chapter 1, I set the stage and introduce some of my participants and share their stories of how they came to be pregnant in prison, detailing the beginnings of their encounters with the maternal web of control. As they explained, no one plans to spend their life behind bars, let alone to be pregnant behind bars, yet this is the reality for thousands each year. In this chapter, I detail some of the experiences of women before their incarceration and show how these early experiences frame their time behind bars and their ability to cope with and process their pregnancy.

In chapter 2, I focus on health and explore how health is governed and subject to control in prison. I discuss the symbiotic relationship between maternal and fetal health and efforts to optimize health, whether through the cessation of drugs or prioritization of nutrition. I argue that the ability to make positive changes in the name of health is limited under the maternal web of control, where incarceration itself threatens health through the inadequacies of prenatal care.

Chapter 3 focuses on preparation for childbirth and motherhood and how these practices are also heavily surveilled and controlled. I show how despite the prison system barring some of the more cultural markers of pregnancy, such as a baby shower or photos that capture a growing "baby bump," women prepare for motherhood in their own unique ways, often collaborating with others to resist efforts designed to strip them of their impending motherhood. I also detail how the practice of separating mothers from their children forces most pregnant women to craft a caregiver plan, detailing where their baby will go after birth.[109]

Chapter 4 is devoted to birth experiences. In this chapter, I show how childbirth in the carceral setting is regulated by both the medical system and the prison system and remains subject to harsh policies and practices that effectively dictate the circumstances of childbirth and eliminate autonomy and the ability to be active participants in birth. I also detail how women come to terms with saying goodbye to their babies under a cloud of carceral control before returning to prison.

Chapter 5 centers on the loss of control throughout the postpartum period. In this chapter, I discuss how women reacclimate to prison life after birth and how they adjust both to the changes in their body and to life as new mothers—without their baby at their side. In doing so, I show how the carceral system transforms the postpartum period, making it difficult for women to access essential postpartum resources, ultimately threatening physical, emotional, and mental health.

Chapter 6 explores mothering both behind bars and in the community after release from prison. I show how the maternal web of control follows women, hindering the ability to parent and receive visitations from their baby while they are still incarcerated, as well as how it affects their reunification efforts after their release from prison. A central part of this chapter focuses on the struggles to demonstrate competency as mothers amid carceral forces that continue to regulate motherhood. Using this focus, I outline how even practices like finding work and a place to live are increasingly complicated for those with young children, threatening the well-being of families and keeping them locked in a permanent underclass.

I conclude the book with a summary of the theoretical framework, discuss the implications of the incarceration of pregnant women, and share recommendations for what social change might look like to better meet the needs of women and their families, creating change both in birth spaces and behind bars. Last, I end the book with an afterword, providing an update on some of my participants today.

Ultimately, I offer this book with the hope of changing the narrative around pregnancy, birth, and motherhood both behind bars and in communities and as a tool to reimagine what reproductive justice could look like and how reproductive oppression operates in the most marginalized of spaces. I aim to fill existing knowledge gaps by centering the reproductive experiences of pregnant women in prison to better understand how incarceration transforms pregnancy, birth, and motherhood for generations to come.

1

Welcome to Prison

Two Pink Lines and the Disruption of Plans

I always wanted to have kids, just not the way it happened.
—Candy

Leslie, a White, fifty-four-year-old woman, was unemployed, homeless, and hungry when I met her. Having served two and a half years in prison on a couple of nonviolent offenses, she was excited to be in the free world again, where she could make her own decisions, though living in the free world was not without its challenges. It was not uncommon for Leslie to have to rummage through the trash cans outside of restaurants and eateries in her small midwestern town searching for food, and it was not uncommon for her to have only a couple of dollars to her name.

On a good day, there would be an opening at her local reentry transition center, a faith-based place where women recently released from prison can stay overnight to have a hot shower and meal. However, given the high number of women vying for these spots, openings at the center were hard to come by. When the center was full for the day, as it often was, Leslie was on her own. And while there were a couple of other transition centers in her community that offered respite for the recently released, these centers only served men—a reality that is the norm in many rural communities.[1] On a bad day, when the center was full, Leslie made a makeshift home for herself under an abandoned overpass bridge garnished in graffiti.

When I asked Leslie about the number of times she had been incarcerated, she told me that before she would tell me I had to promise her I would not get scared. The number was high, and she was not proud of it, so she worried I would think less of her. I do not reveal the exact number to further protect her identity, but it is a number hovering around fifty. Leslie was a self-described "frequent flyer" of the county jail system and was all too familiar with the squeaky brass doors on the local courthouse and the probation conditions that required her to pee on demand. But to this day, she has only been to prison once, which is something she is immensely proud of.[2] It was during one of her stints in jail for drugs and prostitution that she learned she was pregnant with her first child. However, pregnancy was not the only thing she tested positive for that day. She also tested positive for HIV.[3]

As Leslie shared more of her story with me, it was clear she was no stranger to trauma and the criminal legal system. As a small child, she was repeatedly molested by an older family member and witnessed domestic violence on a regular basis. She has no idea who her father is and has only seen her mother a handful of times. Growing up, her mom had more interactions with police officers and parole officers than she ever did with any of Leslie's schoolteachers. Dirty needles, Jack Daniels, and rolled joints were all staples when she was growing up, as was an empty refrigerator. To cope with the pain, Leslie turned to what she knew, first experimenting with marijuana and crack cocaine before later using methamphetamines. To support her drug habits, she turned to petty theft and eventually engaged in more serious property crimes. At the height of her drug addiction, she was also prostituting on a nightly basis.

To say that Leslie was overcome with emotions when she first learned she was pregnant (*and* HIV positive) would be an understatement. At the time, she was "deep into drugs, where it was a struggle just to stay alive on the streets." The news of a pregnancy only complicated matters. Not knowing who the father was made it even more difficult to process the pregnancy, for it could have been "any one of [her] tricks', pimps', or even [her] boyfriend's." In a deep state of addiction and "absolutely scared shitless" to be pregnant, she clung to her faith, hoping to find some answers, remaining steadfast in her belief against abortion.

By the time Leslie was sent to prison, she was two and a half months pregnant and would go on to spend the next year behind bars before being released. As a White woman, she was sheltered from systemic racism, but as a poor woman who grew up in the foster care system, she was already in the crossfires of multiple systems of control, having had frequent interactions with police and child protective services since childhood. Many of the women I interviewed were like Leslie and had some understanding about prison and carcerality well before they came to prison.

Still, to understand any story, and especially this one, it is important to start at the beginning. As several participants told me, *nobody's* journey into the prison system happens overnight—and certainly not by choice either. Rather, as Candy, a White, thirty-seven-year-old mother of two, explained, "Something, *something*, must have gone really wrong at some point in your life to end up [in prison] of all places. Nobody pictures this when they think of pregnancies and having babies." In critically examining that *something*, this chapter focuses on the beginnings of incarcerated pregnant women's experiences with the maternal web of control.

The central argument of this chapter is that the maternal web of control is set in motion well before women ever formally enter the penal system, with structural violence and the matrix of domination channeling women into the hands of multiple systems of oppression and control that eventually converge and intensify to regulate and disrupt pregnancy and motherhood behind bars. In this chapter, I focus on the beginnings of pregnancy and how the maternal web of control affects the ways in which women learn of and process their pregnancy, forcing them to reconcile with their pregnancy while simultaneously dealing with the absence of choice and often ruthless judgment from loved ones.

In discussing the origins of the maternal web of control through a lens of narrative criminology, this chapter answers the bigger question of *what happened*? How do the women I interviewed and the nearly three thousand women like them spend their pregnancy trapped inside both a literal cage and a much larger cage that governs not just their physical body but also the most intimate of matters *inside* their body?[4] As I answer these questions, I provide important information about the backgrounds and early upbringings of those I studied, as a means of further unveiling the *something*, or rather somethings, that land pregnant women, especially more marginalized women, behind bars each year.

Relying on an intersectional framework, I caution readers that while the answers to the question of *what happened* may appear to be more individualized or specific to the particulars, the pregnancy and birth experiences of women in prison are all shaped to some degree by a carceral environment made possible through the convergence of multiple systems of policing, surveillance, and control that are unique to the United States in this time and that all work simultaneously with each other to create a maternal web of control. In other words, the experiences of those behind bars must be contextualized against a larger milieu in the United States, where carcerality is ubiquitous and a social safety net encompassing food, housing, and healthcare is largely absent, especially in rural settings where resources are even more scarce, with the criminal legal system operating in place of a social safety net.[5] Research reveals that "between 2004 and 2014, the number of women in jails increased 43% in rural counties, while declining 6% in urban counties," providing insight into how even larger social problems like the nation's "opioid epidemic" have infiltrated small towns with shrinking economies, few job prospects, and insufficient social services, eventually funneling many into the prison system.[6] Thus, the incarceration of pregnant women is not an individual issue but rather is systemic, influenced by an array of social forces. Accordingly, this chapter sets the backdrop for a much larger story about how carcerality can be found even in places beyond the prison system, trapping women in pregnancy and motherhood devoid of autonomy and control.

A Positive Pregnancy Test

As indicated earlier, although the maternal web of control is set in motion long before women come to prison, the confirmation of pregnancy behind bars assures this control, shaping the ways in which women learn of and process their pregnancy. Yet, women do not always know of their pregnancy before coming to prison. Some may not learn of their pregnancy until they are issued a pregnancy test behind bars. Since early detection of pregnancy is essential for timely initiation of healthcare, delayed detection affects both the health outcomes and the health trajectories of women and babies and the right to exercise full bodily autonomy, including termination—all points I expand upon later in the chapter.

Currently, US state prisons are not required to collect data on pregnancy, so the circumstances through which incarcerated women learn of their pregnancy are unclear.[7] Among the women I interviewed, about half had no idea they were even pregnant *until* they came to prison and were given a health assessment and pregnancy test as part of their prison's intake procedures. Since no universal policies exist for pregnant women behind bars, the practice of pregnancy testing during intake varies widely across facilities.[8] While some institutions issue mandatory pregnancy tests upon admission, the legality of this practice has been contested over the years, with some arguing that requiring women to undergo a pregnancy test is in violation of constitutional and state rights that protect the right to refuse medical care.[9]

From the beginning, healthcare decisions are not made between a woman and her provider but instead require the involvement of the prison system and the navigation of all its many complexities that make it difficult to receive care. While both the American College of Obstetricians and Gynecologists and the National Commission on Correctional Health Care Guidelines *recommend* pregnancy testing to women of childbearing age upon admission to prison, in the most comprehensive survey available, only 64 percent of prisons tested women for pregnancy upon admission.[10] The picture is even more bleak for US jails—only 38 percent of jails issued pregnancy tests to women in their facilities, and 45 percent of jails said they relied on self-report data, only using pregnancy tests to confirm as needed.[11] This data illustrates how the ability to initiate prenatal care is dependent upon correctional facilities—entities that also are laden with red tape and bureaucracy, making it even more difficult for women to receive timely care.

Providing incarcerated women with a pregnancy test during medical intake is especially important given misguided beliefs among many incarcerated women about their ability to even become pregnant because of the combined effects of poor health, inadequate nutrition, and substance abuse. Many of those I interviewed said it was difficult to even remember the last time they had a regular menstrual cycle because of the sheer number of drugs in their body, resulting in a false belief that it was "impossible" to even become pregnant. Yet, incarcerated women have higher rates of unplanned pregnancies and higher rates of fertility than women who are not incarcerated, in part because they face greater barriers to healthcare and experience gendered racism in many healthcare settings, resulting in low contraceptive usage, coupled with lower educational attainment.[12] Even geographical location acts as a barrier to care, where those who live in medical deserts may be forced to travel hours for medical care—a reality that is out of reach for already marginalized women.[13]

It is difficult to speculate on the percentage of incarcerated women in state prisons who used birth control in the months preceding their incarceration, as national data is not kept. However, it is expected to be low given the misguided beliefs about their ability to become pregnant, along with little access to healthcare prior to their incarceration. In a study focused on the reproductive experiences of incarcerated women, only 28 percent of surveyed women reported consistent contraceptive use in the three months before their incarceration—a finding that explains the increasing number of pregnant women in prison.[14]

Early detection is critical for improved health outcomes. An intersectional framework and an understanding of the forces that constitute structural violence explain how early detection is needed even more for more marginalized women, who are more likely to have extensive histories of trauma, having gone years or even decades without healthcare—a fact that highlights the scarcity of available healthcare in the United States, where access and affordability are difficult to come by, particularly for those trapped in poverty living in less populated areas.[15] Given the inconsistent use of pregnancy testing in correctional facilities, to be pregnant behind bars, then, may mean little to no control of or even knowledge about the changes taking place inside the body, greatly undermining bodily autonomy and reproductive freedom and the ability to access proper care.

Processing Pregnancy

When women do learn of their pregnancy, whether behind bars or out in the community prior to their incarceration, pregnancy is marked by any number of strong feelings that require processing and coping. Incarceration may intensify these feelings or set into motion new feelings entirely, including but not limited to feeling overwhelmed, fear, anxiety, depression, and even joy. All responses are valid and are shaped by the backgrounds and lived experiences specific to each person and the degree to which they experience the maternal web of control.

Many women I interviewed acknowledged that their pregnancy was unplanned, which further complicated their feelings, often resulting in confusion, uncertainty, and fear. This is not surprising given that 45 percent of *all* pregnancies in the United States are unplanned—a reality that highlights the lack of healthcare in the United States, where comprehensive sex education is absent, making it difficult for all women, especially more marginalized women in remote areas, to access contraceptives.[16] Women of color report even higher rates of unplanned pregnancies, placing them at greater risk for pregnancy.[17] High rates of unplanned pregnancies among women of color combined with increasing surveillance in low-income neighborhoods means that women of color and low-income White women are especially susceptible to criminalization and incarceration during pregnancy.

Coping with Pregnancy and Incarceration

Intersectionality affects the ability to cope with incarceration during pregnancy. I found that economically marginalized women, across all racial groups, may be more worried about how *pregnancy* would alter their life than about how *incarceration* would impact their life. That is, many of these women were already accustomed to various forms of surveillance and control found both within and beyond the criminal legal system, so incarceration was not viewed as being as life-altering as pregnancy. Pregnancy, on the other hand, entailed a lifetime commitment, as well as physical, emotional, mental, and financial responsibilities that require tremendous work and navigation, especially for those already facing poverty and addiction.

Those who have more education and are in a better economic position may be less worried about the prospect of bringing a baby into the world and more concerned about how *incarceration* would forever alter their pregnancy and life moving forward, for the effects of incarceration on health are deep and the stigma attached to incarceration during pregnancy never seems to quite go away, especially in the smaller towns they were from.[18] In my study, I found that these women are more likely to be in a long-term romantic relationship and have a greater support network, financial and otherwise, to help navigate the complexities of pregnancy and motherhood, for in many ways, pregnancy and motherhood were always a part of their "plan," though certainly under different timing and circumstances. It was *incarceration* that was less familiar and posed a greater threat to health, often acting as a tension point within their social circles—a point I expand upon later in the chapter.

However, even prior experience with incarceration does not ensure a seamless transition to prison life during pregnancy, for each new incarceration entails an understanding of the subcultures and policies and programs specific to each institution. Candy shared how even though she had been pregnant before and had also been to prison before, it was this particular incarceration *during* pregnancy that dramatically altered her feelings about motherhood. According to Candy, "Well, there was a lot going on, so it was like another layer of trauma on top. There was just so much trauma in my life at that time that it was like another piece to the puzzle. If it had been the first time I'd ever been pregnant, I would have been scared to death 'cause I would not have known about being pregnant or what to expect, or if it had been my first time in prison. I always wanted to have kids, just not the way it happened." As was the case with Candy, it is not uncommon for incarcerated women to have extensive histories of trauma.[19] Many are already caught between the trappings of poverty and gendered racism, resulting in significant cumulative disadvantages—and incarceration adds yet another layer of oppression and control, subjugating them even further, making it difficult to view their pregnancy as anything other than connected to the prison system.

Prisons as Places of Refuge

Intersectionality and the convergence of identity markers shape the way women process their pregnancy. In countries like the United States that lack a robust social safety net, it is no surprise that economic concerns quickly follow the news of a pregnancy, especially for those in poverty and in rural areas severely lacking social services.[20] A couple of the women I interviewed who knew they were pregnant before coming to prison disclosed that once they learned of their pregnancy, they deliberately committed a crime that carried prison time with the hope of being sent to jail (and later prison) to ensure that their basic needs were met—a decision that reflects the precariousness of their living conditions. In their eyes, jails and prisons were a safer and stabler environment than the unpredictability of life in the streets because they contain food, shelter, and healthcare—necessities that were not guaranteed on the outside for those without a support network.

Deliberately committing a crime that carries prison time for the purposes of securing basic needs speaks to the larger issue of how jails and prisons act as places of refuge for the most economically and socially marginalized of society, especially during pregnancy.[21] The changing economic conditions in the United States following a post-COVID environment in which wages have remained flat and the costs of goods and services have skyrocketed illustrate the consequences of having little to no social safety net.[22] As medical anthropologist Carolyn Sufrin explains, prisoners are the only population in the United States whose food, shelter, and healthcare are specifically guaranteed in the Constitution under the Eighth Amendment, which specifies that "excessive bail shall not be required, nor excessive fines imposed, *nor cruel and unusual punishments inflicted*" (emphasis added). In other words, correctional institutions *must* provide the incarcerated with basic needs, for incarcerating people without meals and healthcare is a violation of the Eighth Amendment and constitutes cruel and unusual punishment.[23]

When Jasmine, a biracial (Black and White), thirty-five-year-old mother of four, found out she was pregnant, she quickly turned herself in to law enforcement because she was "deep in addiction" and had no means of taking care of herself, let alone a new baby. She had already lost custody of her older children and had no money. In the words of Jasmine, "I was getting hungry, so I caught a charge, so I could get locked up." As a Black woman with only a middle school education and an extensive criminal history, she felt it was only "a matter of time" before she would be transferred to prison—a sentiment that illustrates the prevalence of carceral surveilling forces that marked her life. As predicted, she spent the first few weeks of pregnancy in jail before quickly being sent to prison at the end of her second trimester. While Jasmine and others like her may make a more intentional decision to commit a crime of incarceration, this was *not* something she had ever dreamed of doing; rather, it was a complicated and difficult decision born out of survival needs. The lengths to which poor women are willing to go to ensure that their basic needs are met during pregnancy call into question the prevailing ways in which "good" mothers are traditionally measured according to more middle-class experiences that are often unobtainable to those in poverty, without regard to the unique ways in which good mothering is evaluated in low-income communities.[24] Basic needs during pregnancy are especially critical for those who come to prison already in poor health, providing insight into why incarceration during pregnancy may be less of a concern for some because of the protective benefits it offers.[25] Turning to the criminal legal system in times of crises reflects the state of inequalities in the United States, where economic, neighborhood, and social conditions push the most marginalized into punitive places laced with domination and control exerted under the auspices of care and protection.[26]

Although Jasmine framed her experiences as specific to her personal circumstances and as something that simply happened to her, the growth of imprisonment and other forms of control highlights how her time behind bars was grounded in more structural and systemic causes. As a Black woman living in poverty with few skills and little education, she was already struggling. It did not help that opportunities to earn a living wage in her small town were hard to come by. Without employment, it was nearly impossible to secure housing and healthcare, especially as one of only a few Black women living in a nearly all-White rural community where racism was thick and landlords and prospective employers were even less likely to take a chance on her. For Jasmine, prison provided a chance to be pregnant with some semblance of dignity, increasing her chances of having a healthy pregnancy and improved birth outcomes. In Jasmine's case, prison provided protective health benefits that "gave [her baby] the best fighting chance possible" and removed her from the violence and unpredictability that marked her hometown.[27]

The irony of finding refuge in a controlling and punitive system was not lost on Jasmine and the others I interviewed who turned to the criminal legal system in times of hardship, for while the prison system may offer protective benefits, it also funnels women into a greater web of control that has lasting consequences for their pregnancy, birth, and motherhood, trapping them more deeply into systemic poverty and gendered violence, into a carceral environment that often reinforces the same disadvantages found in the communities they seek to escape.

Prisons as Places of Harm

Incarcerated women from the lower middle class are less likely to view prisons as a place of refuge and instead express more concern about incarceration during pregnancy, despite having a social position that offers more protection. Stacy, a White thirty-nine-year-old, was pregnant with her first child when she was sentenced to prison for her involvement in a white-collar crime. Before coming to prison, she had never been in trouble with the law and was the first in her family to experience incarceration. As a home owner with an advanced degree, she was completely dumbfounded by the news of her incarceration. Having grown up sheltered from the penal system, Stacy suspected that there was "some sort of clause or law or at least something" that granted immunity to pregnant women, especially for those like her with no criminal history. When she learned that this was not the case, she spent much of her time behind bars petitioning her lawyer and correctional administrators for an early release. As Stacy explained, the conditions behind bars were worse than anything she had ever known, making it extremely difficult for her to cope with her pregnancy and incarceration. Stacy's narrative highlights how the ability to come to terms with a pregnancy behind bars is shaped by social background and the extent to which controlling forces are found in communities.

Many of the Black women I interviewed made note of the racial and class disparities embedded in the criminal legal system and acknowledged that there was little to no point in trying to undo or reduce their prison sentence upon learning they were pregnant because "the system" is bathed in inequities that disproportionately favor Whites and those with more income. Ruthie, a Black, thirty-nine-year-old mother of two, shared how some of her White peers who were pregnant "ran to their attorney" as soon as they learned of their pregnancy, fully expecting an early release. Ruthie never considered making the same request of her (court-appointed) attorney because she knew there was "no point" in doing so as a Black woman in a largely White and rural, conservative town with little social support. Ruthie explained, "It's not like I could have went to the staff and been like, 'Oh I gotta get out of here, I got to call my public defender and my lawyer and help me! I got to get out of here!' I didn't do any of that. I don't know. There was just no point in fighting it. I dealt with a lot of racism in my life, so yeah."

Cherelle, a Black, thirty-seven-year-old mother of seven children, had a similar experience and explained how she had grown accustomed to punitive forces from a young age, making it more difficult to process the ways in which gendered racism and structural violence marked the beginnings of her pregnancy and new motherhood. A first-time offender and the first in her family to ever go to prison, Cherelle provided insight into how gendered racism plays a role in sentencing:

> [I] was a first-time offender of a nonviolent offense. I was the first in my family to ever go to prison, [which] lets you know that there was no criminal history. We wasn't criminally minded people. I thought that spoke volumes about my character, but it didn't. When the judge had sentenced me, he was like, "You have to be the example." I was pretty angry because I knew there were other alternatives. They could have gave me the ankle bracelet [or] probation, but they didn't. They sent me to prison because being female and being Black made me double the minority. That played a *very* big part because there were other White women that did the same thing and did not go to prison; they would get probation.

These experiences illustrate some of the larger issues in the US criminal legal system, where Blacks and to an extent Hispanics are disproportionately arrested and incarcerated in comparison to their White counterparts, making them more accustomed to the presence of surveilling punitive forces.[28] Accordingly, these matrices of oppression disproportionately push poor women of color into the prison system, where they are also disproportionately subjected to subjugation during pregnancy and launched deeper into a web of control and oppression.[29]

A Web of Control

The maternal web of control relies on the matrix of domination and structural violence to function.[30] As discussed earlier, although every pregnant woman in prison has her pregnancy controlled through a number of interlocking forces, the effects of the maternal web of control are especially profound for women of color and those in precarious economic positions, often resulting in the news of a pregnancy being accompanied by a fear of surveilling institutions, not only by the prison system but also by other carceral actors like the child welfare system and the medical complex.[31]

As mentioned, many incarcerated women are already in precarious economic conditions before coming to prison. Research reveals that over 70 percent are in poverty—a percentage that is much higher than the national poverty rate of 11.8 percent.[32] It is no surprise that in the wake of a pregnancy, many are concerned that a baby would bring unwanted financial strain to their family, making them more susceptible to the surveilling lens of the child welfare system.[33] Indeed, research finds that most calls to the child welfare system for cases of neglect are due to conditions that stem from poverty yet instead are interpreted as maltreatment and neglect.[34] The child welfare system is a powerful carceral system that has the legal authority to follow families for years, invading their privacy and resulting in unnecessary trauma and harm.[35]

Fears of Carceral Systems

To be incarcerated (pregnant no less) means hyperinspection into the behaviors and decisions of pregnant women not only by the criminal legal system but also by social workers, judges, healthcare workers, and other agents of control who surveil women's parenting long after they give birth and are released from prison. Rhonda, a Black, thirty-seven-year-old mother of three, was already struggling to provide for her older children when she came to prison and had no idea how she would provide for another mouth. She was especially worried that her drug use would negatively impact her baby and feared that as an incarcerated Black woman with a substance abuse history and little in the way of a support system, her pregnancy would be closely scrutinized across multiple systems of control.

Under the maternal web of control, the child welfare system relies on a symbiotic relationship between the prison system and its extensions, including law enforcement and probation and parole officers, as well as other institutions of control like the medical system, to intrude upon the lives of women and surveil and inspect their pregnancy and parenting.[36] This intrusion is significant because these agents of control may work in collaboration with each other to initiate the process of parental-rights termination, inciting fear and trauma among many incarcerated women—a process made easier amid gendered racism and systemic poverty. Black mothers are especially susceptible to the intrusion of the child welfare system, for they are more likely to be reported to the child welfare system than White mothers.[37] Concerns and fear about intrusions from the child welfare system may be especially profound for those who are already mothers and have prior involvement with the child welfare system. Thus, a key concern at the beginning of pregnancy is tied to how pregnancy itself places women at the center of surveilling inspections from the state.

Reverence of Pregnancy and Motherhood

Although the maternal web of control has a powerful hold on women, this does not mean that the prison system has the power to *completely* rewrite the meanings attached to pregnancy and motherhood. For some, a reverence for pregnancy and motherhood may be especially strong no matter where or how the pregnancy takes place.[38] For example, Gloria and her boyfriend had been trying to conceive a baby for five and a half years with no success and had all but given up when Gloria found out she was pregnant during her prison-intake process. To say she was thrilled would be an understatement. Even though her arrest and subsequent incarceration were not part of the plan, both Gloria and her boyfriend remained ecstatic, for the joyous news of a pregnancy overwhelmed any concerns attached to incarceration.

This reverence for pregnancy and motherhood can be explained, at least in part, by research studies that illustrate how motherhood is valorized and remains an important identity marker in the United States.[39] These findings especially hold true among more marginalized women who lack other middle-class markers of success, including a career and home ownership.[40] In a study focused on the motherhood experiences of incarcerated women, one participant, known as "Marlene," is quoted as saying, "We don't have a career or anything. We take pride in our mothering."[41] Marlene's narrative sheds light on why all the women in this study took such a proactive approach to their pregnancy—a finding that offers important insight into the ways in which women contend with a pregnancy behind bars.

I should clarify that all my participants' narratives contained some form of admiration toward their baby. That is, none appeared apathetic or showed signs of indifference toward their baby after birth—a phenomenon that reveals the power of motherhood and its ability to prevail despite carceral forces that dominate and control the mechanisms through which it exists.[42] These sentiments shed light on the limitations of the maternal web of control and its ability to govern women, for even in punitive places designed to disrupt parenthood, women still cling to their motherhood. To be sure, the processing of a pregnancy behind bars is complicated. Although all my participants eventually took a proactive approach to their pregnancy and had a vested interest in their health, sharing stories of the desire to be the "best" mother possible, some acknowledged that they were not exactly enthusiastic about being pregnant in the beginning, and even considered an abortion. Yet, like all matters behind bars, the ability to obtain an abortion is highly regulated.

The Right to an Abortion

Incarceration disrupts not only the way women cope with and process their pregnancy but also their reproductive freedom and the ability to terminate a pregnancy if desired. Before the overruling of *Roe v. Wade*, previous court proceedings have ruled that incarcerated women retain a constitutional right to an abortion, though the realities of incarceration and the maternal web of control make it increasingly difficult to obtain one, as was the case among those in this study.[43] Data on abortions in correctional facilities reveals that only 1.4 percent of pregnancies to incarcerated women resulted in an abortion.[44] Furthermore, in a study involving fifty-three US jails, less than a third of surveyed jails indicated that they even informed women of their right to an abortion.[45] The denial of choice and of the right to even be informed of options highlights how the incarceration of pregnant women is a state-sanctioned form of gendered violence, placing women at an increased risk for harm and in direct opposition to the core tenets of reproductive justice.[46]

Hostile Environments

As mentioned, most of the women I interviewed were incarcerated in the Midwest, where conservative politics, few abortion providers, and restrictive laws severely limit access to abortion, even for women who are not incarcerated.[47] Wichita, Kansas, once known as the abortion capital of the United States, has since become a place that has one of the lowest abortion clinics per female population of any area in the United States.[48] The Summer of Mercy protests in Wichita, which included tens of thousands of protestors, resulted in thousands of arrests over a six-week period, and gave rise to further violence and even repeated assassination attempts of one of the few late-term abortion providers, provides insight into the volatile harassment and violence that make it difficult for even nonincarcerated women to obtain an abortion in this area.[49] In states that are hostile to abortion, even women who are not incarcerated may have to undergo mandatory counseling and ultrasound with a compulsory waiting period before an abortion can take place.[50]

Struggles to obtain an abortion are only amplified in total environments like prisons that are laden with even more bureaucracy, where autonomy is limited and an increasing number of power dynamics are at play.[51] Although each state and correctional facility has its own policies and practices when it comes to abortion, it is not unusual for women to face considerable obstacles before they can leave their facility to have an abortion. Restrictive state laws may also prohibit government (prison) funds being used for an abortion, and the costs of transportation and the overtime pay for correctional officers who must drive and accompany the women to the healthcare facility are passed on to incarcerated women who are already impoverished.[52] In federal prisons, the Hyde Amendment prohibits federal funding being used to cover an abortion, except in cases of rape or incest or where the woman's life is at risk.[53] Yet, funding is not the only barrier, for timing is also a concern.

As mentioned earlier, many who come through the prison system may not even know they are pregnant until well into their pregnancy, and in hostile states, there may be a small window of opportunity in which women can access an abortion, as many states bar abortion late into pregnancy.[54] Even then, an abortion typically entails a mountain of medical and legal paperwork, causing further delay.[55] These hurdles are a prime example of the maternal web of control, providing evidence of how the prison system works alongside other carceral institutions to further infringe on the reproductive and bodily autonomy of women.

That is, the ability to exercise one of the most intimate and personal of decisions resides not with those directly affected by pregnancy but with powerful carceral systems, setting into motion a cascade of further reproductive injustices. The restrictions on abortion in correctional facilities are an outgrowth of the regulation and control that occurs even in communities. In a post-*Roe* world, the maternal web of control has a much stronger hold on women now that abortion is no longer constitutionally guaranteed across all fifty states and instead remains subject to the abortion laws of each state. The overruling of *Roe v. Wade* may also result in an increasing number of women coming into the prison system in places that have criminally outlawed abortion and seek to punish those who do attempt to have one, particularly in places where states are introducing legislation declaring that fertilized eggs, embryos, and fetuses have personhood rights.[56]

The Reframing of Pregnancy

Lora, a White, thirty-nine-year-old mother of three, initially sought an abortion. As a single mother, she already struggled to make ends meet and was heavily involved in drugs. She cared deeply for her children and had a strong desire to quit using, but her addiction was stronger. Just four weeks into her pregnancy, she was arrested on felony drug charges and later sentenced to four years in prison. Lora was dumfounded. "I was using drugs; the baby's father was using drugs, and I'd already had two abortions, and I didn't want to have another abortion, but when I was thinking about this [sighs], I couldn't. We were pretty immersed in that lifestyle, and I just had no way of visualizing something else for us." Lora planned on having an abortion but soon realized that "once you're arrested, there's no deciding whether you're gonna have an abortion because that's not an option on the table at all, so we were having a baby. The only next decision to make was who's going to take the baby?" When Lora realized the abortion was not happening, she too was hopeful that her status as a pregnant woman would mean an early release, but this was not the case. When Lora's abortion fell through, she (re) framed her pregnancy as a "sign" from God that the pregnancy was simply "meant to be."

Lora was not the only one who framed the absence of choice behind bars as "fate." Others shared how in the absence of choice, their pregnancy could only be construed as a "sign from God," representing the unfolding of a new chapter and a "second chance." These spiritual undertones reflect the strong evangelical beliefs often found in the Midwest, where even gross reproductive injustices can be explained as all part of a divine plan from a higher order.[57] Additionally, these faith-based sentiments also reflect some of the more faith-based programming and services that often take place behind bars.[58]

Family Matters

Women who do not know they are pregnant before coming to prison must also contend with telling loved ones the news of their pregnancy—a complicated and difficult matter because of the ways in which a pregnancy also affects families, who may serve as caregivers. Yet, the regulation and control found behind bars make it difficult to communicate news of a pregnancy to loved ones. To begin, there are countless hurdles to visitation and communication. Less than half of incarcerated women ever receive an in-person visit, forcing many to share the news of their pregnancy through a costly call potentially limited to fifteen-minute increments during specific hours in an environment that does not offer much privacy.[59] In some places, phone and visitation privileges may be taken away for virtually any reason and often without warning, further compromising women's ability to communicate with their loved ones, who may act as essential support systems.[60]

Still more, having these conversations with family and other loved ones is difficult, for many families have strong feelings not only about their incarceration but also about a pregnancy and how it may affect them moving forward. As previously discussed, most women in prison are already mothers and have custodial care of their children prior to their incarceration.[61] When they go to prison, family members are often left to bear the responsibilities of caregiving—arduous physical, mental, and emotional work that takes a toll on them. To care for a newborn is another matter entirely, for newborns require additional caregiving responsibilities, causing much concern from family members—an issue I explore in chapter 3.

Difficult Conversations

Most of the women I interviewed said they were extremely nervous about telling their loved ones about their pregnancy—a finding that illustrates how even family members can act as members of the maternal web of control, surveilling and intruding upon their pregnancy. The particulars of how family members contribute to the maternal web of control vary immensely across social positioning and the extent to which incarceration is normalized in their social circles. Those in poverty were nervous about telling their loved ones because they knew they were already struggling economically and would have to potentially shoulder some of the financial burdens of caregiving—heavy responsibilities that were suddenly thrust upon them without much choice or warning. Most of the women I interviewed who were already mothers talked about how their family was already providing care for their other children, so the prospect of caring for another child, a newborn no less, only complicated matters in the wake of financial insecurity.

Processing the news of a pregnancy is complicated and fraught with many feelings, even among family members. The depths of addiction and financial insecurity, especially during pregnancy, may mean that some family members experience a sense of relief when their loved one is incarcerated. As mentioned earlier, although most prisons are far from providing top-notch care, for those in extreme disadvantage, the stable environment of prisons and the access to food, healthcare, and treatment may offer a welcome refuge for those increasingly worried about a loved one living on the margins during pregnancy. As Jasmine explained, "At the time, my grandmother was okay with it [my incarceration] because she felt like that [prison] was the only thing that was gonna keep me sober, so I needed to at least be there. She wasn't upset that I was in prison, she kinda was relieved 'cause she would say, 'Well at least I can sleep at night 'cause I know where you're at, and I know you're not getting high.'"

Families with more money were not as concerned about the pregnancy and the costs of caregiving and were far from relieved about having a loved one behind bars during pregnancy. Amber, a White, thirty-nine-year-old mother of four, said that when she was arrested and sent to jail, her family "bonded [her] out real quick" because she was pregnant, for they were increasingly uncomfortable with the thought of her being pregnant behind bars not only because they were worried that incarceration would threaten her health and pregnancy but also because of the stigma attached to having a pregnant daughter in prison. Although Amber was eventually able to make bail and leave jail, it was not long before she was sentenced to four years in prison and found herself behind bars yet again. Her narrative is yet another example of the social inequalities embedded in the prison system, as those with more privileged backgrounds can escape some of the carceral, controlling forces, even if only for a short time.

The Stigma of Incarceration

Social positioning is important. In circles where incarceration rates are low and incarceration is laced with immense stigma, families may be viewed as guilty by association—and a pregnancy during incarceration is marked by yet a hyper form of stigma, particularly in rural places where there is less room for anonymity.[62] Crystal, a Hispanic, twenty-four-year-old mother of two, said that her family was extremely upset when they found out that she was headed to prison and even more upset after she told them she was pregnant. According to Crystal, "My dad basically told me, 'Is this the fucking life you want to live!?'" In the large, Catholic, Hispanic family where she grew up, "family values" were "everything," and her father's response was predicated on the principle that "good" mothers would never make a "choice" that would land them behind bars and away from their children—a sentiment that illustrates how incarceration is still viewed as an individual issue, removed from the structural elements that funnel women into prison, especially in minority neighborhoods like Crystal's. For some, the stigma that comes with incarceration during pregnancy may be too much, and some may find themselves cut off from any familial support, threatening their ability to cope behind bars.

Maternal incarceration is laden with shame and stigma. Research finds that incarceration is counter to many prevailing ideas about what it means to be a good mother and places a unique burden on women to demonstrate their competency and fitness as a mother, especially in the wake of immense stigma.[63] Melody, now forty-nine and a White mother of six, shared how her family was especially upset with her because incarceration meant making a "choice" to distance herself from her children, disrupting the family unit. As Melody said, "When I told my family I was pregnant, they asked me, 'What the hell am I doing? You're pregnant, you already got kids out there, what was you doing? Why would you subject yourself and your kids and your unborn child to some crazy shit like that and then end up going to prison for it?' They lost total and utter respect for me, but it was like a wakeup call, it scares you." Melody went on to share how her family had an entirely different response when her brother went to prison and became separated from his own children, for his incarceration was not viewed by their family as being as damning as hers. Melody's encounter illustrates the gender inequalities and double standards that exist when mothers are separated from their children, especially in more middle-class circles that adhere to the intensive-mothering paradigm that expects women to always be present and available for their children, while dads are not held to these same rigid standards.[64]

The framing of incarceration as a choice, especially during pregnancy, means that those I interviewed were eager to cast off this stigma and prove to others, and to an extent themselves, that incarceration would *not* adversely affect their pregnancy. If anything, after those I interviewed settled into the idea of pregnancy, all shared how they would use their time behind bars to become a *better* mother by focusing on their pregnancy in a controlled and safe environment and engaging in activities that would optimize their chances of having a healthy pregnancy, including parenting classes, peer support groups, cessation of drug use, and consumption of nutritious foods—issues I discuss in chapters 2 and 3.[65] For some, these were practices they would not have otherwise been able to access beyond prison because of the trappings of poverty in their communities. To that end, some of those in extreme poverty felt that prison was the best place to be during pregnancy because they could lean into these resources and focus on their health and pregnancy— something that was made possible by this newfound "clean slate."

Birth Fathers

In assessing their biggest aspirations and desires for their unborn baby in the wake of pregnancy, some women in more middle-class circles spoke about the desire to have a more traditional nuclear family, complete with the presence of a loving father who could be a source of support. However, for most of the women I interviewed, while they said that in an ideal world, they would love to have a coparent to provide support during pregnancy, they were not concerned about their ability to parent without a partner, for most had grown up in families and communities where single parenting was the norm and marriage as an institution was rare, a reality that has been documented in other research that shows marriage is more prevalent among those with more wealth.[66]

Still, there were those who still yearned to provide their baby with the best foundation possible, and for some that meant navigating a relationship with the birth father, even if they were not romantically involved. However, for many, the ability to give their unborn baby an engaged father was already off the table for a variety of reasons, including not knowing the identity of the father—a source of stigma, especially among those who worked in the sex industry. In other cases, the idea of having a clean slate meant making tough choices about the scope of involvement with their baby's father and entailed coming to terms with the potential of being pregnant with no social support at all.

Among my participants, decisions about whether to disclose a pregnancy to the father, particularly in the wake of stigma from family members, are also complex and only grow in complexity as women consider the long-term implications of coparenting. Those in a committed, healthy relationship were more likely to view their pregnancy in a favorable light and have an easier time coming to terms with their pregnancy, for a partner may provide important emotional support and, in some cases, even help to shoulder some of the foreseeable costs of childrearing, though this tends to be a finding more common among those in the middle class. Still, in most cases, it is a rarity for fathers to be involved at all. About half of my participants said they had no idea who the father was, making it impossible to receive any financial or emotional support from him. Those who do not know the father or who are not in a healthy relationship with him may have a harder time coping with both their pregnancy and their incarceration. In some cases, the birth father may be a codefendant, negating the ability to have any communication, for court proceedings may prohibit codefendants from having communication with each other. Some of the women I interviewed said they felt sad knowing their baby would grow up not knowing the identity of the father, in part because they were all too familiar with the hardships of growing up without a father, presenting difficulties for those wanting to provide their unborn baby with more than they ever had growing up.

Not wanting their baby to grow up without a father, some disclosed that they had considered trying to learn the identity of the father in the wake of their incarceration and pregnancy, if only so their baby could have some resolution later in life. Still, simply knowing the identity does not always mean that this person even wanted to be in the picture. In some cases, the women I interviewed were glad that the father was absent, for they feared that his presence would only complicate matters, a finding that held true across race and class. Several participants were forthright and said that their baby's father was not a "good person," which was typically code for involvement in either drugs or crime. In some cases, it meant he was an abuser. Therefore, they were especially careful about the people they allowed into their life during pregnancy, for they did not want any negative energy adversely affecting their pregnancy—a sentiment that illustrates how seriously women take this newfound fresh start.

Incarcerated pregnant women may be caught between a "rock and a hard place," for while they may want their baby to grow up with a father, they also did not want this person to be around if he was on drugs or involved in crime, both for their baby's sake and because this could signal further intrusion from surveilling institutions of control, including the child welfare system. These women talked openly about their fears that a relationship or even an association with their unborn baby's father could invite intrusion from law enforcement or "DCF" (state department of children and families), especially in cases where the father was already under a surveilling lens of control by the criminal legal system.

Others feared that simply communicating with the father could invite additional forms of surveillance and control, positioning them as targets of the child welfare system, which had the power to threaten their reunification plans after prison. The fear of the child welfare system was widespread and especially pronounced among women of color, highlighting how the child welfare system acts as a carceral system, especially for low-income families of color—an issue I explore throughout the text and especially in chapter 3. For other women, the father of their unborn baby may also be incarcerated, making it impossible to stay connected, for in most facilities the incarcerated are barred from having contact with other incarcerated people.[67] In some ways, having no communication with the father was a strategy some used to proactively guard their heart from pain and suffering, knowing more was soon to come. To my best knowledge, no research has been conducted with fathers of babies born to incarcerated women who were pregnant behind bars, making the need for research and greater understanding all the more pressing.

Conclusion

Incarceration during pregnancy is far from what most women envision for their life, yet this is the reality for thousands of women each year. Starting their journeys as pregnant women behind bars means coming to terms with a new reality and identity as an expectant mother (in prison). The backgrounds and stories of those who are incarcerated during pregnancy are all different and marked by the particulars of their experiences; however, the growth of women's imprisonment reflects the degree to which carcerality is present in society. In the United States, the flourishing of punishment, domination, and control, coupled with a lack of a safety net, means that women are funneled into the criminal legal system, where reproduction and carcerality collide, making them especially vulnerable to the maternal web of control and the multiple interlocking social forces that converge to regulate and disrupt pregnancy, birth, and motherhood.

This maternal web of control is present from the very moment a pregnancy and the penal system intersect. For many, this is at the point of a positive pregnancy test. As indicated earlier, many may not even know they are pregnant until they come to prison and are issued a pregnancy test. Others may not learn of their pregnancy until well into their incarceration—an issue that complicates the ability to receive timely care and resources and to seek an abortion if desired.

Following news of a pregnancy, women may experience a range of emotions as they process and cope with their pregnancy and incarceration. While many are already mothers, for most, the experience of being pregnant *during* incarceration is a new matter entirely and one that requires tremendous navigation. The way women come to terms with their pregnancy is certainly dependent on their background and lived experiences. Low-income women are more likely to frame their incarceration as not all that surprising, for they had already grown accustomed to the presence of punitive systems of control from a young age. For those in extreme poverty, incarceration means access to healthcare, food, and other essentials needed for pregnancy that may not be accessible to them on the streets. Those with a more middle-class background had a different take on their pregnancy and incarceration, for they are less accustomed to carceral systems and do not view the prison system as a place of refuge but rather as a place that threatens their health and pregnancy.

Above all, the early period of pregnancy means the beginnings of being subject to the maternal web of control, devoid of choice and autonomy, where intrusive agents of control pry into their pregnancy and plans for parenting. Additionally, being incarcerated means that the ability to exercise choice is highly regulated, as the bureaucracy and control found in prisons makes it difficult if not impossible to obtain an abortion—a reality that reflects larger social forces wherein criminal punishment is no longer confined to incarceration but instead extends further, holding women captive in their own body.

The incarceration of pregnant women also affects families. For many, it is not unusual to experience shame, stigma, or even open hostility about the news of pregnancy behind bars. There is a tremendous source of stigma attached not only to maternal incarceration but to pregnancy, further channeling women deeper into a web of control. The extent to which women experience stigma is highly dependent on the intersection of their identities, as families in extreme poverty may experience relief, for incarceration means access to basic needs that are essential to pregnancy. Still, many engage in practices to resist this stigma by making a commitment to be the best mother possible for their unborn baby, and that entails making careful decisions about whether to engage with birth fathers. The degree to which birth fathers are involved varies widely and is dependent on several factors that affect communication behind bars, including the nature of their relationship and any criminal involvement the father may have. Even behind bars, pregnancy remains a transformative period for many, as women take their pregnancy seriously and have a vested interest in their health, desiring to optimize pregnancy and birth outcomes—an issue I explore in the next chapter.

2

The Unruly Maternal Body

Struggles to Be Heard

Once you're pregnant, it changes you. It changes your whole mindset about things.
—Melody

Destiny, a thirty-two-year-old, biracial woman, was pregnant with her first child when she was sentenced to prison on drug charges. Although this was her first time in prison, she had been to jail before on a couple of different occasions and grew up with alcoholic parents who were no strangers to the criminal legal system. To say that her childhood and adolescence were rough would be an understatement. Physical, mental, and sexual abuse at the hands of her father was not uncommon, even though both her parents were out of the picture much of the time due to their own incarceration. As a teen, she did not have much of a support system and had no real job or money to her name, forcing her to stay with friends and distant relatives.

To dull the pain, Destiny began experimenting with drugs, first with marijuana and then later turning to harder drugs and eventually petty theft to support her drug habits. Before she knew it, she was getting high nearly every other night. During her cocaine binges, she would go days without eating and sleeping. Hallucinations and delusions became more frequent, leaving her so out of touch with reality that it took considerable time for her to even realize she was pregnant.

When Destiny first found out about the pregnancy, she planned on having an abortion, so she had not given much thought to her own health and continued to use drugs. As Destiny explained, "When you're using, it's a whole other world. I'm not thinking about dates, my health or anything like that—God forbid I wasn't thinking about my baby or being pregnant. I was too busy using." Already on probation and high on drugs, she did not even notice that law enforcement had constructed a sting operation near a local bridge scene—the same place where Destiny purchased drugs. It was near the end of her first trimester when she, along with several others, was arrested and later sent to prison.

When Destiny came to prison, she soon realized the abortion she had been counting on was not happening at all. For one thing, she was very impoverished and had no means of covering the procedure, let alone working knowledge about how to navigate the red tape that comes with an abortion in a correctional setting.[1] With no real choice but to continue the pregnancy, her thoughts then shifted to how she would manage her pregnancy and motherhood. In the words of Destiny, "I was scared. I honestly didn't know what I was gonna do. My whole world was drugs and getting in trouble and that's all that I knew at this point, so when I got to prison it just kinda set in knowing, 'Oh my gosh I'm about to bring a child into this world, how am I gonna do this?' Just playing it through my mind and realizing I'm not where I need to be, but what choice do I have at this point, you know? I'm gonna have this baby, so I better get my shit together."

Destiny, like so many of the women I interviewed, felt that pregnancy, in conjunction with incarceration, resulted in a "wake up call" or turning point causing her to commit to a new prosocial identity of mother. In envisioning motherhood and their hopes and dreams for their unborn babies, a commitment to desistance and prioritization of health were paramount. The prioritization of health stems from both the surveillance of the maternal body and an awareness of a symbiotic relationship between maternal and fetal health outcomes. Although many of the women I interviewed had been pregnant before and some had also been incarcerated before, this was the first time that these two worlds collided for my participants, and it was this particular *intersection*, which some described as "rock bottom," that provided the motivation to strive for improved health, particularly in the wake of stigma from family, who conflated their incarceration, especially during pregnancy, with poor parenting.

This chapter focuses on how incarceration during pregnancy acts as a turning point and a transformative period for pregnant women to reflect on their maternal health and make improvements for the betterment of their baby. A central theme is the desistance of drugs, the consumption of nutritious foods, and a commitment to prioritizing prenatal healthcare. However, throughout the chapter, I show how despite women's best efforts to engage in these practices, pregnant bodies are still heavily regulated and controlled, especially behind bars, where their health is at the mercy of carceral systems of control, making it difficult for them to make many improvements to their health and often perpetuating the same disadvantages found in their communities.

The central argument of this chapter is that the maternal web of control negates the ability to make positive changes to health, for the bodies of pregnant women in prison are heavily regulated and controlled, governed by archaic laws, policies, and practices unique to each state and correctional facility, *in addition* to the policies and practices found in the medical system that prisons partner with during pregnancy. The maternal web of control and its hold on women mean that an emphasis on regulation and order often results in limited care, posing a threat to health. In the wake of fetal-protection laws, as mentioned earlier, the stakes are higher than ever for women to have a healthy pregnancy.

Pregnancy and Prison as a Turning Point

Incarcerated women are often in poor health before coming to prison.[2] Like Destiny, many have experienced some form of generational trauma and various forms of abuse.[3] Poor nutrition, undiagnosed and untreated mental health issues, including bipolar disorder, schizophrenia, and depression, in addition to sexually transmitted diseases may be especially prevalent.[4] Participants talked openly about their struggles with addiction and substance-abuse disorders, and many confided that it had been years since they had seen a doctor—and not by choice either. Much has been written about how access to healthcare is tied to socioeconomic status and how the growing healthcare deserts often found in rural communities limit access to care.[5] Thus, it is not surprising that concerns about poor health quickly follow the news of a pregnancy, driving many to exercise change. This prioritization of health reflects existing cultural narratives that emphasize the importance of health during pregnancy for *all* women, even those who are not incarcerated.[6] As mentioned, just as motherhood is subject to scrutiny, pregnancy is also a site of public surveillance.

Research reveals how even women who are not incarcerated have their pregnancy and motherhood policed—a finding that is especially true for more marginalized women already scrutinized by the criminal legal system and the child welfare system. Sociologists Kathryn Edin and Maria Kefalas describe this process in their book *Promises I Can Keep: Why Poor Women Put Motherhood before Marriage*:[7] "Overnight, her behavior must alter dramatically 'for the sake of the baby.' Even if she does not have the internal drive to make this transformation, the physical evidence her own body provides soon activates a powerful set of social expectations. Suddenly, the penalty for indulging in a drink at the neighborhood bar or a night spent hanging out on the corner with friends is steep, for she must endure the piercing social censure contained in the disapproving glances and contemptuous whispers of acquaintances and strangers alike."

Consistent with Edin and Kefalas's research, every woman I interviewed spoke to the importance of health during pregnancy and the need to reprioritize their health "for the sake of the baby." Many shared detailed descriptions of their attempts to commit to a nutritious diet or exercise regimen and the strong desire to stop using drugs. In some ways, the cultural norms that expect women to modify their health "for the betterment of their unborn baby," including refraining from smoking and drinking and the consumption of nutritious foods, were internalized and reinforced by both the prison system and other carceral systems that scrutinize and surveil the pregnancies of those behind bars.[8]

Pregnancy under Surveillance

For some, the desire and motivation to make changes was born out of these systems of surveillance, for the punishments are steep for those who do not take an interest in their health. Many of the women I interviewed were worried that their poor health would mean that their baby would be born with a disability and that they would be held criminally responsible or that an unhealthy baby would be grounds for loss of custody and the possibility of additional prison time, particularly in the wake of fetal-protection laws that criminalize harm to fetuses. Jasmine said, "I didn't want to have this baby and the state to take it, so I was thinking more about I need to get healthier. I need to take care of myself 'cause now it's not just me, so if I wasn't pregnant, I wouldn't have even thought about those type of things like getting my life together. So, by me being pregnant I had to stop and think I don't want this baby to be in CPS.[9] I don't want it to be in the system." Jasmine's narrative highlights the web of control and the policing that mark women's bodies both inside and outside of prison.[10] While her desire to become healthy was grounded in wanting the best for her baby, it was also in response to a fear of carceral systems and the potential loss of parenting rights.

The policing of women's bodies during pregnancy is an ongoing process that begins with increased scrutiny, where every move is heavily monitored, as noted in Edin and Kefalas's research and through the responses from loved ones, as discussed in the last chapter.[11] Not only are those in prison already under immense scrutiny by the prison system and its multiple forms of surveillance, including by both correctional staff and technocratic forms of video surveillance, but their health is also heavily monitored by the medical system, which acts as a carceral system.

The medical system monitors the pregnancies of women through several tests and exams, taking in a range of numerical data that can later be used against them. The medical system is also fraught with a number of power dynamics, where power and authority remain in the hands of medical staff and women are subjugated to the role of patient.[12] Not only are women monitored by authority figures, but they are also monitored through multiple forms of technocratic surveillance, such as fetal monitors, ultrasonography, and blood pressure screening, to name but a few forms.[13] These elements reinforce the constant surveillance found in a panopticon environment, as women are subjected to the maternal web of control—a network or web of powerful surveillance initiated by both the prison system and its extensions.

These forms of hypersurveillance illustrate the varied ways in which carcerality proliferates. As discussed in the preface, the laws governing reproduction and health are aplenty, and health and pregnancy must fit within narrowly defined boxes, particularly amid a model of medicine that pathologizes pregnancy and allows for little deviation from expected norms.[14]

Accordingly, any instance of subpar health during pregnancy or of failure to seek prenatal care is met with punishment not only from the criminal legal system but also through the healthcare system—for women both within and beyond the prison system. These penalties are grounded in fetal-protection laws that criminalize and punish women for any harm to fetuses, including but not limited to maternal substance abuse and even abortion; cases of miscarriage and stillbirth may also be subject to punishment, criminalizing women for even the slightest instances of poor maternal health.[15] From 1973 to 2005 alone, there were "413 arrests or equivalent actions depriving pregnant women of their physical liberty."[16] Among these arrests are cases where pregnant women were deemed to be unfit or otherwise in poor health: those on drugs were charged with child abuse, and those who failed to seek prenatal care were charged with negligence.[17] Under these laws, even those who experience a miscarriage or stillbirth may be charged with fetal homicide.[18] Women of color and those in poverty are more likely to have their health scrutinized, resulting in further regulation and control, reinforcing the need to prioritize health.[19]

These fetal-protection laws have dramatically altered the ways in which the criminal legal system and the healthcare system operate; their convergence creates a web of control that regulates and limits women's ability to seek care, which ultimately threatens both maternal and fetal health. While framed as coming from a place of concern and care, fetal-protection laws have had profound consequences for women, especially women of color, who are more likely to have their health scrutinized. Consequently, those at the center of oppressive forces may be especially guarded and committed to an improvement in health, for even a miscarriage may be misconstrued as deliberate, criminal, and intentional.

Intersectionality in Health Improvements

The convergence of identity markers, such as race, class, age, family status, and so forth, affects the depth and extent to which women make improvements to their health in the wake of carceral forces. Those who come to prison already in good health may be less concerned about how their *health* would negatively impact their pregnancy and more concerned about the toll *incarceration* takes on health, fearing that incarceration would negatively impact otherwise good maternal-fetal and infant health outcomes.

Consistent with research, the White and middle-class women I interviewed were in better health than women of color and those in extreme poverty—a finding that reveals how health and access to care are tied closely to class and race, especially in the United States, where access to and affordability of healthcare are viewed as privileges rather than rights.[20] Additionally, these women were also less familiar with prison and incarceration, making them especially fearful that their incarceration would adversely affect their health.

Concerns about incarceration are grounded in research showing that the incarcerated face a greater risk of adverse health conditions and infectious diseases than the general population, with new research revealing that incarceration reduces life expectancy and has detrimental effects on physical, mental, and emotional health.[21] Behind bars, access to healthcare is limited, and the stress of incarceration, especially during pregnancy, can exacerbate existing health problems, such as hypertension and diabetes.[22] The COVID-19 pandemic is but one example of how incarceration adversely affects health, with people in prison being five times more likely to test positive for COVID-19 than the general population.[23] The effects of incarceration on health are widespread and continue to affect people long after their release from prison, as indicated through their reduced life expectancy, providing insight into the importance of health during pregnancy.[24]

Having been pregnant before, Melody was well versed in pregnancy and knew the importance of proper prenatal care for improved birth outcomes. In her eyes, the care behind bars was in stark contrast to what she had on the outside, inciting worries that her incarceration would pose a threat to her health. According to Melody,

> Once you're pregnant, it changes you. It changes your whole mindset about things. All of a sudden, it's like, okay, I have to be careful what I eat. I have to make sure I get the adequate amount of sleep. I can't do this. I can't do that. And so, I tried to be very careful, knowing that it's not just you, that there is a baby on the inside of you. So, then it's like, is prison the best environment for me to get sleep, eat healthy? The healthcare in there, let's just say it's not healthcare. I never would have chosen the crap I had to eat, so I was trying to take care of myself, trying to stay calm and not let it stress me out.

Marissa, an Asian, twenty-four-year-old mother of two, shared how in her last pregnancy, she spent considerable time researching the best obstetricians and studying the best exercise regimens and nutritious foods to consume, only to then spend this pregnancy in a place with substandard care devoid of any choice. According to Marissa, "My first thought was that I wasn't going to be receiving the right medical attention. My family felt bad for me. They didn't think I was going to be receiving the correct medical attention and were very worried about my well-being."

Melody's and Marissa's time behind bars and their assessment of their care in prison are tied to their social positioning and their expectations regarding what prenatal care *should* be. In Melody's case, not only did incarceration amplify her stress and remove her from her trusted healthcare provider and support system, but it also limited her ability to consume nutritious foods—a point I discuss later in the chapter. Their narratives illustrate how incarceration itself controls the bodies and health of women through limitations on their autonomy and restrictions on their ability to fuel themselves through nutritious food and proper healthcare and avoid an environment of shouting, commotion, and loud noises that threaten optimal sleep—all essentials for a healthy pregnancy.

The various rules and regulations in place at each facility are structured to support security, with health as an afterthought. The fact that prison count times occur at multiple points per day, well into the evenings and early mornings, illustrates how sleep alone is devalued, despite calls from the American College of Obstetricians and Gynecologists and other leading medical organizations about the importance of sleep during pregnancy.[25] These examples explain how the bodies of pregnant women are punished not just for their criminality but also for their fertility, trapping women into a web of control with lasting consequences.

As discussed in the last chapter, some women experience relief when they are sent to prison because of the food, healthcare, and other essentials that prison provides. Many of these women talked about how they "wanted better" and wished to provide their then unborn baby with more than they ever had growing up—economically, emotionally, healthily, and otherwise. Some even said they were "grateful" to be incarcerated because it meant finally having the time and space to prioritize their health, which is something they were unable to do in the streets, where their concerns were grounded in survival needs—even hypothesizing that incarceration was all part of a "higher plan" or divine order, a sentiment that illustrates the spiritual undertones that permeate rural, conservative pockets, as discussed in the last chapter. The persistence of poverty and even spirituality make it easier for the maternal web of control to operate, as the loss of autonomy is framed as an orchestration from a higher power to have basic needs met rather than as reproductive oppression.

Destiny became excited about the prospect of improved maternal and fetal health outcomes made possible through incarceration because this was the first time in a "long time" when she did not have to think about where she would be staying each night or where she would find food for each day, significantly lowering her stress levels. It was also the first time she had ever had a multivitamin and had access to reliable healthcare and drug treatment. As Destiny explained, "I was healthier when I was in there [prison] because I actually got a lot of sleep and vitamins and prenatals and that kind of thing. I took all that while I was there, so I was probably healthier there than if I wouldn't have been. I probably got more care while I was incarcerated than I did out on the street because I didn't have a doctor or anything like that. I was always running and trying to hustle up money." Similarly, Lacey spoke about how being incarcerated during pregnancy was an "unexpected blessing" because incarceration is what allowed her to obtain resources, including food and prenatal care, optimizing her chances of having a healthy baby. Before coming to prison, Lacey had been homeless and often stayed under a bridge, where she "got high every night." Given her extensive criminal record, the judge who sentenced her did not hesitate to send her to prison *because* she was pregnant and living on the margins. According to Lacey, the judge even said, "I'm going to sentence you to [prison], so we can make sure that baby gets prenatal care." According to Lacey, "Had I not been incarcerated, for sure my son would have been born with cocaine in his system, and I would have been involved with CPS, so it was a blessing in disguise. My mom was even relieved because I wasn't out on the street anymore. I was somewhere safe. They would rather me be locked up than out on the corner doing God knows what, so they were very relieved."

These narratives reveal how race and class converge, affecting access to basic needs and other health essentials. Destiny (a biracial woman) and Lacey (a Black woman) were in poverty before they came to prison, living on the margins with little to no safety net, so their prisons acted as safety nets. Their experiences contrasted with Melody's (a White woman) and Marissa's (an Asian woman), who came from a more middle-class background and were accustomed to quality care in their communities. For them, their care behind bars was woefully inadequate and they were less likely to mention the need to make radical changes to their health, for their concerns were more grounded in maintaining their already good health in an environment known to harm health.

Time to Stop Using

The cessation of drug use, as a component of improved health, is paramount. About 70 percent of women in prison have a history of drug abuse, and new research reveals that 26 percent of incarcerated pregnant women have opioid use disorder.[26] Consistent with these findings, most in my study had used drugs at some point during pregnancy. While many had tried to stop using on their own, their addiction had a powerful hold on them. Although some had been pregnant before and some had even been incarcerated before, it was the unique intersection of pregnancy and incarceration that acted as a turning point in their journey to quit using.

Stigma of Drugs

The strong cultural norms regarding the behaviors of women during pregnancy encourage and even expect women to cease drugs during pregnancy, invoking much fear in those who do not. Health concerns and the threat of losing parental rights were motivation for most of the women I interviewed. Most worried that their baby would be born addicted to drugs or have a physical or mental disability, and this compelled them to want to quit using.

Yet, the lack of affordable and accessible treatment programs, specifically designed for those in pregnancy, particularly in rural regions where specialized care is even more sparse, means that some may turn to the criminal legal system, believing that imprisonment is the best way to access care to ensure a healthy pregnancy. Amanda, a White, forty-six-year-old mother of five, was on drugs with a warrant out for her arrest when she found out she was pregnant. Although she tried to quit on her own several times, her addiction was stronger. Amanda explained, "You see, I was a shitty mom to my other kids by leaving them for drugs." Adamant about wanting to "get things right" this time around, she intentionally turned herself in to law enforcement to access treatment programs behind bars. According to Amanda, "I was on drugs, and it was really hard to quit. I tried to quit on my own first, but then that's why I turned myself in so I wouldn't harm my baby. I just did what was best for her, well for me too."

Some women like Amanda, with no way to quit on their own in the community, view correctional institutions as ideal environments in which to get clean, crediting correctional facilities as places that offer treatment, structure, and support. As Amanda explained, drugs are a contraband and not permitted in correctional institutions, and while they definitely still make their way behind bars, some argue that they are more difficult to obtain in prison than in the communities they call home, making the urge to use more difficult to satisfy.[27] Incarceration can also make it easier to sever ties with friends who are known drug users, helping to reduce the urge to use. However, the most standard approach for care during pregnancy behind bars entails medication, including methadone and buprenorphine.[28] Yet, research reveals that most prisons are ill equipped to provide pregnant women on drugs with the medications and supports they need to get clean—despite medical research revealing that it is safe to use medication for opioid use disorder during pregnancy.[29] Although women may express the desire and motivation to cease drugs, they may not be given adequate supports behind bars.

Drug treatment programs in prisons have experienced substantial cutbacks in state funding over the years, further complicating women's ability to access care and make improvements to their health. Beyond treatment, prisons can offer specialized peer support groups for women wanting to get clean; however, the decision to attend peer support groups is complicated because of the stigma attached to drug use during pregnancy, even behind bars.[30] Also, the availability and quality of programs and support groups vary widely across institutions, for each prison has differing levels of funding, resources, support, and staff.[31]

While each prison has its own unique subculture, Jasmine shared how it was not unusual for the pregnant women on her floor to be ostracized by other women in prison for using drugs during pregnancy. As Jasmine explained, "They [the other women and staff] was talking about me and felt like I didn't care for my baby with the drugs and stuff, like why I couldn't get it together before, why did it take going to prison being pregnant, being the lowest in there to change."[32]

The stigma attached to drug addiction during pregnancy, even in carceral settings where drug use is common, is a reflection of the stigma and regulation attached to pregnant women on drugs even among those who are not incarcerated.[33] This stigma is reflected in the "crack baby epidemic" in the United States, in which Black babies exposed to drugs in utero were thought to be born with mental and physical disabilities and addicted to drugs. This "epidemic" was expected to create a surge in the number of people addicted to drugs, overwhelming schools, hospitals, and social services and creating a permanent "underclass" in inner cities. Although this prediction was later deemed to be unfounded, it provides insight into how pregnant women on drugs, especially Black women, are vilified during pregnancy.[34]

Drug Testing

The stigma and legal punishments attached to drug use during pregnancy often threaten the ability to get needed care and to access treatment programs, making it more difficult to quit using and funneling women deeper into a web of carceral control, particularly amid fetal-protection laws that punish those with substance abuse issues.[35] The particulars of how this happens begin with drug testing. During pregnancy, incarcerated women and nonincarcerated women alike are routinely asked to give samples of their urine to healthcare providers to screen for health complications like preeclampsia, urinary tract infections, and diabetes.[36] Yet, a component of these tests also includes screening for drugs. Under a medical system that works alongside the prison system, any traces of drugs may be used to further punish and criminalize women.[37]

This hesitancy to seek prenatal care during pregnancy due to the fear of a drug screening illustrates the power of the maternal web of control and the ways in which carcerality has become increasingly embedded in the medical system, creating a web of surveillance and control over women and their families.[38] As a result, women may avoid encounters with the medical system, further compromising both maternal and fetal health—a finding that has been documented in other research.[39]

While drug tests may be performed throughout pregnancy, perhaps the ultimate fear is the drug testing of the baby at birth. Many feared that if they did not stop using, their baby would also test positive for drugs, cascading further surveillance and intervention from the child welfare system, which works alongside the courts to initiate the termination of parental rights, with the power to impose additional prison time onto their sentence. These concerns are not unfounded, for in the United States, mothers may be charged with additional crimes, such as child endangerment or other forms of abuse, in the event that their baby tests positive for drugs at birth, setting into motion the termination of parental rights and the potential for additional prison time.[40]

Furthermore, under the Adoption and Safe Families Act (ASFA, enacted in 1997), custodial rights may be stripped if a parent is not physically present for fifteen of the preceding twenty-two months (including because of incarceration), which means that women may be at risk of losing their children when their sentence exceeds fifteen months.[41] While the ASFA was intended to reduce the time frame and number of children in foster care by placing them in more permanent homes, a consequence is that it has torn apart hundreds of thousands of families, including those touched by maternal incarceration.[42] Although the ASFA and the practice of drug testing infants may be framed as coming from a place of care and protection, the ASFA is also laced with regulation and control, creating adverse consequences for pregnant women.

Women of color are more likely to experience this maternal web of control, in part because of the racial disparities embedded in the medical complex. Although pregnant women across all backgrounds are potentially screened for drugs at healthcare appointments, Black women are more likely to have their urine samples tested for drugs than their White counterparts (at a rate of 11.3 percent in comparison to 4.2 percent among Whites).[43] They are also more likely to face "legal consequences for prenatal drug use, including incarceration and the loss of custody of their child immediately postpartum."[44] These startling disparities illustrate how structural gendered racism is nestled within the healthcare system, the child welfare system, and the prison system, creating a web of control over women and their families.

Still, even with support, quitting drugs is far from easy, and not everyone is able to quit entirely. Those on harder drugs like cocaine or methamphetamines are more likely to struggle with quitting and may turn to softer drugs like marijuana instead. Some may be unable to quit at all and instead may make improvements in their health in other ways. Barbara, a Black, twenty-nine-year-old, self-described "crack addict," was pregnant with her fifth child when she came to prison. She tried to quit drugs as soon as she learned she was pregnant but quickly realized her drug addiction was stronger. Unable to quit or limit crack, she did "everything else" in her pregnancy. For Barbara, "everything else" entailed implementing practices to limit her stress, eating healthily, and exercising regularly, for she hoped to do everything in her power to offset her drug use.

Finding Food

Central to concerns about health during pregnancy is the importance of nutrition. Leading medical organizations have made clear that proper nutrition is critical for optimal maternal-fetal and newborn health.[45] Yet, despite calls for nutritious foods during pregnancy, no national standards specifically addressing the nutritional needs of incarcerated people, including pregnant women, exist.[46] Even the National Commission on Correctional Health Care fails to provide specific information about the nutritional needs of pregnant women—a concerning matter that illustrates how correctional institutions are ill equipped to provide for the unique nutritional needs of women during pregnancy.[47]

Inadequate Nutrition

A lack of control over food during pregnancy is yet another example of how the bodies of pregnant women are controlled behind bars. In the United States, there is no universal law or policy that governs the health and nutritional needs of women across all fifty states. As a result, health matters may be decided not by those in the maternal health field but instead by the prison system—a system that has no training in or understanding of the unique nutritional needs during pregnancy and has no financial incentive to make nutritious foods accessible.[48] In many ways, the various rules and regulations of the prison system severely limit access to sufficient and nutrient-rich foods, leaving many women to go hungry. Although pregnant women in prison may be focused on the optimization of health outcomes, including having a strong desire to consume nutrient-rich foods, their ability to consume these foods is limited.

The consequences of inadequate nutrition are profound, greatly undermining women's ability to have a healthy pregnancy. Furthermore, in a country that regulates and penalizes poor health during pregnancy, any signs of poor health may be used as justification for further punishment, ultimately locking women more deeply into a web of control, where they are devoid of choice and subjected to further harm. A central aspect of the maternal web of control is that women experience oversight and regulation from both the prison system and its affiliates, including the medical system and the child welfare system—as described previously. These entities work in concert with each other to scrutinize the health of women during pregnancy, especially in places that have fetal-protection laws, where inadequate nutrition during pregnancy may be grounds for charges of child endangerment.[49]

Additionally, the restrictions on food behind bars place women at risk for a number of health concerns. Research finds that poor diet during pregnancy has been linked to adverse birth outcomes that can impede brain development, resulting in a low birth weight, neural tube defects, and even preterm birth—issues that are all concerning, especially given that many incarcerated pregnant women are already food insecure and in poor health before coming to prison.[50] In the absence of national standards governing the nutritional needs of pregnant women in prison, some states have implemented their own policies and practices; however, thirty-one states currently lack any policy or guidelines.[51] Even states that have outlined provisions for the nutritional care of pregnant women have vague and ambiguous policies, leaving much room for inadequacies.[52] At the time of this writing, California is the only state to provide *detailed* guidelines regarding food for incarcerated pregnant women—a fact that reflects (again) how prisons are not equipped to care for the unique needs of women and pregnant women in particular.[53]

Unsurprisingly, very few of the women I interviewed were incarcerated in facilities that provided clear guidance about nutritional needs during pregnancy. Some facilities may provide a "pregnancy snack," in addition to three meals a day; however, these snacks are still largely inadequate to meet the recommendations set forth by leading medical institutions, often consisting of a single carton of milk and on occasion an extra piece of fruit.[54] Even then, access to a snack may be highly controlled, dependent on staff and the availability of food on any given day, further illustrating how even in the wake of a desire to have a healthy pregnancy, the lack of nutritious food behind bars threatens women's ability to make improvements to their health, often adversely affecting their likelihood of having a healthy pregnancy.

Tiana, a Black, twenty-seven-year-old mother of four, said, "I was kinda upset with them [correctional staff] because when you're pregnant and incarcerated, you're supposed to get three meals a day *and* the snack, but sometimes they just didn't. When they forgot to give me snacks, I just went without." Tiana's narrative is important because it shows how even in facilities with specific rules governing the care and treatment of pregnant women, these rules are not always followed.

In a study examining the nutritional needs of prisoners in South Carolina, researchers found that the food served in South Carolina correctional facilities failed to meet the recommended dietary needs for women during pregnancy, including the absence of fruits, vegetables, and milk; in other instances, the food contained higher amounts of sodium, sugar, and cholesterol than what is recommended.[55] These findings are not surprising, given that South Carolina spends just $1.13 *per* prisoner per *day* on meals.[56] When one considers the more specialized nutritional needs for pregnant prisoners, the findings from the South Carolina study are even more alarming.

A lack of autonomy with respect to food and health is a concern, especially to women like Gloria, who, prior to prison, had the means to access sufficient and nutritious food with relative ease. Much of Gloria's narrative centered on the frustration and lack of control she felt over being in a place that offered classes and books about pregnancy and childbirth emphasizing the importance of proper nutrition during pregnancy and yet limited access to nutritious food. As Gloria explained, "I read the books and everything from the library about what all you should be doing and then I wasn't able to do that. So, it was kinda nerve-racking to me 'cause like you should be drinking this much milk and you should be eating vegetables, and I'm like they should really have vegetables and milk on commissary or give us that balanced fruit or something. But they didn't bother to care, you just had to live with it, so it brought on a lot of anxiety because I definitely did not get what I should have." As with all matters, the nutritional experiences of pregnant women in prison are tied to their background. While Gloria was upset that she did not have sufficient and nutritious food, others may be grateful to have food at all—regardless of whether it was healthy or adequate.

Serena was thirty-two when she came to prison pregnant with her fourth child; a Black, single mother of young children, she was extremely impoverished and struggled to provide food for her family. In Serena's words, "I was very malnourished when I come in. With my other pregnancies I be out on the streets lookin' for food, this one I be locked up eating a lot of food. So yeah, it was good to not have to worry about food in there."

As related earlier, some of the women I interviewed turned to the prison system to have their basic needs met after learning they were pregnant, highlighting how prisons have become places of refuge amid extreme poverty and the absence of a robust safety net. Prior to her incarceration, Jasmine worked as a sex worker and shared how she struggled just to get by, growing hungrier by the day. When Jasmine learned of her pregnancy, she knew that her work would grow increasingly difficult, making the search for food more daunting as her pregnancy progressed. Although the food was worse than what she expected, it was better than no food at all. Others who intentionally turned to the prison system for their basic needs found that it was worse than expected or still insufficient to meet the specific nutritional needs of pregnancy. Kia, a Black, twenty-four-year-old woman pregnant with her first child, talked about how the food at her particular prison was often inedible, heavily processed, and high in sodium, starch, and cholesterol—so much so that she lost weight. Her pregnancy eventually ended in a miscarriage, making her wonder still to this day whether the lack of sufficient and nutritious food was a contributing factor.

Perceptions of food and nutrition during pregnancy are intersectional. Those with more education and money may be especially critical about the food behind bars, for they tended to have a greater understanding about the importance of nutrition during pregnancy and were used to having some control over their food choices. Their narratives even focused on how incarceration limited the ability to have their pregnancy "cravings" fulfilled, a concern that went unmentioned by the more marginalized women I interviewed—an irony given that their economic background afforded them more freedom to have some choices in their food behind bars and to secure food in times of inadequacy. Their social positioning meant they were more likely to have loved ones send food care packages and place money on their commissary account, making it possible to purchase additional food, even if the food for sale behind bars is largely unhealthy, consisting mostly of bagged chips, candy, and cookies, and more expensive than what one might pay for the same item on the outside, with research reporting that prices may be five times higher behind bars.[57]

The inequities in prison that affect health are deep. Although incarcerated women can earn money through their work assignment, allowing them to purchase food in times of scarcity, the pay is often meager, and the gender pay gap persists even in prisons, making it even more difficult for women to earn money. Private industry companies that employ prisoners are less likely to have contractual agreements with women's facilities, in part because of the nature of the manual work involved and because women's prisons tend to be located in more rural areas, making any work assignments difficult for employers to oversee.[58] Pregnancy itself contributes to these inequities, as it is not a stretch to say that some facilities may bar those who are pregnant from working, making it difficult to earn any money and significantly limiting the means through which women can purchase items behind bars that could optimize their health, particularly amid little financial support from loved ones.

Collective Efforts to Find Food

The importance of nutrition during pregnancy was taken very seriously among my participants. All shared stories about their efforts to obtain food in times of scarcity, and many talked about how they relied on their peers and engaged in collective care through the creation of networks of support that offered avenues for sharing their food and commissary money or even the exchange of institutional knowledge and insight regarding roundabout ways of accessing food, including befriending someone who worked in the kitchen or requesting a work assignment in the kitchen, where it would be easier to obtain food. Peers may also offer institutional knowledge about which correctional officers are more lenient with prison rules regarding the stashing and trading of food, making it easier to obtain food.

While each facility is different and has its own unique subculture, Lacey provided insight into why at her prison, pregnant women benefit from a higher social status that granted her collective care from her peers, who would do what they could to ensure she did not go hungry. According to Lacey,

> Everybody treats the ones who are pregnant usually way better. Everybody's bringing you something to eat or something different because of the cravings. When you're pregnant, everybody's usually more willing to share with you. Like when we had baked potatoes, usually somebody would give me theirs. I might have two of those stashed or something to eat on another day if I didn't like. I had to make sure I had enough to eat, especially 'cause everything just kinda made me sick. You're not supposed to keep your food, of course, but some weeks I would sneak it depending on the guard.

Marissa offered insight into why so many women may be willing to come together to offer support during pregnancy. According to Marissa, "I think people feel sorry for the pregnant women in there, well for the baby that is. You were untouchable while you were pregnant. You gotta remember in prison there are women who have life sentences or are long termers, so when they see someone pregnant or a woman with a child, it opens a very soft spot for them because they haven't been around this type of circumstance for a while. If there's a woman who's pregnant or elderly, it's like a community coming together, everyone kinda helps that person." Marissa's narrative illustrates how punitive places can lead to the creation of support networks among the incarcerated to ensure basic needs are met during pregnancy.

Similarly, although Kia grew increasingly discouraged about her struggles to obtain food, she was particularly touched by the number of women who helped her out in times of scarcity in her journey to make improvements to her health. Kia said, "So many women were like, 'I'm gonna take you under my wing as a daughter or as a sister. I'm going to take care of you and make sure you're eating certain foods'—you know, offering their food and saying things like 'find a job in the kitchen 'cause you don't want to go without food.' I think it would be a lot harder if it was just me by myself." Stacy had a similar experience and shared how her cellmate, whom she referred to as her "guardian angel," helped her not only obtain food but also acclimate to both her pregnancy and her incarceration. Although Stacy was particularly close to her cellmate, not every woman is around others during pregnancy, for some may be housed in solitary confinement, locked into their cell for twenty-three hours or so a day, making it difficult or all but impossible to access support networks.

These narratives bring to light the ways in which women may resist the maternal web of control through collective action and through the circumvention of rules, especially in the absence of policies or provisions addressing the nutritional needs of pregnant women. Still, the subverting of prison rules through the stashing and sharing of food in times of pregnancy demonstrates how pregnant women are subjected to additional forms of punishment in ways that men are not. Although prisons are punitive places, particularly during pregnancy, they also contain countless examples of the human spirit, highlighting how women come together with others to resist the maternal web of control and provide collective care.

Prenatal Healthcare

Beyond the cessation of drugs and the acquiring of food, healthcare is essential for optimal pregnancy outcomes. Yet, the various rules and regulations that govern prisons mean that many pregnant women in prison may experience inadequate or delayed healthcare, as security is the leading concern. While leading organizations like the National Commission on Correctional Health Care (NCCHC) have outlined some health standards for pregnant women, including but not limited to the availability of prenatal care, assessment and treatment for mental health disorders, and lab work, correctional institutions are not required to adhere to these NCCHC pregnancy standards, leading to significant disparities in care.[59]

While some prisons are considered "model" institutions, complete with comprehensive prenatal and postpartum care, including doula care and dedicated lactation spaces, other facilities fail to provide women with the most basic care, forgoing specialized maternity care altogether.[60] Research from the Bureau of Justice Statistics reveals that only 54 percent of incarcerated pregnant women receive routine prenatal care in prison—a startling number that indicates the need for greater care during pregnancy.[61]

Even in places of routine medical care, women may still be unable to access care and must first be believed—an issue I expand upon throughout the chapter. Faye shared how her cries for help were dismissed by correctional officers because she did not have physical symptoms in the wake of a debilitating migraine. According to Faye, "To get medical attention in prison you either had to have an appendage coming off, gushing blood or damn near dying, literally, to get any kind of medical treatment or medical help. Because I was not throwing up or bleeding, they would not help me. They said, 'Go back to your unit, you're fine.'" Faye's experience illustrates how women must first be believed before they can be seen—a difficult feat given the power dynamics that keep women subjugated.

The inadequacies of maternal healthcare in prisons are a consequence of the maternal web of control, wherein the bodies of pregnant women in prison are held hostage, as security needs override health, and the red tape and bureaucracy inherent in total institutions like prisons means that access to health providers is regulated and controlled. According to Amanda, "The medical was always fighting the security, like that's always the fight. Medical can say what they want to say, but if security overrides it, then that's that. It's not supposed to be like that, medical is supposed to be the end-all be-all but obviously it's not." Amanda's narrative reveals the power of the penal system and how it governs the healthcare experiences of women.

Hurdles and Consequences of Medical Care

Many of the women I interviewed explained how accessing medical care behind bars involved filling out a medical request that would then need to be approved by correctional staff before they were able to see a healthcare provider. Lengthy delays are not uncommon, due to overcrowding, staff shortages, and paperwork that could be lost or processed incorrectly. These delays can have devastating consequences for both women and their fetuses, particularly given the importance of timely care among those with a high-risk pregnancy.[62]

Latrice had severe abdominal pain and heavy vaginal bleeding and was worried that she was having a miscarriage. When she asked a correctional officer if she could be released from her cell to see her provider, she was told no because she did not have prior approval. It took four weeks for Latrice's paperwork to get approved. As Latrice waited nearly a month to be seen, she described how the wait was akin to sitting "on pins and needles" not knowing whether she was still pregnant or whether she had suffered a missed miscarriage.[63] As Latrice explained,

> It took four weeks to get approval before I could be seen. They took me to the ER. The ER said that because I was sixteen weeks pregnant, they couldn't see me there, I needed to see an OB doctor, and then I had to go see a specialist because I was over thirty-five years old, so now we got to submit another request, wait another four weeks for the approval. This time, they took me to an OB doctor's office, but the OB needed to do an ultrasound immediately to see what my status was, well they couldn't take me to the ultrasound because the approval was not for anything but to see your doctor, so I had to go back, wait, wait for them to send in another request for the ultrasound.

Latrice's baby was ultimately born stillborn, and to this day, she still wonders if her baby would have been born alive had she had more timely medical care. As Latrice explained, "I'm like if you clearly see that

I'm having a problem how can you just walk past me and tell me that I have to wait until you hear back from somebody?" Through tears, she went on to share how her prison lacked some of the most basic medical instruments like a fetal doppler, an instrument that monitors fetal heartbeat. The extent of miscarriages and stillbirths among incarcerated women is difficult to know, as national data across state prisons is not kept. However, the most comprehensive study to date examining the pregnancy outcomes of incarcerated women across twenty-two state prison systems and the Federal Bureau of Prisons found that 6 percent of pregnancies of incarcerated women resulted in miscarriage and .5 percent of pregnancies resulted in stillbirths.[64] Latrice's experience and the lack of existing national data reaffirms how prisons are also gendered organizations designed to serve men, without regard to the unique needs of women, confirming the need for correctional facilities to have greater staff and even the most basic of medical instruments to properly care for pregnant women.[65]

Latrice's experience highlights how the incarceration of women during pregnancy results in a powerlessness that can have grave consequences for both maternal and fetal health. Not only is the ability to see a provider highly controlled, even in cases of emergency, but healthcare information and the ability to use the Internet to "Google" symptoms or to even use the library is also tightly controlled, leaving women in the dark about the changes happening to their body—an issue I discuss in more detail in the next chapter.

To be sure, perceptions of health are complicated and influenced by a myriad of historical and social processes that govern the lives of individuals and communities. While *all* the women I interviewed talked about the importance of prenatal care and the desire to have the best care possible, concerns about the inadequacies of care were especially salient among the Black women I interviewed. Many of the Black women I interviewed were also more likely to speak about their distrust of the "system," where the "system" referred to both the prison system and any other system that works to govern and control the lives of poor, Black women, who were worried about placing their health in the hands of systems that historically have not had their best interests in mind.

A distrust in both a historically White medical care system and a historically White criminal legal system is not surprising, given the extensive histories of abuse and mistreatment, including unlawful and unethical medical practices, such as sterilization and medical experimentation performed on Black, Hispanic, and Indigenous women both within and outside US prisons in medical settings.[66] A couple even made mention of these abuses as a source of their distrust, also calling attention to the long-standing history of discriminatory practices and the glaring racial disparities found in maternal mortality rates, with Black women being three times more likely to die from pregnancy-related issues than White women.[67] These inequities illustrate how the maternal web of control may be especially pronounced for Black women, with gendered racism proliferating in medical settings, causing further harm.

Kia, a Black woman, shared how her pain was frequently dismissed by correctional staff, making it nearly impossible for her to see a medical provider. Her narrative highlights the consequences of dismissing medical concerns among Black women during pregnancy and how gendered racism in an environment laced with carcerality and surveillance can have life-and-death consequences, especially for Black women. As Kia explained, "There was another [Black] woman who was pregnant at the same time as me, and she complained about not feeling well, and they dismissed her, and she wound up having a miscarriage, just like me, and I wonder a lot about how often there's a cost associated with being dismissed, whether that's your death or somebody else's or irreversible damage that's done because people think you're faking it, and they don't want to take you seriously and do what they need to do to make sure that you're okay." Kia's narrative reinforces existing research that shows Black women's concerns are frequently dismissed or minimized, due to systemic racism and false beliefs that are rampant in society about the pain tolerance of Black women, often resulting in delayed treatment or the absence of care altogether.[68] While this dismissal of health concerns among Black women, especially during pregnancy, is well documented outside of prison gates, it becomes magnified in correctional settings where women are stripped of their humanity and subjugated to the status of prisoner, making it easier than ever to exert control and authority.

The White, lower-middle-class women I interviewed also expressed concerns about their quality of care; however, these concerns were tied more closely to comparison with the care they had in the "free world." Many of them already had a care provider in the community and felt that their care behind bars was abysmal in comparison. Candy shared how her incarceration resulted in the denial of choice over her medical care and explained how if she had not been incarcerated, she would have had greater control over her medical care. According to Candy, "I would have been able to take myself to the doctor like I've done in the past with my other pregnancy, so the worst part was the lack of control because I knew that if I tried to knock on the door to medical, I'd go to the hole. That's how bad it was, so the level of powerlessness was overwhelming."[69]

The race and socioeconomic background of women greatly affect their experiences with care. The more marginalized White women I interviewed had a somewhat different take on their prenatal care, for they were less likely to express concerns about their care behind bars and instead shared how grateful they were to have any healthcare at all, as many of them had gone years and even decades without it. Amber explained, "I felt good about it. I felt like I wasn't missing out on nothing, they were taking care of me. I didn't feel like I was being mistreated medically. I was just glad to have prenatal care 'cause had I not been in there, I probably wouldn't have had it."

Strip Searches

Even the availability of medical care behind bars does not mean that women are not subjected to harmful and degrading invasive strip searches and sometimes even cavity searches to ensure they do not have contraband as they go to and from their medical appointments off prison grounds.[70] Although these searches are framed by prisons as central to ensuring security and order, they are harmful and represent yet another obstacle that women must undergo in order to receive care. As previously mentioned, many incarcerated women have extensive histories of trauma and abuse, and the practice of pat-downs, strip searches, and especially cavity searches, may ignite triggering memories of painful abuse, as well as frustration and embarrassment.

Searches in the name of security highlight how women may be subjected to state-sanctioned gender-based violence, punished in ways that incarcerated men are not, in their effort to access necessary care to improve their health. Cavity searches, especially those not performed by a medical provider, can introduce infection into both the rectal and the vaginal area, causing further harm to both maternal and fetal health.[71] Cavity searches performed by medical authority illustrate how the medical system is complicit in this process, even as it threatens health, further revealing how the medical system also acts as a carceral system and participant in the maternal web of control.

As mentioned, there is much variation across facilities, for each prison and state has unique laws, policies, and practices. While some states have brought forth legislation to ban or restrict invasive searches during pregnancy, only permitting them under certain circumstances, these practices are still commonplace.[72] At the federal level, the Prison Rape Elimination Act has also placed restrictions on cross-sex searches. Still, the use of cavity searches comes with much discretion—a practice that is frequently racialized, where Black women are more likely to be perceived as "criminal" or "threatening," increasing the likelihood of having an invasive search performed. Those incarcerated in more rural areas that lack specialized maternity care on site may be subjected to more searches, as they may leave the facility more often to access care. These experiences illustrate how incarceration itself causes harm and how access to healthcare is laced with carcerality.

Conclusion

Central to an understanding of health during pregnancy are the intentions that many women express about wanting to be the *best* mother possible, doing everything in their power to optimize pregnancy and birth outcomes in preparation for motherhood. For many, pregnancy during incarceration acts as a turning point, placing a renewed emphasis on health through the cessation of drugs, the consumption of nutritious foods, and healthcare. However, health itself is subject to control and regulation, as incarceration not only perpetuates existing health inequities but also causes new harm to women and their fetuses.

The nature of incarceration and the emphasis on rules and regulations in the name of security mean that even with the best of intentions and efforts, the ability to get clean, access nutritious food, and receive prenatal care is often beyond women's control, as they are under surveillance and control from the prison system, the healthcare system, and the child welfare system, trapping women into a subjugated, controlled state with limited decision making and autonomy to exercise power over their health, sometimes resulting in devastating, lethal consequences.

Although leading organizations and researchers have issued recommendations for the care of pregnant women behind bars, no national standards have been adopted, resulting in large disparities in care.[73] While some women speak highly about their care behind bars, including access to drug treatment programs and support groups, nutritious foods, and healthcare, others are quick to share how their healthcare behind bars was inadequate and substandard, placing them at further risk of harm. These differences in experiences are tied not only to the institution women are incarcerated in but also to the intersection of their social identities.

White women in poverty are more likely to credit their incarceration for their ability to access drug treatment programs, food, and healthcare—all essentials for a healthy pregnancy that they did not have access to in their communities. Many of the Black women I interviewed were quite skeptical about their healthcare experiences behind bars and shared how they distrusted both the correctional system and the medical system. Those with a more working- and middle-class background were less likely to view the prison system as a place of refuge and instead made mention of the inadequacies of care and how this care is laced in control, particularly in comparison to the care that they had known on the outside. Not only is healthcare highly controlled behind bars, but other cultural elements that women engage in to prepare for birth and motherhood are also subject to immense regulation, forcing women to improvise and make changes to, in some cases, long-held visions of pregnancy and motherhood—an issue I explore in the next chapter.

3

Pregnancy 101

The (Un)Making of Mothers

You start getting excited and makin' plans for the baby, but then it's like hold up 'cause you can't really get ready—at least not how you want to.
—Marissa

Judith, a Black mother of four, was thirty-four and pregnant with her fifth child when she came to prison. Having been pregnant before, she knew what to expect when it came to pregnancy and motherhood. She was well versed in Braxton Hicks contractions and knew exactly what foods triggered her nausea and morning sickness. A single mother of young children, she found it hard to make ends meet, for the money she earned through sex work was never quite enough to make rent on time. Despite the hardships, Judith still considered herself "blessed." A devout Christian, she was grateful for her church family, who helped in times of scarcity and had a close relationship with the church elders who were already planning a baby shower for her. Knowing this was likely to be her last pregnancy, she looked forward to the shower, wanting to savor every moment of her pregnancy. However, five months into her pregnancy, the plans for the big shower fell through after she was sent to prison for violating her parole.

Having already served five stints in jail and two in prison on various drug trafficking and prostitution charges, Judith was familiar with prison count times and knew just how much items cost at the commissary store. She knew healthcare and communication with those on the outside were hard to come by, and after watching countless pregnant women come through the prison system over the years, she thought she had a firm understanding about how incarceration would affect her own pregnancy. However, what she did not yet know, at least at the time, was just how different (and difficult) a pregnancy behind bars would be.

Not only would she be away from her children (again), but she soon discovered that incarceration meant missing out on the pregnancy experience she had envisioned, including the last opportunity to wear cute maternity tops and to have a baby shower thrown on her behalf. No longer would she be able to watch her pregnancy unfold through the eyes of her children or take photos of her growing baby bump. The farm-themed nursery she planned on having in the corner of her third-floor apartment bedroom was now out of reach.

Like so many of the women I interviewed, Judith had already endured a painful goodbye to her older children before coming to prison and was distraught about the thought of having to say goodbye all over again to a baby she did not yet have a chance to fully know. Though she knew the impending separation would be painful, she was grateful to have an extensive support network and was confident her family would happily fill the role of caregiver while she finished serving her sixteen-month sentence. But, to her surprise, they all said no. Judith was stunned. As her family explained it, they were already burnt out and stretched too thin raising her four other children. Not only were they physically and emotionally exhausted, but they were drowning economically as well.

Desperate, she called everyone she knew, hoping to find at least one person willing to provide care. With no luck, she even reached out to the father of her unborn baby, even though they were not in a relationship and barely knew each other. With no one to come forward, she eventually had no choice but to inform a social worker at her prison that she would place her baby in foster care—something she never wanted to do. In the end, the excitement and joy she had about the baby shower and the farm-themed decor were replaced with sadness and anger over the loss of the pregnancy experience she thought she would have. As Judith explained, "Had I not been in there, I would have been extremely happy, excited, and enjoying every minute, but I couldn't. There was and always will be a black cloud over that pregnancy. I didn't have a chance to get out my clothes, I didn't have a chance to get my crib out. I didn't have a chance to pick out my receiving blanket. You know, I didn't even get to pick out a diaper bag."

When I interviewed Judith and the other women in this study, a central theme entailed the loss of the pregnancy experience and the makings of motherhood they had long envisioned, as they were stripped of the ability to engage in important cultural elements that bring humanity and dignity to pregnancy. As noted earlier, pregnancy entails more than biological phenomena but is grounded in important cultural aspects that humanize the experience of pregnancy, particularly for women who are incarcerated and largely dehumanized.[1] While there is no one single or defining cultural aspect of pregnancy, pregnancy may be marked by any number of cultural components and rituals. Some of the more common rituals in the United States include the selection of a name, a baby shower and/or gender reveal party, participation in childbirth classes, the securing of diapers and bottles, and the reading of materials about pregnancy, childbirth, and parenting, as well as a commitment to health, as evidenced in the last chapter.[2]

Still, engagement in these arguably more middle-class activities varies considerably, for motherhood unfolds differently across cultural and social settings. Some I interviewed were forthright in acknowledging that they were too depressed to engage in anything pregnancy or baby related, while others went out of their way to ensure they had at least some form of a baby shower.[3] Regardless of the ways in which women prepare for motherhood, carcerality permeates all elements behind bars, including the cultural elements of pregnancy and motherhood, effectively stripping women of anything that does not uphold and support the control and order of the prison state. Yet, despite the prohibitions on the more humanizing elements of pregnancy that women attribute to the making of their motherhood, allowing them to parent with dignity—a core tenet of reproductive justice—this does not mean that incarcerated pregnant women do not prepare for the birth of their baby behind bars; rather, the ways in which they prepare all unfold differently.

In this chapter, I explore how incarcerated pregnant women prepare for birth and motherhood behind bars in an environment designed to strip them of their humanity and all other elements that recognize their role as mothers rather than prisoners. I detail some of the cultural practices women engage in behind bars—whether those entail reading pregnancy and birth materials, taking childbirth classes, or creating caregiver plans. I specifically examine how women adapt to the loss of the pregnancy experience they thought they would have, while recognizing that for some, incarceration acts as a unique way to engage in and access some of these more cultural elements that are otherwise inaccessible in their communities.

Just as incarceration during pregnancy acts as a turning point for women to commit to being a "better" or "good" mother by prioritizing health, engagement in these cultural practices is also seen as an important step in the journey to be good mothers. Lastly, this chapter focuses on how women participate in the one preparation task that the carceral state imposes on women through forced separation from their babies: the creation of a caregiving plan for their baby—an arduous task that signals a separation will soon follow.

The central argument of this chapter is that like other aspects of pregnancy, the ability to prepare for pregnancy and motherhood is limited and heavily regulated and controlled by the carceral state and its extensions, resulting in a web of control that envelops women, their births, and their babies. I show how carcerality extends to the maternal domain, limiting the ability for women to prepare for birth and motherhood in a dignified manner characterized by choice. The elements of control, surveillance, and criminalization inhibit the ability to engage in these cultural practices and force mothers to create a caregiving plan that undermines the maternal-infant bond and is fraught with complexities and trauma. Throughout the chapter, I show how incarceration extends beyond the punishment for crime and carries over into all things pregnancy, birth, and motherhood, with reverberating consequences for women and their families.

The Loss of an Experience

Coming to terms with the life-altering news of a pregnancy is an ongoing process accompanied by a range of emotions—a pregnancy that unfolds behind bars is another matter entirely. As described in chapter 1, women experience a range of responses to the news of a pregnancy behind bars, a sensitive subject marked by complexity. Many of my interviewees explained how in prison they had an abundance of time—time to think about their visions for motherhood and their now-disrupted plans for their motherhood.

Most of the women I talked with said they had dreamt about motherhood since childhood and had long yearned for a blissful, carefree pregnancy complete with a decorated nursery and an elaborate baby shower, highlighting the power of cultural norms and widespread marketing. And while these dreams were already out of reach for some, due to family circumstances, addiction, or the trappings of poverty, incarceration all but ensured the complete erasure of these dreams, leaving most with painful tears and scars. The forced separation of families also means that women must begin the process of making caregiver arrangements during pregnancy—a task that further signifies their subjugated status as prisoners and mere case numbers within the child welfare system.

Sociologist Harold Garfinkel has written extensively about how individuals are stripped of their dignity, humiliated, and subjugated through a process that he calls the "degradation ceremony."[4] Degradation ceremonies punish people through the stripping of elements that bring dignity and through the integration of new elements that support the new deviant identity, as individuals are denounced from society. Much has been written about the degradation ceremonies that the incarcerated undergo, including the use of shackles, a prison jumpsuit, the use of a number instead of a name, and a mugshot photo published for all to see, signifying the transformation from individual to prisoner.[5] For pregnant women in prison, the denial of these cultural elements that bring dignity to pregnancy, such as a baby shower, supports the degradation ceremony, making it clear that these women are not mothers but rather prisoners first and foremost. The requirement to create a caregiver plan represents the new introduction of an element that reaffirms the prisoner status and the stripping away of motherhood.

Marissa shared how incarceration left her unable to document her pregnancy in the ways that she would have liked, for she was not able to take photos of her growing baby bump or create a pregnancy scrapbook as she had done in her previous pregnancy, due to rules at her specific prison that prohibit the incarcerated from having cameras and personal cell phones. In the wake of an emphasis on order and security, pregnant women are denied the ability to access some of the more normalizing elements of pregnancy and motherhood, such as the use of photos that could later be passed down to their children, keeping them at the periphery of pregnancy and motherhood circles. As Marissa explained,

"I was more upset 'cause I couldn't really do much. With my first child, during my pregnancy, we had a baby shower. I did a scrapbook for her and was just able to take photos all the time documenting my pregnancy. And with my second one, I couldn't really do it like I wanted. You start getting excited and makin' plans for the baby, but then it's like hold up 'cause you can't really get ready—at least not how you want to." Marissa's experience highlights how carcerality not only affects matters of health but also limits the ability to engage in important practices that help women connect with their (unborn) baby, ultimately strengthening family bonds that would have allowed them to resist some of the elements of the maternal web of control and the degradation ceremonies that mark imprisonment.

The prohibition of cameras among pregnant women, even to document the growing changes in the body, is ironic given the constant lens of surveillance that exists behind bars, where cameras are ubiquitous. Although prisons have countless images and videos of women during their pregnancy, capturing their every move, even when no human is present, most incarcerated pregnant women have no photos of themselves during their pregnancy, limiting their ability to access important rituals during pregnancy and hindering the means to have a pregnancy with dignity, making pregnancy itself a site of punishment.

The emphasis on order and control means that women are often unable to prepare for their pregnancy in the ways that they would have liked and in the ways that society expects them to, as was the case with Marissa. And yet, many of the interviewees described instances of innovation, resistance, and on occasion even hope, as they did their best to reaffirm their identity as a(n expectant) mother, preserving some of the cultural markers of pregnancy in the face of extreme regulation and control. For example, it was not uncommon to hear about how other women in prison hosted a baby shower for them or helped to educate them about the particulars of pregnancy to provide a semblance of humanity and normalcy in the cold and impersonal environment of prison.

As mentioned, although most of the women I interviewed were not in a relationship with the father of their baby at the time of their incarceration, those who were shared how incarceration meant the erasure of their partner's involvement in the pregnancy, forcing them to prepare for new motherhood on their own without the support of a partner.

The destruction of family ties is yet another example of how women are stripped of their humanity during pregnancy, removed from their roles not only as expectant mothers but also as wives, girlfriends, and partners, undermining the family.

Despite the physical barriers that come with incarceration, those in a *healthy* relationship may try to involve their partner (if they have one) as much as possible, whether that entails sharing updates on the phone (arguably a practice that still benefits those with more money) about the changes in their body or their plans for parenthood. Lora talked about how it was difficult to decide on a baby name because she wanted her partner's input and yet had limited means of contacting him. Being incarcerated means that even important cultural aspects of pregnancy like the choice of a name are forced to take place in a particular way that adheres to the minutiae of prison life and its many rules and regulations about contact, greatly limiting the ability for women to talk freely with loved ones about important matters.

Wanting to make the most of her time on the phone, given her limited funds and long waiting lines, Lora wrote letters to her partner ahead of their few calls and included several names on a sheet of paper for her partner's consideration in the hope that this would expedite the discussion about names. According to Lora, "I would send him self-addressed envelopes in a form style, where check yes or no on this, and here are some names, circle ones you like and send it back to me, that way we could make the most of our time on the phone."

Another woman, Susan, forty-four at the time of our interview and a White mother of three, shared how she tried to involve her partner in her pregnancy by reading his letters aloud to her unborn baby. As Susan explained, "I had headphones, and I would put the headphones on my belly, and I know they can hear things and whenever I would have a minute, I would read [my partner's] letter over and over and over again out loud so that way [my baby] could at least hear from her daddy." Although Susan remained disappointed that her partner could not participate in her pregnancy as she had wanted, reading his letters aloud allowed her to reclaim some control over certain aspects of her pregnancy that were thwarted by the carceral state.

Those who were close to family shared how they tried to involve them in any way they could, for they knew their incarceration also took a toll on their family. Some shared how they felt badly that their family was unable to feel the fetal movements of their unborn grandchild or unable to see their growing baby bump—all-important elements of family involvement that end with the incarceration of women, providing insight into how incarceration affects not just those behind bars but also loved ones.

Those with a more middle-class background, who were predominantly White, were more inclined to talk about the loss of the pregnancy experience they had envisioned outside of prison. That is, their socioeconomic status afforded them the ability to dream a bit more and to embrace even the more detailed elements deemed central to "good" motherhood, such as baby shower decorations, nursery décor, and all things baby gear—experiences that are in stark contrast to those in poverty. For them, phone calls with loved ones focused more on the preservation of these preparatory elements of pregnancy, allowing them to take back some control over their pregnancy and motherhood and to exercise a modicum of autonomy in a place devoid of choice.

Low-income women were less likely to frame their time behind bars around the *loss* of a pregnancy experience, in part because their pregnancy was not tied as closely to these more middle-class practices like scrapbooking and the acquiring of various baby items. For them, pregnancy even outside of the carceral setting would not have necessarily entailed plans for an elaborate Pinterest-planned baby shower, the decoration of a dedicated nursery space, or the creation of a baby registry at Walmart. Instead, they were more likely to suggest that prison was an ideal place to prepare for motherhood and the birth of their baby. In many ways, this was the first time they had ever had sufficient access to food, childbirth classes, pregnancy educational materials, and healthcare, while for others, this was the first time they had a support system of people who celebrated their pregnancy alongside them.

Getting Educated

As discussed earlier, pregnancy, particularly in the prison setting, can act as a turning point and source of motivation for women to be the best mother possible, with a focus on optimizing maternal and fetal health outcomes. Given the poor health of many women in prison, it is not unusual for many to have serious concerns that their poor health would adversely affect their pregnancy.[6] Becoming educated about pregnancy and childbirth was a way to optimize both maternal and fetal health and allowed them to take ownership of their pregnancy and exert autonomy over their body, particularly in a system that denies them this freedom.

To be clear, pregnancy is a unique period marked by several changes. The ways in which women are expected to prepare for and educate themselves about these many changes are numerous; whether it entails researching the maternal body and becoming knowledgeable about the many bodily changes taking place, practicing breathing techniques for labor, or studying developmental milestones, pregnancy remains a transformative period in which women are expected to make provisions to welcome their baby into the world.[7]

Knowledge as Power

The extent of planning and preparation that women undergo during this period is viewed as a marker of their parenting fitness, particularly in the United States, where "good" moms are viewed as subscribing to the Western intensive-mothering paradigm focused on high levels of parental involvement in all things pregnancy, birth, and baby.[8] A failure to immerse themselves in these matters may be perceived as disinterest or a lack of care, especially among more marginalized women, who were already under increased scrutiny and surveillance under the maternal web of control.[9]

Yet, incarceration often hinders the ability to engage in these practices, despite the fact that imprisonment often presents women with more time to focus on their pregnancy and prepare for the birth of their baby—something that some of my participants said they were unable to do in previous pregnancies, when they were more focused on survival. Wanting a "do-over," many of my participants shared how they wanted to learn as much as possible about pregnancy, birth, and motherhood to both be *and* be seen as the best mother possible, even if they were imprisoned.

When Candy was pregnant with her first child, she acknowledged that she was "not in a good place," unable to focus on her pregnancy. Resolved to be more engaged this time around, she looked for ways to become educated about pregnancy and the many changes taking place in her body. According to Candy, "There was just so much trauma in my life at that time. The lights were off in my house, so I couldn't even think about those things, but with this pregnancy I really wanted the opportunity to learn how to be a good mother before I was back on the street again with my kids, so I knew it'd be a long process to get my kids back and that the laws were so strong and so archaic and so not family friendly, so I really wanted to learn this time."

For women like Candy, having the opportunity to learn about pregnancy and parenting in preparation for motherhood is important because it not only enhances their confidence in their parenting abilities but also acts to resist some of the carceral system's attempts to deny them their motherhood. That is, it allows them an outlet to (re)affirm their role as mother in a place that is intent on the denial and erasure of all identities except that of prisoner. For pregnant and birthing women, having knowledge about birth and motherhood serves as an outlet through which to take back control and ownership over their pregnancy and birth experiences. Indeed, research finds that having access to knowledge and information about childbirth and "what to expect" can increase women's sense of control over and satisfaction about birth.[10] For women under a web of control and at the center of multiple matrices of oppression in an environment rife with high maternal mortality rates, it can also ensure their survival.

Having knowledge about parenting also acts as a way for women to demonstrate to those working in the carceral system that they did indeed care about their unborn children and were fit to be mothers—something that would later prove to be important in the fight to retain or regain their parental rights.[11] Candy shared how she knew the road to regaining parental custody would be a long one and she wanted to be able to show to attorneys, parole board members, and the judge that she had used her time behind bars to better herself and prepare for her new role as mother.

Candy was keenly aware of the stigma attached to incarcerated mothers and the insinuation that incarceration was not compatible with motherhood. For her, getting educated about pregnancy, birth, and motherhood through childbirth and parenting classes and reading materials was a way to mitigate some of this stigma by showing others how she was indeed capable of mothering and that any criminal involvement was not reflective of her mothering ability.

Denise, a White, forty-three-year-old mother of two, also said it was important to "take the time to learn everything about being pregnant, really take charge on the healthiness of it, really take charge on what to expect when you have a baby, just to learn, learn everything you can while you're pregnant to have a healthy baby, you must take care of yourself because everything you do affects your baby. And so yeah, of course I wanted the best for my baby but also, I didn't need people thinking I didn't care about my kid just 'cause I was in prison. So, hopefully, hopefully, they saw that I was tryin' real hard." Denise's narrative shows how incarcerated pregnant women are subject to intensive-mothering expectations that permeate the maternal web of control. While Denise's commitment to preparation came from a place of wanting the best for her unborn baby, it was also in response to a cultural paradigm that expects women to prioritize their pregnancy above all else and in response to the stigma attached to maternal incarceration.

However, the maternal web of control restricts access to education, limiting the ability for women to become fully informed about pregnancy and childbirth, making it easier for the maternal web of control to operate. Not every woman I interviewed had access to pregnancy educational materials and classes—in fact, most did not. Programming and materials are largely dependent on the offerings at each specific facility and even dependent on the attitudes of correctional staff. Programs specific to pregnancy care may be scarce to begin with, as most prisons, including women's prisons, are designed with men in mind and ignore the unique needs of women, particularly in rural areas that are often slower to change. As much as some want to prepare themselves for pregnancy and parenthood by reading various materials, some discovered that their prison restricted materials and programs, often reserving what little was available to those enrolled in parenting classes or those approaching reintegration, denying them the ability to be informed about pregnancy and birth and the ability to advocate for themselves if needed.

Others explained how it was difficult to demonstrate their competency as a mother to actors in the maternal web of control when educational materials and pregnancy and parenting classes behind bars are so heavily restricted. For Candy, not only was her body heavily regulated and controlled behind bars but the denial of information and resources also served to regulate her mind, restricting important knowledge about pregnancy. To no surprise, those incarcerated in more rural facilities with fewer pregnant women were less likely to have resources specifically on pregnancy and parenting, primarily because the demand for these materials was lower. At the time, Amber was the only one who was pregnant at her prison, which meant that the specific needs of pregnant women like herself were an afterthought.

Jada, a Black mother of two, was just twenty when she went to prison, and although she had been pregnant before and had some knowledge and previous experience to rely on, she was anxious to learn more but soon discovered that her prison had nothing in the way of resources or educational materials on pregnancy—leaving her with many questions and few answers. As Jada explained, "The library don't have like pregnancy books where you can go and read about being pregnant. Yeah, if you have any questions, you just must wait to ask the doctor at your next appointment; there's nothing that you can do in the meantime. There's nothing to read. There was no Lamaze classes, there was no pregnant mom classes, none of that stuff, so I was just afraid 'cause I didn't know what was going on." Additionally, Lora shared how the lack of available materials was in stark contrast to their availability during her first pregnancy, in which she read pregnancy books and regularly consulted them when she had a question about the changes in her body. A lack of pregnancy materials and services in prisons is not random but rather reflects the patriarchal structure of the carceral system and its primary focus on men.[12] The denial of information is intentional and further serves to suppress and control incarcerated women, as knowledge is power, and the absence of this knowledge makes it easier to control the maternal bodies of those behind bars. As Rhonda explained, "They don't like it when you know what's going on."

Being incarcerated may also mean no access to the Internet, further denying the means to access information and to have answers about health concerns—a disturbing reality in this increasingly tech-driven society, where even many nonincarcerated pregnant women regularly rely on the Internet to find information and support during pregnancy.[13] In a national study of women who had just given birth in the United States, research revealed that 82 percent of them used the Internet at least once a week during pregnancy to access information about pregnancy and birth.[14] A lack of programming and resources becomes even more concerning when one considers its relation to health, as pregnant women in prison may not have reliable access to a trusted provider and instead must rely on information in its absence to self-diagnose issues, especially in the wake of poor health. Above all, the denial of education and information ensures that women remain relegated to the status of prisoner, uninformed and unable to advocate for themselves, making it easier to lean into the maternal web of control and the decisions made by more powerful forces.

Those I interviewed who did have access to educational materials shared how they would frequently consult these materials to determine whether a symptom was "normal," especially in the absence of timely healthcare—a norm at many prisons.[15] In cases where women are unable to access educational materials, they may be forced to innovate and rely on the knowledge accrued from any previous pregnancies or from their peers to decipher whether their symptoms were "normal." As Rhonda said, "We know our bodies, and so with my other pregnancies I knew what to look for and 'cause I knew around the fourth month I always get these cramps in my legs, so I knew, I'm like, okay it's that time again."

Those new to pregnancy and without educational materials or childbirth classes may be especially anxious about the unknown, for they do not have any previous experiences from which to draw.[16] The lack of educational materials is increasingly important given that narratives around pregnancy and childbirth emphasize a loss of control and the need to expect the unexpected—a reality that may be especially true for incarcerated women, who must navigate birth within the confines of multiple, interlocking systems of control.[17]

Peers as Educators

In the absence of information and classes, women may be forced to rely on their peers to learn about pregnancy and childbirth. In line with extant research, most women I interviewed said their peers were already mothers, so many were eager to share (both solicited and unsolicited) advice about pregnancy and baby matters, helping them to become educated about pregnancy and childbirth.[18] In the words of Candy, "The girls in there didn't see me as a bad mom for getting pregnant and being in prison. They knew it was just a really bad year. The people that I knew scattered like leaves. They were just gone, so I relied on the girls a lot to learn about my pregnancy." Although everyone I interviewed was surrounded by peers during their incarceration, this may not be the case for everyone, particularly for those housed in solitary confinement.

Not only may other incarcerated women provide information and support, but they may also help celebrate a pregnancy by hosting a baby shower, helping to reaffirm a woman's identity as an expectant mother rather than prisoner. Bonnie said, "I was so grateful; they were so kind and did their best to throw me a shower with what we had, like they made a cookie cake with a spread, typical prison stuff." To be sure, not everyone in prison is friendly or supportive of pregnancy and eager to offer advice and support, though most of the women I interviewed spoke fondly of their peers and said that being pregnant, at least at their facility, largely meant occupying a special status that sometimes came with extra privileges and care.[19]

The availability of pregnancy and birth resources varies greatly across prisons. Some facilities offer several opportunities to participate in childbirth and parenting classes, in addition to having a dedicated "pregnancy corner" in the library that contains a wide array of pregnancy and parenting books. There are other correctional facilities that do not have a single book or pamphlet about pregnancy that women can read and feel more prepared about pregnancy, birth, and motherhood.

Marissa was incarcerated in a large facility that offered a prison nursery program and ample opportunities to check out books about pregnancy; she also had the ability to enroll in a six-week pregnancy and childbirth-preparation class. When the six-week program ended, those enrolled in it were able to participate in a baby shower hosted by the childbirth educator, a social worker employed by the prison. Marissa was extremely grateful for these classes, as they allowed her the opportunity to learn about pregnancy and the chance to establish friendships and support with some of the other pregnant women on her floor. Marissa went on to share how helpful these friendships were in easing her depression and fears.

Similarly, Barbara came from a larger prison and was able to attend peer groups specifically designed for pregnant women. These self-directed groups provided an opportunity to learn about pregnancy and prepare for motherhood in an informal and supportive environment devoid of judgment. Since Barbara used crack cocaine throughout her pregnancy, these groups were particularly important in equipping her with knowledge about how to best offset her drug use and optimize health outcomes in a nonjudgmental setting with other pregnant women who were also focused on recovery—something that was important to Barbara given the stigma surrounding pregnancy and drug use. It was this unique setting that equipped Barbara with the confidence to give birth and the means to feel empowered and validated in her motherhood journey.

Doulas as Educators

A growing response to the incarceration of pregnant women is to provide women with doulas—professionals trained to support women during pregnancy and beyond. Angel had access to volunteer doulas who came to her prison and spoke highly of their support. According to Angel, "The most literature that I got about my pregnancy, how my baby's forming, what I should eat, drink, how to keep myself calm, the doulas, they're the only ones that provided us with any information. The doctors there didn't provide us with nothing." Angel spoke fondly about the volunteer doulas who came to her prison, in part because they helped her exert her agency in a place that otherwise limited her autonomy. Angel made a sharp distinction between the volunteer doulas who came to her prison and the medical staff who worked at her prison, as the correctional healthcare staff failed to provide her with important information about how to have a healthy pregnancy and birth—something she desired, given her high-risk pregnancy. Angel went on to share how the doulas taught a Lamaze course and provided hands-on comfort measures that helped her while she was in both early and active labor. In her own words, "They made me feel more secure and more prepared for that day. I even got to pick out some calm music and we got to pick out the smell of what we wanted in the hospital room, the little aroma stuff, so I had a lavender smell." The use of doulas may be especially important amid the regulation and control that emanate from both the prison and the medical systems.

It is difficult to speculate about the extent of pregnancy program offerings and doulas in correctional settings, as national data is not kept—though in my research I found that those incarcerated in larger facilities had greater access to offerings. Angel was the only one I interviewed who was incarcerated in a facility that provided doulas to pregnant women.[20] However, a growing number of both prisons and jails have expanded the use of doula services because of the cost savings associated with them.[21] Doulas are critical in improving maternal and infant complications and mortality rates, particularly among women of color, while also decreasing the need for interventions and cesarean sections. Research has found that the physical and emotional support that doulas provide, especially in correctional settings, can help women feel more informed and empowered in an otherwise dominating and controlling environment.[22] The use of doulas may be especially important to incarcerated women, who are often forced to give birth alone without the support of a partner, a point I discuss in the next chapter.[23] Through education and programming, women are equipped with the tools needed to better navigate birth behind bars and the means to resist the maternal web of control.

Families as Educators

In the absence of doulas and even peers, some may rely on conversations with loved ones to become educated about pregnancy. Destiny, pregnant for the first time, shared how her mom acted as an important resource in helping her feel more educated and at ease heading into birth. In Destiny's words, "My mother sent me books to read to prepare me for motherhood, and I just tried to prepare myself the best I could, so I was all ready for my little boy. At that time, I was able to call her, and she would come visit me, and we were able to kinda discuss the changes in my body and the things that I was going through so that was helpful, but a lot of these other women don't have that."

As Destiny noted, and consistent with extant research, many incarcerated women do not have visitors or contact with those on the outside from whom to learn about pregnancy and what to expect during childbirth, particularly given that the prison system operates as a total institution, where information about even pregnancy and birth is tightly surveilled and controlled by the carceral state, restricting the availability of resources for women.[24] Middle-class women are more likely to have visitors and phone calls, making it easier for them to access information, equipping them with greater resources to defy the maternal web of control and to have improved health outcomes.

Still, not everyone who is pregnant in prison wants to actively engage in pregnancy- and baby-related activities, for a variety of reasons; some may be too depressed, and the thought of taking a birth course or reading pregnancy materials may be too painful. Others shared how these activities would only fuel their depression, as they knew it would only be a matter of time before they would be separated from their baby at the hospital.[25] According to Taylor, a White thirty-five-year-old who was pregnant with her first child, "I know this sounds bad but the only preparing I could do was to mentally prepare myself to say goodbye." Others shared how they prepared for birth by keeping a safe distance away from all pregnancy-related topics and did their best to protect their heart from the painful separation that was soon to come. In my study, those with longer sentences were less likely to participate in some of the more traditional means of preparation. Many shared how there would be "no point," for they would be incarcerated for years to come, unable to implement their knowledge in practice. For these women, preparation for motherhood meant making a methodical effort to distance themselves from any potential heartache.

Who's Gonna Take My Baby?

Not only does incarceration during pregnancy entail the loss of important cultural rites that mark motherhood, but it also means the introduction of new practices that are unique to the control of pregnant women in prison. Given that few prisons in the United States have mother-baby programs, often called prison nursery programs, that allow a woman's baby to stay with her after birth through the duration of her imprisonment, most pregnant women in prison will be separated from their baby shortly after birth, necessitating the appointment of someone else to provide care.[26]

Carcerality infiltrates this practice as well. Not only does the appointment of a caregiver necessitate the involvement of another punitive system—the child welfare system—but women are also forced to make this difficult yet monumental decision in a controlling and invasive environment, where the ability to speak freely with potential caregivers is often limited and conversations over caregiving plans are expected to adhere to specific time frames and rules as established by each prison. It is acknowledged that this practice varies immensely across prisons. I interviewed some who said that phone calls about caregiving plans were treated no differently than their other phone calls and were still expected to be limited to fifteen-minute increments, and that phone calls and even visitations could be taken away for any number of reasons, while others were able to speak freely at length with potential caregivers in a more private setting.

The Separation of Mothers and Babies

Indeed, the process of separating mothers from their babies is certainly specific to time and place and is a direct response to the ever-changing views of women, crime, and punishment. In the United States, the carceral system and the maternal web of control punish not just pregnant women but also their loved ones and children in the most extreme of ways. This forced separation of mothers from their children provides insight into the cruelty and domination inherent in the prison system and is yet another direct violation of reproductive justice, leaving mothers unable to parent with dignity. Interestingly, many participants were convinced that if they lived in any other country, they would not be incarcerated at all or at the very least would not have to be separated from their baby at birth.

Prior to the 1900s, societal views on women acknowledged and even emphasized the importance of families, as reformatories encouraged incarcerated women to bond with their children and to cohabitate with their newborn baby in prison (similar to modern-day prison nursery programs), effectively eliminating the need to appoint a caregiver at all.[27] At the time, baby bonding was deemed essential to preserving the all-important family ties, resulting in the first prison nursery program opening in 1901 at the Bedford Hills Correctional Facility in New York—other states soon followed.[28]

By the 1950s, thirteen states had established prison nursery programs; however, the criminal legal system as a whole and corrections in particular took a different approach in the 1970s when states shifted away from reform to a more punitive approach and introduced legislation that effectively eliminated many nursery programs in the United States.[29] Throughout the 1990s and 2000s, much has stayed the same.[30] At the time of this writing in 2024, only eleven states in the United States have prison nursery programs in place, which means that most incarcerated pregnant women have no choice but to spend their time behind bars in search of a caregiver.[31] In Kansas, lawmakers are considering a pilot plan for the creation of a nursery program, fueling optimism that these programs are expanding, even in rural areas.[32]

In the absence of nursery programs, the process of appointing a caregiver is messy, complicated, and influenced by a myriad of social factors, including but certainly not limited to race, socioeconomic status, geography, and just about everything else in between. Suffice it to say, selecting a caregiver is not an easy task and is often emotionally taxing and extremely difficult because it holds such significance.[33] Depending on the length of the sentence, caregivers may be asked to provide care for anywhere from a few months to a few years or, in some cases, a decade or more, while women remain behind bars.

Crafting Plans

The process of appointing a caregiver entails women coming to terms with the stark reality that someone else will be raising their baby—an unsettling thought for many. Even having a close relationship with someone in the community did not always mean that that person would be the caregiver. In fact, few participants said they automatically knew whom they wanted to appoint, in part because caregiving, especially of a newborn, is a major commitment and not only includes emotional and physical labor but also entails financial responsibilities, with little to no financial support.[34] Caregivers may also be asked to foster communication and visitation, effectively serving as gatekeepers between mothers and their children.[35]

Melody shared how she had a "rocky relationship" with her family for years and was apprehensive about asking them to provide care, for families also act as surveilling agents of control. Others were quick to acknowledge that they came from a "dysfunctional" or "toxic" family, where abuse, alcohol, drugs, and crime were considered a way of life, leaving many to feel uncomfortable about placing their baby in this same environment. Even in cases where love and affection are present, some family members may be unable or unwilling to provide care, as was the case for Judith.

There were a few like Taylor, who acknowledged that she had a relatively easy time finding care. As an only child, Taylor was especially close with her parents and said she never considered anyone else as a potential caregiver because her parents were in a financial position that made it possible for them to provide care. According to Taylor, "I don't even think that was a question in their mind that they would take her. They held a lotta guilt about me, they thought it was their fault I was locked up and what could they have done different? I think they might have seen [my daughter] as their second chance to do things differently."

Taylor was the rarity, however. Most of the women I interviewed were at a complete loss in terms of who would provide care, and several described the process as akin to searching for a "needle in a haystack." Not only is it difficult to ask someone else to raise a baby full-time, but to raise one against the backdrop of the carceral system is another matter entirely. For many, in an ideal world, it was important to select someone who was economically stable and who lived close to the prison they were incarcerated in because proximity increases the likelihood of visitation.[36] Women who also have older children may want to appoint the same caregiver for their older children so their children could be together.[37] For most, one of the biggest factors that weighed into their decision was who would keep their baby out of the foster care system and who would nurture a reunification after their release from prison.

Finding a caregiver who was economically stable may be especially important to those living in poverty, for many shared how they did not want their baby to go without basic needs like food and shelter, funneling them further into the hands of the child welfare system, where impoverished people are more likely to be targeted. Others shared how they wanted their baby to be able to have experiences they did not have in their own childhood, like trips to the local zoo or swimming pool. Concerns about money and how it would impact caregiving were especially salient among the Black women I interviewed, for they were more likely to be impoverished, in which case necessities were not always guaranteed, due to cumulative disadvantages that stem from systemic racism and structural poverty, among other issues.[38]

Jasmine was quick to reach out to her grandmother to inquire about the possibility of providing care because her grandmother was economically stable and had lived in the same house for decades. Because she wanted stability for her baby, her grandma made the most sense because she was the one person in her life who "didn't bounce from place to place every other month." According to Jasmine, "I knew the best thing I could do was to keep [baby] from moving from house to house to house 'cause my grandma could give a stable house of discipline, not just beating them or nothing like that but structure." Though Jasmine was thankful that her grandmother agreed to be the caregiver, she also worried that her grandma would struggle to provide care given her advanced age—a concern that never really went away and worsened with time.

Still, simply having a loved one who was economically stable does not always mean that person is fit to serve as caregiver. Denise explained how even though she was "born and raised in an upper-middle-class family," she knew from the beginning that her family would not be a suitable match. According to Denise, her family was "not nice at all and completely wrote [her] off" when she went to prison, including withdrawing financial support. They were embarrassed and disappointed that she was incarcerated—let alone pregnant and incarcerated. Fearing that her family would take their anger out on her unborn baby through the withdrawal of necessary financial support, she made an adoption plan. As Denise explained, "I've burned all my bridges, my family has completely written me off. I placed my baby for adoption because I wanted what was better for her."

Although research indicates that some pregnant women in prison consider making an adoption plan, few ultimately place their baby in adoptive care.[39] Only two of the women in this study, including Denise, made an adoption plan—and only after the realization that their own family would be unable to provide care. Denise explained how the decision to place her baby in adoptive care was one that generated pushback from her friends, including those who were also incarcerated, as they viewed adoption as akin to infant abandonment. Even though she was hurt by the insinuation, she still moved forward with her plans for the adoption, knowing this was the best arrangement for her baby.

Not only did Denise encounter resistance from her peers, but she also felt that the correctional staff at her prison did not support her decision to place her baby in adoptive care. Although she hoped to have some assistance from a social worker, Denise said that the only social worker at her prison was either aloof or unsupportive of the adoption plan, in part because adoption was messier and more complex than other arrangements, including foster care—at least from a paperwork perspective. Determined to move forward with the adoption plan, with or without help from prison staff, she used her designated phone time to contact an adoption agency. According to Denise,

> The prison, they never helped whatsoever. They didn't help at all, in fact they tried to prevent me from getting assistance in making these plans. So, what I did is you can request to look at phone books and then you put that request in and several days later you get called out. And I wrote down the number of every adoptive agency I found in the phone book, which is how I found the family that she's with. But I was only able to find the adoption agency and do what I did because I have enough intelligence and ingenuity to get those phone books and then place those collect calls. But most people that are inmates, to tell you the truth, don't know how to go about doing any of that.

Denise's experience illustrates how even her caregiver plans were tightly regulated at her prison, while at the same time her experience sheds light on the resolve and ingenuity of women defying the carceral system. It is no surprise that Denise was not the only one who encountered resistance from her prison in making caregiver plans. Others shared how prison social workers were quick to encourage the use of the foster care system above other arrangements, including arrangements involving grandparents and the birth father. In some ways, encouraging incarcerated women to use the foster care system above these other arrangements was racialized in that women of color were more likely to encounter false narratives suggesting that they or their family members were not fit to provide care, a phenomenon that has been well documented by legal scholar Dorothy Roberts.[40]

Still, appointing a caregiver who lived near their prison was also important to many of the women I interviewed because it meant an increased chance that their baby would be able to visit them.[41] Longer travel distances, especially in rural areas with little public transportation, may also necessitate added expenses, such as a car rental, food, and lodging, which may be out of reach for many families of the incarcerated.[42] In other cases, caregivers may be unable or even unwilling to drive the baby and any older children to visit their mother in prison for many reasons, such as having tight work schedules that make it difficult to accommodate limited visitation hours.[43] Those sentenced to several years in prison shared how it would only be a matter of time before their unborn baby would grow into a curious toddler with many questions about incarceration—questions that had no simple or easy answer—and in that case, they did not want the caregiver to be the one left to explain the particulars of such a difficult topic.

Angel was pregnant with her third child and sentenced to three years in prison, so she knew early on that she would miss many milestones in her baby's life; however, she was not embarrassed about having her children see her behind bars and instead wanted to see them as much as possible. For Angel, finding someone who was willing to foster this visitation was especially important. And as she considered her options, she felt most comfortable with the father of her unborn baby providing care. After all, they were happily married, and she knew he would be willing and able to bring their baby for a visit.

But not everyone in Angel's social circle approved of the arrangement. Many of Angel's family and friends did not approve of a man raising a baby, at least on his own, and felt that her husband would be too incompetent when it came to parenting. According to Angel, "My family kept saying, 'A man doesn't know how.' 'How is he gonna raise her?' [They said,] 'You were the one who is supposed to care for your child, you were selfish and not thinking about your baby to wind up pregnant in prison, and now she has to be raised by him.'" When I spoke with Angel, she confided that she also shared some of her family's concerns about her husband's ability to raise their daughter by himself. But, as she considered the matter further, she felt strongly that her husband would be the best person to provide care because he lived the closest to prison and would be in a better position to bring their baby for a visit.

Although the father of Angel's baby was in the picture, most were not. Some fathers lived "in the streets," leaving them unable to provide care. Lora talked about how she wanted nothing more than to have her boyfriend—the baby's father—be the caregiver; however, he had several warrants out for his arrest, and Lora knew it would only be a matter of time before he would be arrested and sent back to jail and, later, prison. For the most part, the women I interviewed were more likely to designate the father as a caregiver if they were already in a committed relationship.

One participant, Crystal, made plans to utilize a nursery program at her prison—something she was excited about because it meant that her baby would get to stay with her in prison until she was released. Research on prison nursery programs finds that both incarcerated women and their babies have better health outcomes and a strengthened mother-child relationship when they are allowed to stay together, especially during the first year, as nursery programs may also equip women with parenting resources and support as they transition back into the community following their release from prison.[44]

For Crystal, the nursery program was an ideal arrangement because it allowed her daughter to stay with her. And although Crystal theoretically avoided the need to appoint a caregiver, she was still forced to contend with the stigma that accompanied not only being pregnant in prison but also raising her daughter in a nontraditional setting (i.e., a correctional facility). Crystal explained how her family looked down upon her decision to use the nursery program. According to Crystal, "They frowned upon me. I get it, I was labeled as an inmate or a bad person for keeping my baby in prison, but at the end of the day, I am a human being and a woman who just wanted to be with her child." Although Crystal's use of the prison nursery program was viewed as nontraditional and even unacceptable for some, for Crystal, the ability to be with her baby, regardless of the particulars, was important to her.

Gloria was also incarcerated in one of the prisons in the United States that had a nursery program, and although she had initially planned on utilizing the program, she quickly discovered that, at least at her prison, it cost $350, which was far too expensive for her and her family.[45] The cost of prison nursery programs varies widely for the incarcerated in the United States. Gloria reasoned that "I would rather have my baby's dad, my boyfriend, keep that $350 dollars and just him be home with him and buy the stuff that he needed. I mean, I probably would of used that if I were rich or something. I only had three months left in prison, so I was like I'll be alright. I knew I had family that would take care of my child, so I thought I was doing what was in the best interest of my son." Those with older children talked about how important it was that their baby be placed with older siblings, thinking that their older child(ren) could "watch out for" the baby, acting as surrogate parents in some cases. The placement with an older sibling also meant that the older sibling could possibly teach the baby about their mother—something that was especially important to participants serving a longer sentence, who would be separated from their baby for a considerable period. Melody had older children who were already in foster care, so she approached her children's foster care mother about providing care. As Melody explained it, "It felt a lot more reassuring that [my baby] would be in with my other kids." For Melody, the decision to place her baby in foster care made the most sense because it meant that her children could remain together. However, despite Melody's satisfaction with this arrangement, she experienced pushback and stigma from her peers about her decision to use foster care, especially among her peers of color, for they were more likely to view the child welfare system as a policing system.

A Carceral Child Welfare System

This resistance stemmed, at least in part, from a long-standing history of the US child welfare system removing poor children of color from their homes in the name of "protection," at rates that are disproportionate to their White counterparts, leaving Black children to be overrepresented in the child welfare system.[46] Although Black children make up 14 percent of US children, they account for 23 percent of the children in foster care, with research revealing that most of these children are removed from their homes due to "neglect" arising from poor living conditions that often stem from poverty without regard to the structural causes of these conditions and the role that sexism and systemic racism play in the creation of these living conditions.[47]

To be sure, much has been written about how the child welfare system operates like the prison system to "monitor, regulate, punish, and devalue Black mothers," as child protective services tend to be in poor communities, making poor families more likely to experience surveillance and increasing the likelihood of their being accused of maltreatment.[48] The maternal web of control that emanates from the foster care system and the criminal legal system are already familiar to many poor families of color, as a system predicated on providing care does not always serve to protect children but rather functions as a carceral system by separating children from their families, providing insight into why Melody, a White woman, felt more comfortable with the idea of placing her baby in foster care, in comparison to some of the Black women I interviewed.

Race is a contributing factor in the creation of caregiver plans. Most of the Black women I interviewed were more likely to express serious reservations about the child welfare system as a viable outlet and partner in their search for a caregiver. Many shared how some of their older children had previously been placed in foster care and that it had been extremely difficult to regain custody once their children entered the system, especially as a Black woman, with institutional racism and structural poverty making it nearly impossible to demonstrate competency as a parent to a group of largely White child welfare workers.[49]

Tiana, a Black woman, said, "It's tough with the system 'cause it's their *job* to catch you and terminate parental rights. The extreme that you must go through to get your kids back is like death and darkness closing in more and more." Like Tiana, many did not trust that the child welfare system had their best interests in mind and were skeptical about placing their child in the hands of this system, a response that is consistent with findings from other research.[50] Similarly, several other women I interviewed shared how they had been "in the system" as a child and experienced sexual and emotional abuse at the hands of a foster parent, which did little to ease their anxieties around the child welfare system. For Tiana and many others, the child welfare system represents a great deal of pain and a source of family separation. The mistrust many participants had about the child welfare system speaks to the larger issue of the US carceral environment, where policing, punishment, and control are no longer limited to the criminal legal system but instead extend to other systems, including the child welfare system and even the medical system, a point I discuss in the next chapter.

Conclusion

While being pregnant in prison was far from what most women ever planned or imagined, most resolved to make the most of their time behind bars and wanted to use the excess time on their hands to prepare for the birth of their baby. To that end, pregnancy behind bars entails many forms of preparation. For some, it involves reading books or pamphlets about pregnancy, childbirth, and parenting, while in other cases, it means attending pregnancy classes offered in select prisons or relying on peers for information and support. For others, preparation means making a concerted effort to distance oneself from all things pregnancy and baby to protect themselves from further heartache. As much as the women I interviewed wanted to shelter themselves from the pain of an upcoming separation, nearly all had no choice but to select a caregiver—a task that was fraught with heartache and anxiety.

The ways in which pregnant women in prison approach preparation depend on a variety of factors, including their socioeconomic status and race, as well as family dynamics and other factors, such as the number of children they had and the proximity of loved ones. Those with a higher socioeconomic status were more apt to talk about how incarceration effectively prohibited their ability to engage in some of the more common, albeit middle-class, cultural practices of preparation like a baby shower or the decoration of a dedicated nursery space. This was in stark contrast to the experiences of most of the low-income women I interviewed, who talked more about how incarceration served as a window into educational resources and programming and even into a support system that they would not otherwise have had if they had not been behind bars. However, even in the act of preparation, women are not immune to regulation and control. For one thing, access to reading materials and classes is heavily regulated and dependent on the offerings of each prison and even the attitudes of correctional staff. Second, caregiver plans are also not immune to the regulation and control found in a correctional setting, leaving some to decide on a caregiver plan within a heavily regulated environment with countless rules and procedures that make planning difficult. The creation of a caregiver plan may necessitate involvement with the child welfare system, a carceral system that most wished to avoid because of the power it has to separate families.

Still, despite the regulation and control found in a correctional environment, the narratives around preparation also included instances of resistance and even hope. Denise's narrative of self-advocacy, as described earlier in the chapter, through the requesting of phone books in order to move forward with her adoption plan, provides insight into the ways in which women resist power and control from the rules and regulations that govern motherhood behind bars. In a place intentionally designed to keep women devoid of choices that affect their motherhood and from the rites and rituals of pregnancy, many shared how they turned to others on their floor to learn about pregnancy and parenthood, especially in the absence of more formal education. Accordingly, in a punitive environment, where women are stripped of their joy, some were able to find it in the celebration of a makeshift baby shower or other forms of support.

Perhaps Lora said it best when she explained how in an otherwise hopeless place, in a place where "everybody's under a lot of stress and everything is completely out of your control, where you feel helpless and just so depressed about all you're missing out on, . . . some of the most amazing examples of the human spirit can be seen in these rooms, women who threw me a baby shower or taught me about what to kinda expect."

Although preparation certainly looked different behind bars and even entailed additional tasks, like the creation of a caregiver plan, even in a system of control designed to strip women of their motherhood, they were still (expectant) mothers at the end of the day—a unique status that even the carceral system could not fully erase, nor could it negate the desire and willingness many have to prepare for their baby. For after these practices were finished, the only thing left to do was give birth—a phenomenon that I discuss in more detail in the next chapter.

4

The Ultimate Cage

Birth as a Site of Surveillance and Control

With my first, my baby's dad was there and got to cut [the] umbilical cord and put [the] first diaper on, so it wasn't the same this time.
—Angel

When Jada, a Black, single mother of two, came to prison, she was "young, naïve, and didn't know what to expect." A first-time offender at just twenty, she had never been in trouble with the law before. And even though she lived in a "rough neighborhood," where drugs and crime were present, she stayed away from trouble and immersed herself in her studies. A nearly straight-A student in high school, she was determined to make something of herself and enrolled at the local community college, where she majored in clinical therapy and behavioral studies with the dream of becoming a social worker.

While in college, Jada met the man of her dreams, and they quickly fell in love and moved in together. She was excited about the future and was ready to get married and settle down after she completed her degree. But, after a night of "one too many drinks," she became pregnant, though she was still determined not to let the pregnancy adversely affect her schooling. Her boyfriend found work at the local manufacturing plant, wanting to provide the best for their baby, and they settled into life as a family of three. Yet, just six months after giving birth, she became pregnant again.

Her boyfriend was unhappy about the latest pregnancy and, worried about their ability to make ends meet with another mouth to feed, encouraged her to have an abortion. A self-described "strong Christian," Jada never considered an abortion and was committed to making things work. Yet, as finances grew tighter by the day, her boyfriend began to drink more—what was once a couple of beers after work quickly turned into full-fledged alcoholism. Before she knew it, her boyfriend was unrecognizable, raising his voice at her nearly every day—and sometimes his fist.

Jada was torn. Still pregnant with their second child, she loved the idea of a nuclear family and convinced herself that their relationship would improve once she finished her degree and became more financially stable. According to Jada, things were *only* "really bad" when he drank. And even though she had concerns about bringing their then unborn baby into this volatile environment, her boyfriend was always apologetic and quick to offer promises of a better tomorrow. Jada resolved to leave the relationship once she finished school and was in a better position to support herself and her son. After all, she was only a couple of months away from graduation—or so she thought.

It would end up being decades before Jada would earn her degree, for on a rainy Saturday in September, things turned increasingly violent when her boyfriend unleashed his anger and his fist—though this time not just at Jada but also at their young son. To protect her son and her unborn baby, Jada "snapped" and grabbed a kitchen knife, and "that's when everything went black." Less than an hour later, she was in the back of a police car headed toward county jail, before she was later transported to prison on a twenty-year sentence for taking the life of her abuser.

Jada experienced a range of emotions behind bars. She missed her son terribly and struggled to understand why she, a battered woman, had to serve time at all.[1] As she neared her due date, she looked forward to giving birth and meeting her new baby but agonized over the thought of having to say both hello and goodbye to her baby in such a short period of time—something that no book or class could ever prepare her for. Although she had never been to prison before, she grew up watching those from her neighborhood cycle in and out of prison and knew that childbirth in the prison system would be different from anything she had ever known, a stark contrast to her last birth.

As a Black woman incarcerated in a nearly-all White rural community, she knew she remained especially vulnerable to mistreatment, abuse, and even death.[2] As a result, she distrusted both the prison system and the medical system and knew that her identity as a Black woman from a rough neighborhood meant that she would have little power and autonomy over her birth experience. As a student of social work, she was familiar with the racial disparities in maternal mortality rates and knew that Black women are three times more likely to die from pregnancy-related causes than their White counterparts, due to causes that are mostly preventable, including institutionalized racism, systemic poverty, and a number of implicit biases that permeate the US modern medical system.[3]

As Jada explained, "I was in a White town scared to death, so as the only African American in the hospital, I'm like, 'Oh no, I can't have my baby in *this* hospital.'" But Jada had no choice, for she was incarcerated, which meant having no say in her medical care. The loss of control she experienced during childbirth was nothing short of "horrific," for she was subject to regulation and control from both the prison system *and* the medical system, with decisions being largely made *for* her rather than in consultation with her, making her feel like a mere spectator in her birth experience. Jada's experience is hardly unique, as thousands of incarcerated pregnant women are stripped of their bodily autonomy and dignity, unable to make decisions about the most intimate of matters—a reality that has lasting effects on the health of women and their children.

This chapter focuses on the birth experiences of incarcerated women and the varied ways in which they are controlled and surveilled during childbirth and through the first twenty-four hours following birth. I examine how the prison system and the medical system work together to exert control over women. Whether it is through the denial of information, the use of shackles, the surveilling watch of correctional officers and healthcare providers, or the forced separation of women from their babies, every aspect of birth is tightly controlled and subject to punishment. This chapter provides a rare chronological portrait into some of the more unique complexities that govern birth behind bars, as I show how incarcerated pregnant women are punished at every point during the birth experience.

Throughout the chapter, I show how the medical system acts as a carceral system, fraught with rules, surveillance, and control, working alongside the prison system to exert a web of control and authority over women. This web continues to function even during birth, producing a unique type of control that punishes women and their families in ways that incarcerated men and even nonincarcerated women are not punished. I argue that just as prisons consider the maternal bodies of women to be state property, in need of containment, the maternal bodies of women also belong to the medical system, in which they are monitored and surveilled further. To be pregnant behind bars, then, means to be punished by multiple carceral systems across multiple ways: whether it is through the use of shackles that restrict movement during birth or through the surveilling presence of a correctional officer in the room during the intimate act of childbirth or through forced, unwanted cervical exams or through continuous fetal monitoring that records a range of numerical information that can then be used to further restrain women in the ultimate cage, childbirth is yet another site of punishment.[4]

Laboring

The paternalistic model of medicine that permeates the United States is grounded in the notion that the maternal body is out of control and unruly—dangerous to the women themselves and to their fetuses.[5] Childbirth, then, is viewed as a medical event that must be controlled and managed at a hospital through the skillful intervention of medical experts and through a range of (sometimes unnecessary) medical procedures and instruments, including the use of forceps, anesthesia, and cesarean sections. This medical model of care is in stark contrast to the woman-centered model that dominated through much of the seventeenth century, an approach that viewed birth as a normal, natural phenomenon, a site of empowerment, where women were encouraged to lean into their intuition, attended by a skilled midwife, surrounded by a close circle of support.[6]

The move away from a woman-centered model of care to a medical model that frames birth as a dangerous medical event that inherently entails a loss of control has had lasting effects on the way childbirth is treated still to this day.[7] The framing of birth as a violent, unpredictable event not only contributes to the trauma and fears surrounding childbirth but also creates the expectation for women to willingly lean in to trusted medical experts who "know best."[8] As a result, birth is marked by a number of power dynamics that view medical providers as the trusted experts, even over those who are pregnant, removing the power and authority of women and redirecting it to medical providers who then deliver the baby, erasing the mother entirely.[9]

While even nonincarcerated women experience a lack of control and surveillance during childbirth, the effects are especially pronounced for those behind bars, who remain especially vulnerable to the maternal web of control and multiple matrices of oppression. Although there is a wide variety of birth experiences, women are often left in the dark and not told about the particulars of what is to come, including but not limited to the nature of procedures and practices that will be performed on them (often without their consent), as well as matters such as *where* and even *when* they will give birth—a stark contrast to those outside of prison who may have some semblance of understanding about what is to come, even engaging in childbirth classes that may include a tour of the hospital. Most of all, many are left not knowing how much time they will have with their baby before they will be forced to say goodbye. According to Jeanine, thirty-one and a biracial mother of five, "They don't explain nothing to you because they don't want you to tell anyone else on the outside of the wall. So, I was kinda scared because I was worried like how I was gonna have my child. Whenever I went into the nurses' station in the prison, I was like, 'Oh my gosh, am I gonna have my child here?' Or, 'Am I gonna have to have my baby with my hands being in handcuffs or stuff like that,' so they don't explain nothing like that to you, so it's scary not knowing." In the absence of information and educational materials, as discussed in the last chapter, women remain especially powerless, unable to exercise full autonomy, making it easier for the maternal web of control and human rights violations to proliferate.

Forced Inductions

Although each prison has its own unique policies and practices when it comes to childbirth, nearly all the women I interviewed said they were forcibly induced rather than allowed to have their labor occur spontaneously, even in cases where an induction was not deemed medically necessary. Correctional administrators, as well as medical providers, did not consult with them on whether they wanted an induction, nor did they communicate with them about *when* the induction would occur, resulting in great uncertainty as women did not know when they might be retrieved from their cell in the middle of the night and taken to the hospital or even to what hospital they would be transported for labor and delivery. As Angel explained, "They don't tell you when they're coming to get you to take you to have your baby, they just come take you at night, so I never knew."

Melody was especially upset that an induction was performed at all, for it was not medically necessary, and she never consented to the procedure. As Melody said, "There was no way to challenge that because my body was property of the state and they can't have liability, so I had to interrupt the natural rhythm of which my child was to come out in the world. I had to give birth and have it artificially induced, so it was a huge violation, a cosmic violation, because I didn't really want to induce. I've never had a labor induced. I've only had natural, so it was very disturbing, and I had no control of it." Correctional administrators argue that to inform women of their induction date as well as other important matters, such as location, could present a "security risk," where the incarcerated could theoretically connive an escape attempt with people from the community.[10] Correctional administrators also argue that inductions allow them time to ensure they have adequate staff to transport, as well as general security provisions at the facility—yet another example of how the emphasis on security and order trumps the medical care of women and their fetuses.[11]

The medical system is complicit in this practice, for the prison relies on the medical system and its interventionist medical model of care, in which even women who are not incarcerated are routinely offered inductions and many times encouraged to have them beginning around thirty-nine weeks of pregnancy—an outgrowth of the lack of autonomy over birth decisions.[12] While women who are not incarcerated may experience inductions against their will, they have more power to decline an unwanted induction and to seek alternative care because they are not incarcerated and under the maternal web of control.[13] While inductions can be medically necessary and an important tool, particularly in cases of preeclampsia, they can also carry significant risks, including infection, hemorrhage, and uterine rupture.[14] Research shows that inductions (and cesareans) may be preferred by medical providers because they offer more convenience and predictability to providers' schedules.[15]

Physicians may frighten women into having an induction, citing fears of a large baby or the need for a cesarean section, unnecessarily pressuring women into procedures they do not want or need.[16] Furthermore, research finds that inductions do not require formal written consent and that even outside of prison, consent is explained to women in ways they do not fully understand, leaving women with little understanding about their choices in childbirth.[17]

Yet, because medical providers are viewed as experts over pregnancy and childbirth, any questioning of medical authority may be perceived as a failure among women to consider the safety and care of their baby—reaffirming the notion that they are not "good" mothers. These sentiments are especially profound for incarcerated women, particularly women of color, who are caught in this web of control and expected to continuously demonstrate their fitness as mothers, with "bad" mothers being demonized not only by the medical system but also through the prison system.

Delayed Care

There are some who go into spontaneous labor on their own behind bars. Even during a critical point of labor, the maternal web of control proliferates, as women remain subject to the various policies and practices that govern life behind bars, where order and security reign supreme. In cases of spontaneous labor, women must first locate an officer—something that is not always easy to do given staff shortages and prison overcrowding. Even then, incarcerated women, particularly Black women, are not always believed, a reality that has been documented extensively in research.[18] Consequently, officers may hesitate to give the okay for a woman to be seen by the prison medical staff, who act as gatekeepers regarding whether a woman should be taken to a hospital in the community where she will give birth. Even then, correctional staff must first be located to perform a strip search on women before they can leave the facility, and a vehicle and staff must also be secured before women can be transported by staff to the nearest hospital. At any point, women may experience repercussions for "faking" their need for medical care or for perceived impoliteness, as even during labor, women are expected to issue pleasantries to staff.

The nature of prison and the need for frequent security "counts" means that it is not uncommon for women to experience considerable delays in their transport and medical care, in some cases having to wait until count is finished until they can be transported to a hospital.[19] And since prisons are often understaffed and overcrowded, it may take considerable time for a count to finish, resulting in the delay of medical attention—a reality that can have life-or-death consequences for both women and their unborn babies. Delays at any point can pose serious concerns for women and their fetuses, as timely medical care is important for optimal birth outcomes.[20]

Faye discussed how she had to wait between two and three hours before an officer became available to drive her to the hospital, and in the meantime, she was left in excruciating pain. According to Faye, "It was so horrible. I called out, 'Please help me.' Well, I had to sit there for two, three hours in labor because they had to wait till count cleared till they could do anything. I'm sittin' here in labor, active labor for two and a half hours in labor with nothing. No medicine, no nothing. And then, I'm sitting there crying, freakin' out all alone." For Faye, it was already a challenge to have her pain taken seriously—to issue a call for help only to have it fall upon deaf ears was exhausting and only led to more distress. Suffice it to say, Faye was angry that a routine practice like "count" trumped her need for medical attention, yet another example of how prisons are ill equipped to handle pregnant women.

A failure to transport women in a timely manner is especially concerning given that incarcerated women are at a higher risk for health complications, due to a culmination of health risks and underlying health needs, as previously discussed.[21] And while Faye went on to give birth to a healthy infant, there have been documented cases where a delay in transportation resulted in a life-threatening situation.[22] Concerns about making it to the hospital on time were especially felt among those who went into spontaneous labor and were incarcerated in more remote areas away from major highways and hospitals.

Research reveals that in maternity care deserts, like many of the rural prisons the women were incarcerated in, women may have to travel hours during labor to receive care.[23] Those in remote areas may have to travel 3.7 times farther than those in places that have more access to care, highlighting the importance of timely care behind bars.[24] In Faye's case, the nearest hospital was an hour and a half away from her prison, which made for a long drive that was made all the more painful as she was restrained at her ankles and wrists throughout the car ride. According to Faye,

> That was a horrible car ride, and they shackle you head to toe for the whole drive, so you're pregnant and you're big, fat, and you're shackled. And they put you in a van. And your feet are shackled with handcuffs, and they're put together so you can only move so much. And tryin' to get in the van and get out of the van is horrible, it's pain. You have pain everywhere, in your hands 'cause you're shackled like this around your waist. And you got the handcuffs and the shackles on your wrists and around your feet. You have pain in your ankles 'cause the damn thing's too tight.

While making it to the hospital in a timely manner may be a concern that is also felt by pregnant women even outside of prison, this concern is arguably magnified for the incarcerated, who must navigate additional layers of security before they can even leave for the hospital.[25] Even then, once women arrive at the hospital, there is often a delay before they can be seen. Their status as prisoner only contributes to this delay, as obstetric staff are often inexperienced in the unique provisions that come with the incarcerated. Once they arrive at the hospital and are processed through the medical system, the medical system works in collaboration with the prison system, exerting its power and authority to regulate women even further, stripping them of their bodily autonomy.

Birthing

Carceral control is intensified at hospitals, as women are subject to yet another layer of control by the medical system, positioning them deeper into a subjugated status of both patient and prisoner. Childbirth in a medical interventionist model of medicine is grounded in gendered racism, where birth is a medicalized event that must be managed through increasingly technocratic care from both humans and machines, as patriarchy, institutions, and technology proliferate.[26] Under this model, birthing women are reduced to mere vectors, subjugated and infantilized, while medical providers go to work in an assembly-line-like fashion to produce the ultimate product—a baby.[27]

Medical anthropologist Robbie Davis-Floyd eloquently illustrates how women are subjugated during birth, stripped of their power during the most intimate and transformative of moments. According to Davis-Floyd,[28]

> If we stop a moment now to see in our mind's eye the images that a laboring woman will be experiencing—herself in bed, in a hospital gown, staring up at an IV pole, bag, and cord on one side, and a big whirring machine on the other, and down at a huge belt encircling her waist, wires coming out of her vagina, and a steel bed, we can see that her entire visual field conveys one overwhelming perceptual message about our culture's deepest values and beliefs—technology is supreme, and you are utterly dependent on it and on the institutions and individuals who control and dispense it. The lithotomy position, in which the woman lies with her legs elevated in stirrups and her buttocks at the very edge of the delivery table, completes the process of her symbolic inversion from autonomy and privacy to dependence and complete exposure, expressing and reinforcing her powerlessness and the power of society (as evidenced by its representative, the obstetrician) at the supreme moment of her own individual transformation.

Incarcerated women are controlled even further, as the prison system assists the medical system in this process, controlling and supervising every move, ensuring that women submit to the process. Not only are they surveilled through the watchful eyes of medical providers, technology, and correctional officers but the use of restraints at the ankles, wrists, and belly in a practice referred to as shackling adds yet another layer to this surveillance, providing a visual sign that incarcerated women are dangerous, unruly bodies in need of this ultimate cage.

Obstetric Violence

In this assembly-line model, the power is in the hands of institutions, as individual choice is removed, and decision making is nearly nonexistent. Matters such as cervical examinations, where providers insert their fingers through the vaginal opening, the placing of the Foley bulb into the cervix, and who is and is not permitted to be in the birth room when these intimate procedures are performed are all decided *for* women rather than in consultation with them.[29] Consent is an afterthought and in some cases not deemed necessary at all, for the bodies of pregnant women belong to the state, just as much as (if not more than) they belong to women.

The erasure of consent, especially when a number of power dynamics are present, means that mistreatment and abuse happen with relative ease in a phenomenon known as obstetric violence.[30] At its core, obstetric violence is a form of institutional violence and gender-based violence in which mistreatment or harm at the hands of medical personnel occurs to pregnant, birthing, or postpartum women.[31] Routinized and forced procedures performed without consent and dignity, like cesarean exams, cervical exams, membrane sweeps, inductions, and episiotomies, can easily become obstetric violence, leaving women with substantial birth trauma and little legal recourse.[32] While all women remain susceptible to obstetric violence during birth, the potential for violence is arguably amplified among the incarcerated, particularly for racial and ethnic minorities, where additional layers of surveillance, control, and authority exist.[33]

Leslie explained how consent and autonomy were absent during her birth, leaving her with significant birth trauma. According to Leslie, "There was no talk about what type of labor I wanted or if I wanted to use the labor chair or if I wanted a natural, it was just a pretty cold procedure, it was just 'we'll do a C-section.'" The lack of choice made her feel "robbed of [her] birth" because she wanted to give birth naturally in a birth pool at a birthing center, but her prison would not allow it and instead deferred to the more routinized and technocratic care that comes with a medicalized-model approach.[34] Leslie said, "I didn't have an amazing birth. It was just we'll do this; we'll do that. There was nothing that was discussed with me. I didn't want the hospital, but I didn't have those choices about my birth because I was a piece of property of the [State] Department of Corrections." Freestanding birth centers are growing in popularity, particularly in the wake of the US maternal-mortality crisis, with more women, especially women of color, turning to these centers not necessarily to have a more empowering birth but to *survive*.[35]

Ruthie was also vocal about her birth experience and explained how she was forced to have a cesarean section, even though she did not give consent. As Ruthie explained, she had already had a cesarean section and wanted to have a VBAC (vaginal birth after cesarean) this time, but the hospital her prison transported her to had a policy that prohibits VBACs. VBAC bans are a common practice among smaller, rural hospitals that do not have access to robust maternity care, including round-the-clock anesthesia if needed, and there is also a scarcity of providers who are willing to accept patients who wish to have a trial of labor after cesarean (TOLAC).[36] The placement of prisons in remote rural areas shows how the prison system is intentionally designed to limit choice even further, while simultaneously keeping otherwise floundering economies afloat. Research reveals that VBAC bans are more likely to occur in hospitals that also serve a larger percentage of women on public insurance and with lower educational levels—a disturbing reality that demonstrates the disparities in birth experiences and how marginalized women even outside the prison system experience an erosion of reproductive freedom.[37]

Though many of the birth stories of incarcerated women certainly contain descriptions of trauma, obstetric violence, and barbarism, not every woman who is incarcerated views her experience this way. As with other aspects of pregnancy, race and socioeconomic status matter a great deal. Some of the impoverished White women I interviewed were simply grateful to have healthcare at all, particularly given their poor health and history of drug abuse. Although some discussed the problems in their healthcare, they were quick to issue a caveat expressing their gratitude for simply having healthcare at all, when they were previously accustomed to having none.

These experiences contrast with those of women from a more affluent background, who knew that even as incarcerated people, they were still entitled to be treated with dignity and to be informed about their rights and granted choice during childbirth. As a result, they were more apt to vocalize their concerns and understood the importance of self-advocacy. Many of the Black women I interviewed were also painfully aware of the harms that limited their choice and governed any decision making in the birth space and felt that their concerns were not taken seriously;

however, as Black woman, incarcerated no less, they also face more consequences from carceral systems for "speaking out."

That is, when Black women give birth, especially while incarcerated, they must contend with the gendered racism that permeates the birth space and paints Black women as unruly or difficult.[38] The effects of these "controlling images" are profound. Although mistreatment has been documented among women across all backgrounds, it is higher for women of color.[39] Recent research reveals that one in three Black women experience mistreatment during birth, in comparison to one in five for mothers overall—startling statistics that illustrate how institutionalized racism and obstetric violence converge to produce adverse consequences in birth, making it harder for Black women to exercise agency, especially in historically White institutions.[40] The presence of surveilling correctional officers with the power to impose disciplinary actions when women deviate from the expected obedient and infantilized status of patient and prisoner only contributes to the loss of power and autonomy at birth.

Shackling

The use of shackles at the waist, ankles, and wrists adds yet another dimension to surveillance and control, for women are literally chained to ensure they are compliant in their submission, reinforcing the notion that they are out of control, unruly, and violent. The use of shackles on women during pregnancy, labor, delivery, and postpartum recovery and during transportation (to a medical facility or court, as examples) is a practice unique to incarcerated pregnant women. Shackling women during labor and delivery is a prime example of how the medical system collides with the prison system to impose additional punishment. Although leading medical organizations, such as the American College of Obstetricians and Gynecologists, the American Medical Association, and the American Public Health Association, have all denounced the practice of shackling because of how the use of shackles threatens not only fetal health but also maternal health, the medical system is complicit with the prison system in this practice when women are shackled during birth, strengthening the power of the maternal web of control and its hold over women.[41]

Research shows that freedom of movement is central to the birthing process and that the use of shackles can interfere with women's ability to access medical care in a timely manner.[42] In cases where an emergency cesarean section is needed, the use of shackles could delay the cesarean section, as a correctional officer must also be at the ready to remove the shackles prior to surgery.[43] Any delay in an emergency situation is significant in that it could cause a number of health complications, including brain damage or even death.[44] Legal scholars and advocates have also argued that the use of shackles violates the Eighth Amendment to the US Constitution, which states that "excessive bail shall not be required, nor excessive fines imposed, nor cruel and unusual punishments inflicted," in addition to violating many international laws protecting humans from cruel and inhumane treatment.[45]

The extent of the use of shackles on pregnant women is not fully known, as national data is not kept; however, it is a practice that continues to exist because of long-held beliefs that frame shackles as necessary to prevent an escape or to restrain potentially violent women.[46] However, research shows that most incarcerated pregnant women are serving time for nonviolent offenses and do not pose a security risk, especially while in the vulnerable state of labor, as described earlier by Davis-Floyd.[47] Furthermore, even women serving time for violent offenses do not pose security risks during the vulnerable state of childbirth.[48] To date, there have been no documented cases of escape attempts among incarcerated pregnant women, reinforcing the notion that this practice is used not for security and protection but rather to further subjugate women.[49]

While the Federal Bureau of Prisons prohibited the use of shackles in 2008 for those incarcerated in federal prisons and codified this prohibition into law in 2018 under the First Step Act, at the time of this writing, only forty-one states have implemented *restrictions* on shackling—nine states, including some of the states my participants were incarcerated in, have no antishackling laws in place at all, meaning that the use of restraints can be imposed at any point, even during labor and delivery.[50] Even in states that pose restrictions on shackling, there is a disconnect between the law and the realities of actual practices. Furthermore, all states that have antishackling laws still have loopholes that grant correctional officers the authority to shackle women during pregnancy if they are deemed a threat, for there is not a single state that has outright banned the practice of shackling women, closing these legal loopholes.[51]

In the absence of legislation barring shackling, the practice is subject to much discretion, as it is largely up to the attending correctional officer to make a determination as to whether a woman appears "dangerous" and "threatening" and in need of restraints—a practice fraught with racial disparity, with women of color being more likely to be perceived as a threat that must be restrained to protect the mostly White healthcare providers and correctional staff.[52] The uniqueness of having an incarcerated patient means that even medical providers who may be against shackling often defer to correctional staff about the particulars of shackling, for the use of shackles and the presence of a correctional officer reaffirm women's danger. Shackling pregnant and birthing women relegates them to a submissive state with little to no power or legal recourse and with their bodies being subject to the authority and control of these systems.

It is no surprise, then, that many of the women I interviewed also questioned the need for shackles during childbirth. As Denise said, "Like where am I going? I'm in labor *and* you have a CO in there, so where are you going?[53] I couldn't move. I was numb from my breasts down; I couldn't get off that table and run if I wanted to." Women who opted for epidurals or underwent cesarean sections were especially taken aback about the "need" for shackles, as their lower bodies were numb. Gloria shared how the very idea that she would connive an escape attempt while in the hospital undergoing a cesarean section was "ludicrous" and "insulting." According to Gloria, "They had me handcuffed to the bed like I was just gonna get up and run away with a seven-inch incision. It's like it was bad, they had me handcuffed to the bed while they were giving, having surgery on me, they had one leg and they had one arm. They also had this female CO in the room the whole time when I was having my surgery."

There were even a few women I spoke with who were shackled during the active or pushing stage of labor. Stacy shared how she was shackled to the bed at the wrists, ankles, and waist as she labored and gave birth to her baby, making her feel like an animal. The use of shackles inhibited her ability to labor and push because she could not move freely and change positions—something that is often viewed as beneficial and even necessary in labor, as it helps the baby get into an optimal position, avoiding unnecessary interventions, including a cesarean section.[54] In the words of Stacy, "I had shackles around my feet and hands. It was just degrading, and it's like do you not see that I'm carrying this child. I mean I guess it's protocol, but I was shackled to the bed while I was delivering my baby. You feel shamed, and it makes you feel unworthy, and it just puts a stigma on you. I had waist chains, and I couldn't move through the contractions, so the actual part of being shackled to the bed, I felt like an *animal*." In the age of fetal-protection laws that are framed as necessary for the protection and care of fetuses, the babies born to incarcerated women are not given these same protections, for the carceral practices imposed on the mothers also threaten babies' health.

Even in places where shackling is outlawed, women may still be shackled because it remains such a long-standing practice. In these cases, women are in an uncomfortable position where they either risk punishment for speaking out or remain quiet, ensuring the continuance of harm. Rhonda, for example, was incarcerated in a state that permitted the use of shackles during childbirth only among those with a higher, more serious custody level. The rules at her specific prison permitted those placed on minimum custody (like herself) to remain unshackled during childbirth. However, during childbirth, a correctional officer still tried to shackle her. According to Rhonda, "They did try to shackle me, but again, you must know your rights and because they kept trying to shackle me to the bed even when I was going to have the baby I said, 'What are you doing with those handcuffs?' She's like, 'We have to shackle you just in case I have to go to the restroom,' and I said, 'No ma'am.' I said, 'Check my reports, check my file. I am not to be shackled at any time,' and she checked my file, and she said, 'Oh, you're absolutely right.'" Rhonda's encounter speaks to the importance of both knowledge and self-advocacy, while also highlighting the risks that come with speaking out. As Rhonda told me, to some degree, she felt "lucky" that the attending correctional officer listened to her, for she feared that her advocacy could easily be conflated with disobedience, especially for a Black woman like her who must contend with controlling and racialized tropes like the "angry Black woman" that characterize Black women as aggressive and threatening.[55]

Surveilling Correctional Officers

Adding yet another layer to this surveillance is a correctional officer who always accompanies women during their hospital stay, sometimes staying directly at the foot of the bed, making it more difficult for women to labor. The surveilling presence of a correctional officer is yet another way that women are degraded during birth, where even their most intimate organs are on full display, stripping them of any dignity, increasing their stress and anxiety and inciting trauma. To be clear, research highlights the importance of a calm and relaxing environment during birth, as labor relies on a complex interplay of hormones, wherein stress can hinder the production of oxytocin, the hormone necessary for the stimulation of labor.[56] Having an officer in the room and in some cases while they were already shackled, devoid of any movement and freedom, is a prime example of how women are punished not just for their crimes but also for their reproduction and womanhood, for they are punished in ways that incarcerated men are not.

Stacy explained how the presence of correctional officers (especially men) can incite further trauma for survivors of sexual abuse. Stacy's experience was "horrible" because it brought back painful memories of abuse. As Stacy said, "See that was horrible, and a lot of women who are in prison are sexually abused. I was too, so that brings up a whole 'nother list of issues because it was another trauma to have to give birth with a guard constantly in the room the whole time. It was just embarrassing, it was embarrassing." Stacy was not alone in her sentiments. Research finds that maternity care may be reminiscent of sexual abuse for survivors.[57] Given the high rates of sexual abuse among incarcerated women, they may be especially susceptible to birth trauma, making the need for trauma-informed care even more important.

Ruthie's narrative about feeling exposed during birth, as multiple male officers watched her give birth in varying stages of undress, triggering painful memories of abuse, was especially poignant:

> It was very embarrassing and uncomfortable. It was like I couldn't even lay on my bed and try and relax and get some rest because they was sittin' right there in my face. When I gave birth, it felt like they was all up on me. And I had to have a cesarean, so my stomach was all open, and it was

like this other person that's controlling me right now is gonna go up in my insides. And I felt that way, really like I felt the officers goin' inside my body. So, it was like you're in my private space, like it was just really, really uncomfortable. I really hated it. I mean, they were so bad; I couldn't even eat my food because I was so scared and violated.

Ruthie's narrative illustrates that even when women are on an operating table, physically unable to move and escape, even if they wanted to, they are controlled and surveilled, highlighting the punitive nature of these practices. In Ruthie's case, the attending officer saw more of Ruthie, including her internal organs, than Ruthie did of herself. Thus, having a correctional officer in the room during such an intimate act as childbirth has less to do with mitigating risk and more to do with regulation and control, reaffirming the power of the carceral state.

Welcome to the Family

Not only do incarcerated women have no control over whether a correctional officer attends their birth; the prison system also controls whether loved ones are able to be present during labor and delivery, regulating women's ability to access support at a time when they arguably need it the most. The research is clear—women who have a support system at birth have improved health outcomes all around—including fewer childbirth complications and decreased rates of postpartum depression and anxiety.[58] Although each prison and hospital has its own set of rules and regulations regarding having a companion person and visitors at birth, many of the women I interviewed shared how their family and friends were unable to be there for their birth, leaving them without support—whether that was because of restrictive rules and regulations from either the prison or hospital that forbid a support person or due to the many logistical barriers that made it all but impossible for loved ones to be physically present.

Support Companions

Given the uniqueness of incarcerating pregnant women, prisons may have little to no guidelines or formally written rules when it comes to visitors at birth, yet this does not mean that women have a great deal of autonomy and freedom over who can attend their birth. In many cases, I found that a prison may defer to the visitation policies that are in place at their respective facilities that may limit visitation to an hour or less and only to those who have previously been approved by the prison—a process that may take weeks or months.

Even then, logistical barriers make visitation at the hospital difficult if not impossible for low-income families without the means to travel, especially if their loved one is incarcerated far from home, as was the case with most of my interviewees in remote, rural areas.[59] Given that many are not informed in advance of their induction date or even the name of the hospital where they are to give birth, this adds yet another layer of complexity that makes it difficult for loved ones to come to the hospital, let alone to be there in time to be of support during labor. Still more, visitors are also subject to the visitation rules at each hospital, which may limit the number of visitors and place limits on the hours of visitation.

Angel explained how she was allowed to have visitors but only *after* her baby was born. Even then, she was not allowed to personally call her husband to inform him that their baby was born; an attending correctional officer told her that only staff could place this call because of "prison rules." Angel went on to share how the attending officer was so slow in calling her husband that by the time the officer reached her husband, she was on the verge of being discharged from the hospital—leaving her husband (who lived out of state) with little time to make it to the hospital before she would be discharged and sent back to prison. In the hours leading up to her husband's arrival, Angel was going "stir-crazy" wondering whether he would make it to the hospital in time, for she had no way of calling him to determine his whereabouts. According to Angel,

> They didn't even call [my husband]. They didn't even call him until after I had [my baby] and then they gave him a time frame of how long to get there, how long he had to get there until [my baby] *would* go through social services, and he was traveling over eight hours away, so I was nervous, really nervous because I didn't have a clue if he was gonna make it or not. I didn't know. With my first, my baby's dad was there and got

to cut [the] umbilical cord and put [the] first diaper on, so it wasn't the same this time.

As Angel indicated, one reason she was particularly worried about her husband making it on time is that she had designated her husband as the caregiver. Caregivers may be given just a short time before the baby is placed with a social worker only to then be placed in foster care—an arrangement that terrified many, especially for those with lived experience in the foster care system. Angel's narrative illustrates the power of the child welfare system and how it works in conjunction with the prison system to disrupt families.

Jeanine explained how her mom lived in a different state from where she was incarcerated and hospitalized, and just like Angel, she too experienced anxiety as she waited for her mom to pick her baby up from the hospital. As Jeanine explained,

> I called my mom as soon as they let me, and she left that same day. [By the time she got here,] she showed up maybe thirty minutes before they were gonna take my child and put my child into the shelter and stuff, so they don't even give you enough time to try to plan out . . . like, whenever I was in labor they could have let me call my mom and be like, "Hey, mom, be here tomorrow by this time so you can come grab her" or anything like that. They didn't try to let me plan it out. It was just a last-minute thing, and I don't think that's fair to women 'cause there was one lady, her child got taken away because of that . . . but it's prison, if you don't do things on their time, you gotta play by *their* game.

Arguably, caregivers and families with more money have an easier time navigating the visitation rules of the prison system, the medical system, and the child welfare system, which means that they are likely to arrive sooner because they do not have to navigate the complexities that come with securing transportation, as well as securing possible lodging and childcare. These delays can easily be viewed as grounds to place a baby into the child welfare system and do not take into consideration the structural barriers that make it difficult for impoverished families to come to the hospital in a timely manner, particularly for those in remote areas—making even caregivers targets of the child welfare system.

Above all, the rules and regulations that come with visitation make it difficult for women to have the support they need during the critical period of childbirth, thwarting their ability to attain optimal birth outcomes and to parent with dignity—a core tenet of reproductive freedom. The emphasis on regulation and control, including over visitation, means that even infants are welcomed into a carceral world, where rules and procedures dictate the circumstances through which families can be together, forever altering familial ties.

Saying Goodbye

Most of all, the maternal web of control governs the forced separation of families. Typically, incarcerated women are discharged from the hospital about twenty-four hours after a vaginal birth and about forty-eight to seventy-two hours after a cesarean birth.[60] Suffice it to say, this is an emotional time, as women are forced to say both hello and goodbye to their baby in the same period, only to then place their baby in the arms of a caregiver—all while under the surveillance and scrutiny of correctional officers, medical providers, and even social workers, which means little to no privacy in which to have heartfelt conversations and quality, uninterrupted time. There was a consensus among the women I interviewed that the hardest part of their entire hospital stay was when they had to say goodbye to their baby and head back to prison. Nearly all the women I interviewed became visibly emotional and shed tears as they talked about their heart-wrenching goodbye. As Faye said,

> No woman wants to give birth in prison. No woman wants to sit there and hold her baby while being handcuffed and having shackles on her feet. No woman wants to have to sit there and look at how beautiful her baby is and know in two days you're gonna have to give him away. I had known the entire time that this was what was going to happen, that I was going to give my son to another woman, and I thought that I had a firm understanding of that and that I was okay with that, and when it came time to leave the hospital, I could not stop crying, that's all I could do.

In some cases, women who had a cesarean section said they were grateful to have a cesarean birth rather than a vaginal birth because it typically meant a longer hospital stay. And while nearly all the women I interviewed said they had "mentally prepared" for this moment and took some solace in their placement plan, it did little to ease the pain of saying goodbye.

Bonnie shared how she "broke down" in the hospital when it was time to leave. Wanting to preserve every detail of her baby, she asked if she could keep her baby's receiving blanket and was told that she was not allowed to take the blanket back to prison, for it too was considered contraband and subject to the rules of the prison system. As Bonnie explained, "I'll never forget when I was leaving the hospital to go back to the prison after my last visit with my baby. [My baby's] receiving blanket had been left in the room with me and I wanted to take it back with me, and [the officer] would not let me, and I cried my eyes out, and she would not let me take it back with me. She's like, 'If I let you take it back, everybody's gonna think they can bring back their baby blanket, and I'm sorry I just can't let you do that.'" The receiving blanket was especially important to Bonnie, as she had no other keepsakes from her baby's birth, such as photos or the treasured hospital wrist bracelet—keepsakes she likely would have had if she had not been incarcerated, making her feel further robbed of her birth experience. Although Bonnie understood the institutional rules that governed contraband in her prison, she was still hurt by the varied ways in which domination, control, and surveillance marked nearly every aspect of her birth, funneling her into a deep depression. These narratives highlight how pregnant women in prison are punished not just for their crimes but also for their reproduction.

Resisting the Maternal Web of Control

While the maternal web of control is at its peak during childbirth, this does not mean that women do not engage in various forms of resistance, advocating for a better birth experience, or that there are not people inside both the prison system and the medical system who go out of their way to provide care or compassion at a time when it is needed most, circumventing rules from both systems to provide women with a semblance of dignity. This is not to say that every woman experiences compassion nor even obstetric violence during childbirth, for there is much variation in birth experiences.

Among my interviewees, Cherelle shared how she developed close relationships with the nurses who took "exceptional" care of her during her two-month-long hospital stay because of health complications, making her feel especially loved, giving her back a semblance of dignity and humanity. Because Cherelle needed such a long hospital stay, her prison did not have enough correctional staff to be able to stay with her throughout the duration of her hospitalization, so they relied on hospital staff for supervision. As Cherelle explained, the care and attention the nurses gave her was only made possible because prison staff was not present:

> I had really good nurses. I was really, really, really blessed at that hospital . . . [begins to cry] They didn't see me as a prisoner, all the nurses on that floor gave me a baby shower. They sent home over one hundred pounds of clothes, T-shirts, Pampers, they mailed it to my grandmother's house. One nurse would come in every morning around seven o' clock, pass me her cell phone, and I was able to call my grandmother every day. They would do all kinds of stuff they weren't supposed to do with me, and I was very grateful for that. Those ladies could have lost their jobs. I'll never forget it.

There were others I interviewed who said their attending officer stayed just outside their hospital room rather than *in* it out of respect for their privacy, even though the rules at their prison facility specified that they were to be in the room. Others offered to purchase something for them from the hospital vending machines. Some women shared stories about specific officers who allowed them to remain unshackled, even when their facility rules required them to be shackled. Cherelle's narrative highlights both the tremendous risk and the generosity of individual staff who circumvent rules to provide care. Context is important in that although hospitals are still carceral places, fraught with surveillance and control, they usually contain less surveillance than prisons do, leaving healthcare staff and even correctional officers with more freedom to provide care than they otherwise would have been able to provide behind bars.

Angel shared how she found an advocate in her doula, a trained, nonmedical person who provides support to pregnant, birthing, and postpartum women, allowing women to mitigate some of the maternal web of control.[61] Angel said, "I'll never forget my doula's name 'cause if it wasn't for her, I don't even think I would have made it through. She was questioning them COs (correctional officers) about stuff and always asking them, 'Why are you doing this?' If it wasn't for her, they could do what they wanted to do. Nobody would be accountable for it. Nobody would have been there to witness it."

The importance of doulas among both incarcerated and nonincarcerated women cannot be overstated, for research finds that doula support decreases both maternal and fetal health complications, as well as the need for interventions, including the use of a cesarean section, resulting in a more pleasant and empowering birth experience all around—something that may be especially important to incarcerated women, given how regulation and control mark much of their time behind bars.[62]

Doulas can play a critical role in resistance of the maternal web of control, for they can provide both physical and emotional support to women—something that is particularly important in the absence of a support partner.[63] Doulas may also be particularly beneficial given that many incarcerated women have underlying health conditions and little to no prior healthcare, leaving them at particular risk for health complications at birth.[64] Because of these benefits and more, including cost savings from a decrease in medical complications, volunteer doulas are starting to work more collaboratively with prisons, yet doula programs are still a rarity in most correctional facilities in the United States and largely at the mercy of doula prison projects—grassroots organizations whose members volunteer their time.[65]

Miscarriage and Stillbirth

In discussing birth behind bars, it is important to note that not every woman experiences a live birth—some women have a miscarriage or stillbirth. The most comprehensive study to date found that 92 percent of pregnancies to incarcerated women ended in a live birth.[66] Yet, for women who experience a miscarriage or stillbirth, the maternal web of control adds yet another layer to their grief, for prison and hospital rules dictate how a death is handled, with women again being erased from the conversation and expected to fall back in line as if nothing had happened, forcing them to grieve under a carceral lens that allows for little expressions of grief.

Candy gave birth to a stillborn baby and explained through swollen eyes and tears the grief and trauma she experienced at the hospital. When she gave birth to her deceased daughter, she did not have adequate time or privacy to process her grief or to make arrangements for her baby's body before falling back into the minutiae of prison life. The details of burial and funeral planning were made not by her but by the prison and medical systems, without her consent. According to Candy,

> I was chained to the bed, and it was bad, I was sitting in the hospital and they're like, "We will send [the baby] down to the morgue, and they'll take her down to the funeral home, and she'll be cremated," and I was like, "Okay, none of that's going to happen. First of all, you're making a lot of decisions and a lot of assumptions. And none of that's okay," and so I only had twelve hours before they were gonna ship me back to the prison, so I had to get a hold of my family to get a hold of a funeral home that was willing to come up and transport her down and do a burial, and I mean the whole thing was just so awful.

Candy's experience illustrates how the various rules and regulations of both the prison and medical systems, including the routinized, assembly-line model of "care," affected not just her pregnancy but also the aftermath of her stillbirth, removing choice even when it came to decisions regarding after-death care. This approach means that as women are erased from the birth experience, unique supports after cases of miscarriage or stillbirth, such as grief counseling, are often afterthoughts, as neither prisons nor hospitals may know how to proceed in the aftermath of loss among incarcerated women.[67] In this way, the regulation of women behind bars highlights a complete disregard for the unique needs of women during pregnancy, childbirth, cases of miscarriage and stillbirth, and even during the postpartum period, often unleashing further trauma.

Conclusion

Childbirth within the context of the prison system means that institutional rules and regulations, from both the prison system and the medical system, dominate all aspects of care, trapping women into a cagelike setting where they lack autonomy and decision making over nearly all matters related to birth. Under the maternal web of control, the prison system and medical system collide to dominate and control women, reducing them to mere spectators during the pivotal and transformative moment of birth.

The power dynamics inherent in both the medical system and the prison system leave many feeling like outsiders looking in, as they are subject to a range of (unwanted and unconsented) procedures, including but not limited to inductions, cervical exams, and even cesarean sections. The power dynamics embedded in interactions between both correctional officers and medical providers make it difficult, if not impossible, to exercise agency, for the prison system and the medical system work alongside each other to exert the highest form of regulation, surveilling and regulating women across multiple layers, each of which becomes stronger with the introduction of another layer, reinforcing how power is constituted behind bars.[68] Whether it is through correctional officers or medical providers watching their every move, the use of shackles to impose physical restraint, or the use of machines recording every piece of medical information imaginable, women experience carcerality during childbirth.

As a result, the narratives regarding birth are varied and come with a range of emotions—from excitement over finally meeting one's baby to frustration and anger over the lack of autonomy at birth to sorrow and anger, as women are forced to say goodbye to their baby and return to prison within days of giving birth. To be sure, giving birth as an incarcerated person is an experience like no other, for many of the circumstances regarding birth are suffused with regulation and control.

Birth experiences are also influenced in large part by the interactions women have with other people—people who can either impose or lift additional forms of control. At times, correctional staff ease forms of surveillance and control, away from the watchful lens of prison, allowing women the ability to freely call loved ones or even to remain unshackled during labor and delivery—actions that demonstrate empathy and resist the carceral control of women. Certainly this is not the case everywhere, however, as other officers are far less inclined to break the institutional rules set forth by the prison system. In other cases, giving birth as a prisoner means being stripped of one's dignity, forced to welcome new life in a cold and uncomfortable environment amid the watchful surveillance of an officer and with shackles leaving women with little privacy and dignity at a time when it is most desired.

Most of all, giving birth as an incarcerated person entails a painful goodbye, as women are separated from their infant and sent back to prison—an experience that was perhaps the most trying part of their hospital stay. Not only did many of the women I spoke with experience grief over the loss of the birth experience they thought they would have, but some, like Candy, were also grieving the death of their baby, as carceral rules permeate even the wake of death. However, in many ways, the grief and trauma women experience at the hospital are only the beginning, as most must also contend with the many struggles that have come to mark the "fourth trimester," or the first twelve weeks following birth.[69] At points, the women I spoke with said they truly wondered how they would go on without their newborn baby by their side, as the postpartum period is often dark and marked with emotional intensity. Despite the loneliness and despair, women do their best to secure postpartum care and focus on their recovery, both emotionally and physically—all topics I address in the next chapter.

5

Silenced Cries

Punishment in the Postpartum Period

You never really get over having to say goodbye to your baby.
Nothing can ever prepare you for that.
—Alice

Rhonda, a Black woman, was thirty-seven and pregnant with her third child when she was sentenced to twenty months in prison on drug and theft charges. Although Rhonda had been pregnant before and had also been incarcerated before, this was the first time that the two worlds would collide—though, in some ways, Rhonda was surprised she had not been pregnant behind bars before. She grew up in poverty against a backdrop of drugs and crime, with tough times not only for her and her family but for nearly everyone else who came from her small rural town.

The manufacturing plant, which was once the largest employer in town, had all but closed its doors, relying more on outsourcing and technology over the years, making the once-bustling little town now nearly empty. Vandalism and dirty needles now replaced the sidewalk chalk and flowers that used to line the small businesses on Main Street. Determined to leave town and to make something of herself, Rhonda enrolled at a nearby community college. And like Jada, she also dreamed of becoming a social worker and wanted to help those back home recover from drug addiction.

However, it was Rhonda who would end up needing help with addiction, for just a year into college, her grandmother's health declined, forcing her to return home. Back at home, Rhonda reconnected with some old classmates and an old flame from high school, who, like others in town, sold methamphetamines in times of economic hardship. In the wake of her grandmother's passing, she found herself in a deep depression and soon began "getting high just about every night" to dull her pain. It was not long before she became pregnant with her first child. Upon word of her pregnancy, she got clean a bit and made ends meet by waiting tables at a local diner—the same place where she later met a different man who propelled her further into the drug scene. A few years later, she was pregnant again and found that singly mothering two young children was anything but easy. Not only was Rhonda physically and emotionally exhausted, but she was drowning economically as well.

Over the years, she started to use again, hoping the meth would give her the energy and relief she needed to make it through each day. There were occasions when her odd, erratic behavior caught the attention of local law enforcement, especially as one of just a few Black women in town, resulting in her spending a weekend or two in jail on occasion. In the words of Rhonda, "my addiction had a hold on me"—so much so that her children went to live with their grandparents. In her drug-addicted state, Rhonda stole from her friends and occasionally from the diner, though always with a promise of righting matters once her financial situation improved. However, as time went on, the drugs and thefts continued, and Rhonda was ultimately sent to prison, a place where she would stay for the next twenty months.

When Rhonda came to prison, she was still high on drugs and never considered the possibility that she was pregnant—something she only found out when she took a pregnancy test during intake. Still in shock about this third pregnancy, Rhonda reasoned that her time behind bars would not be "all that bad." She already knew some of the women in prison and was grateful to have healthcare and three meals a day—something she did not always have outside of prison. She passed the time by doodling and journaling and reasoned that the next twenty months would fly by. To some extent, it did. Before long, she had reached the end of her pregnancy and was in the hospital, where she gave birth to a son. Although much of her narrative centered on the difficulties of being pregnant in prison, she acknowledged that the period *after* the birth of her son was the hardest, for the days away from her newborn and her other children seemed to stand still. Not only was Rhonda severely depressed, but she also found herself contemplating suicide in the aftermath of her son's birth—something she had never considered before. As Rhonda explained,

When they took me back to the prison after I left the hospital, I kept praying to myself, "Lord, please do not allow me to break down in front of all these officers." Because that's the name of the game, they want to see you broke. And again, I just lost my son. Even though he wasn't dead, it felt like he was dead to me, and as I was walking in, all these guards was asking me, "Hey, how's it going?" And I didn't speak, 'cause if I had spoke, I would have broke down. And I'm like okay, I just need to get to my room. And it seemed like forever because once you come back, you have to get undressed, they have to check your breast, they have to check your anal area to make sure you haven't brought anything in. So, when I finally made it to my cell, I just let it all out. I never ever cried so much. My pillows were so wet with tears I had to keep turning it over. And then my pillows became so wet on both sides that I had to get a coat to lay on because my pillows were wet. Mind you, the coat became wet because that's how much I cried. That's when I understood suicide. Right there, I understood it.

In addition to her emotional pain, Rhonda experienced physical pain that she attributes to vaginal tearing and the absence of postpartum care. While Rhonda was familiar with the pain following the days and weeks of childbirth, this was a different type of pain and one she had not experienced before. Hoping to find some answers, she sought an appointment at the medical unit in her prison but found that postpartum healthcare in prison was not as accessible as she had thought. Any time Rhonda spoke of her pain to correctional officers, it was dismissed, and she was told that she could not see a provider—an experience not uncommon for Black women both in and outside of prison who seek medical care.[1]

Still in pain and hoping to have some answers, Rhonda looked forward to her postpartum appointment, a standard appointment she knew she would receive six weeks after birth.[2] But, the postpartum appointment in prison was in stark contrast to the postpartum care she had in the community after her first pregnancy. The appointment she had looked forward to for weeks was over in a matter of minutes, leaving her with no answers but also with the shallow suggestion to simply follow up with her care provider after her release from prison—one she had not been able to see in some time because she was impoverished. As Rhonda explained,

As women, we know when something's not right with our body. I did not heal the way I thought I healed because I felt a tear, and I didn't get anything, I didn't get *anything*, and so once you have the baby, you're supposed to have this postpartum checkup six weeks after you have a baby. Well, I'm back at the prison, so I sat on the table, she [the provider] took a flashlight, she shined it in my eyes and said, "Okay, you're good to go." So, see, that's not a checkup. I said, "Ma'am I deserve a six-week checkup. You're not going to check me to make sure everything's in place?" She tells me, "No, you're going home in a few months, follow up with your primary care physician." So, I was like, first of all, how do you know I have a primary care physician? I deserve a six-week checkup.

Rhonda's vaginal tear grew more severe by the day, resulting in excessive bleeding, leaving her with no choice but to create a makeshift pad out of a T-shirt to collect the blood from her vaginal area. According to Rhonda, "Even to this day, it's like at times, certain things don't feel right down there, so I knew that it was because of the birth of my son which I should have got stitches for that. I didn't, so the medical portion, it's horrible. It's horrible." The prison system that once provided some respite for Rhonda in the form of rest and food turned into a unique hell, for being under correctional control meant having no answers to questions about her health. As Rhonda explained, had she not been incarcerated, she would have had the ability to seek answers from a healthcare provider about her pain. She would have been free to seek support in the wake of her postpartum depression, and she would have been able to enjoy new motherhood with her baby at her side.

As Rhonda's case illustrates, the unique needs of postpartum women are largely overshadowed by the routinization and control that mark both the prison system and the medical system. The convergence of control that emanates from both systems exacerbates the physical, emotional, and mental health of women, affecting family relationships for years to come. For many, the postpartum period behind bars is dark and marked with depression, engorged breasts, and the absence of a familial support system, making it difficult to separate pregnancy and birth from these carceral systems.

In this chapter, I focus on the fourth trimester, or the twelve weeks following birth, often referred to as the postpartum period, and detail women's experiences after they are discharged from the hospital and return to prison. What happens to women after they have their baby and return to prison is largely unknown, as the postpartum period has still been overlooked by scholars. Consequently, both the prison system and the medical system fail to consider the unique needs of incarcerated women during the postpartum period. As mentioned, women have about twenty-four hours with their baby at the hospital before they are separated and sent back to prison—an emotionally charged and surveilled process that results in significant birth trauma and postpartum depression. When women return to prison, they may find themselves with inadequate postpartum care, with little to no provisions in place to support unique needs such as lactation, often resulting in painful breast infections that harm their health and hinder the ability to breastfeed upon reintegration with their baby. These harms exacerbate already existing health issues that threaten the safety and well-being of both women and their children, making it clear that prisons are ill equipped to meet the needs of women in the aftermath of childbirth.

I argue that the maternal web of control follows women even after they give birth, further regulating their access to care. Not only does the maternal web of control produce birth trauma and depression, but the power and control that emanate from carceral systems make it difficult for women to access the support they need. Much has been written about the inadequacies of maternity care in the US medical system and the disregard for the care of women, as the primary focus remains on the successful delivery of the product—the baby.[3] Just as women are erased from their birth experience, so they are erased in aftercare as well, with even nonincarcerated women having unmet postpartum health needs. Postpartum health concerns are only amplified behind bars, where control and regulation are ubiquitous, making it all but impossible for women to access care and to survive, let alone thrive, behind bars, especially women of color, who also encounter varying forms of oppression. Ultimately, I argue that the disregard for women in the postpartum period extends beyond the punishment for any wrongdoing and instead penetrates the familial arena, punishing not only the health and safety of women but also that of their families.

Returning to Prison

After saying goodbye to their baby at the hospital, most women are quickly transported back to prison, where they stay for the duration of their imprisonment—often shackled during transportation, too.[4] No longer pregnant, they are treated like any other prisoner and forced to fall back in line with their peers, expected to carry on as usual as if *nothing* had happened, despite the magnitude of events that just transpired. The cold, sterile environment of prisons, which is fraught with much surveillance and little support, makes it difficult for women to recover from childbirth and to process the pain and trauma they have just endured. Those I interviewed who had given birth before shared how their postpartum period in prison was distinct from their previous postpartum periods, when they were able to savor the sweet smells of their newborn—a sharp contrast to their experiences this time, when they came "home" to barbed wire, a metal cot, engorged breasts, tearful eyes, and no baby.

Absent Postpartum Care

The patriarchal technocratic medical system described in the last chapter almost exclusively focuses on babies, failing both incarcerated mothers and nonincarcerated mothers alike. Given the failures to provide women with adequate care, even in the community, it comes as no surprise that for many women in prison, their postpartum health needs are only abysmally met through the ingenuity and benevolence of other women in prison and only made possible through the circumvention of rules rather than through any institutional support. The lack of concern for the postpartum healthcare needs of incarcerated women is especially apparent at the point of hospital discharge. Women who have just given birth may experience excessive bleeding, vaginal pain, incontinence, hemorrhoids, and engorged breasts, among other issues.[5] The postpartum recovery period typically lasts six to eight weeks, though it may take longer.[6]

Behind bars, women are asked to conform to the minutiae of daily living without the necessary supports in place to facilitate their recovery. A failure to consider postpartum needs means that it is not unusual for many to still be in pain and to be slow to move around in the days and weeks after birth, especially those who have had a cesarean section. As a result, women may need additional assistance with navigating daily tasks, such as getting in and out of the shower, climbing up to their bed, and walking to the toilet—tasks that in some communities may be handled by close family, friends, or even doulas.

As Faye said, "The nurses [at the hospital] they helped me out to the fullest, getting in the shower, getting out [of] the shower, helping me clean my incision, everything. They had a lot of compassion, but once you get back to that prison, you're shit out of luck there, buddy, because they don't want to do *shit*. They don't care." While there are some doula programs in prisons (and jails) that provide support and accommodations for the unique needs of pregnant and postpartum women, helping women with these tasks, these programs are not in every facility and are often at the mercy of volunteers and funding—which tend to be in short supply.[7]

Ruthie shared how after her cesarean section, a correctional officer yelled at her for her slowness and struggles to move around and perform everyday tasks, such as getting out of bed and walking to the bathroom. According to Ruthie, "I had a cesarean, and I was tryin' to get out of the bed, and she [the correctional officer] was not tryin' to help me, I had to get up on my own, go to the bathroom, and then when I got in the bathroom, as soon as I sat in the bath, 'you need to hurry up, what are you in there doin'?' and 'that's why you got your kid taken away now,' and I mean she just went on and on the whole time, and I mean I was so scared to come out of that bathroom."

Ruthie's narrative highlights the disregard for the importance of the recovery period, especially for women who undergo a cesarean section, a major abdominal surgery. In Ruthie's case, not only was she yelled at for being slow, but her slowness was also characterized as a reason for the loss of child custody. In Ruthie's case, her punishment for wrongdoing went beyond incapacitation, as even her parenting and biological responses were under fire.

New recommendations from the American College of Obstetricians and Gynecologists released in 2018 recommend that postpartum women should have twelve weeks of support, including an examination three weeks after birth, marking a move away from the previous recommendations, which outlined the need for a single visit at six weeks postbirth.[8]

These changes come in the wake of research revealing that most maternal and infant deaths occur within the first month after birth.[9] Tailored postpartum screenings are important for improved health outcomes for both mothers and their babies, as mothers may be screened for any number of several serious and life-threatening conditions, including postpartum depression and postpartum psychosis, as well as issues like hypertension and diabetes.[10] These screenings are especially important for incarcerated women, who may already be in poor health, in part due to systemic racism that contributes to health disparities, placing women of color at an increased risk for developing a number of health complications.[11]

Health Consequences

Although incarcerated women may leave the hospital with discharge instructions outlining the importance of taking care of their health and following up with a healthcare provider, a lack of coordination and facilitation between the medical system and the prison system often means that women are not seen at all and that their care ceases at the point of discharge. This comes as no surprise given that the US medical system fails even women who are not incarcerated, as a third of women have health problems after childbirth.[12] Moreover, research reveals that 40–50 percent of all women do not receive postpartum care, despite recommendations from leading medical organizations.[13] This number is even higher for women of color and impoverished women, who are less likely to have access to healthcare—a reality that highlights how institutionalized racism and systemic poverty are embedded in maternal healthcare.[14] Black and Indigenous women are especially at risk, as they have higher rates of maternal deaths than their White counterparts—disparities that have only worsened in the wake of the COVID-19 pandemic.[15] These findings demonstrate the devastating consequences for those who are already vulnerable to interlocking systems of oppression and control.

The extent of postpartum care for incarcerated women is not known, as national data is not kept, a telling finding on its own. However, in 2004, the most recent year of available data, only 54 percent of pregnant women in prison received *prenatal care*; thus, it is likely that *postpartum care* is also much lower, as conversations about health in the postnatal period are almost always focused on the baby.[16] Although postpartum care is recommended by ACOG for all women, medical care behind bars is highly regulated and entails the navigation of institutional rules and procedures from both the prison system and the medical system, making it difficult for women to access care. While the rules and procedures of each prison vary, accessing care often involves a series of steps that begin with the securing of approval from correctional staff who act as gatekeepers to medical care. Correctional officers are trained in security and often do not have specialized training in the assessment of postpartum care, resulting in far too many women having their health concerns dismissed, increasing the likelihood that serious health issues go undiagnosed and untreated.[17]

To be sure, the reliance on correctional officers to facilitate postpartum care is also fraught with racial and class inequalities, as women of color are more likely to have their pain dismissed—a phenomenon that is grounded in misguided beliefs that still infiltrate both the medical and the nonmedical community regarding racial groups and pain tolerance.[18] Several participants shared how their pain was dismissed by correctional officers, as they were told they were "fine" and only seeking "attention." Bureaucratic issues, among other concerns, may mandate that women adhere to a number of procedures in order to receive care.[19] As a result, it is not unusual for women to experience a lengthy wait time, as a single facility may have only a couple of healthcare providers on staff at any given time, a reality that is likely to be exacerbated for those incarcerated in more remote areas.[20] Even then, these providers may not have the specific training to be able to offer specialized maternal care.

Angel received fifteen stitches as part of her unplanned cesarean section and later encountered a problem when her stitches opened as she climbed up to the top of her bunk bed. When she went to the medical unit inside her prison to receive care, a correctional officer told her to "go back into [her] unit, there was nothing they could do." Angel's narrative illustrates the emphasis on order and security, even over health, as her pain was dismissed by correctional staff.[21] Angel explained how, "after that, my roommate traded spots with me as far as the bed, she got on the top bunk and [my cellmate] would help me clean it [the incision area] or put whatever we could on it to make it heal." Since she was unsuccessful in obtaining cream at the medical unit in prison, she was forced to rely on her cellmate, who helped her make a "homemade" topical cream to apply on her wound. Although the cream offered some relief, the problems with her stitches continued, as they were left in "entirely too long." As a lay person with no medical training, she was at a complete loss and unable to exercise any control, for her body was at the complete mercy of the prison system, and even the most intimate areas of her body were under correctional control.

When her stitches were finally removed, her body was infected and completely covered in scabs. As Angel's narrative illustrates, a lack of preventative care can contribute to larger issues that become more complicated to treat over time, threatening maternal health.[22] For Angel, the best care she found behind bars was the care tied to individual people like her cellmate rather than to any care embedded in institutional policies or practices from either the medical system or the prison system. The incarceration of postpartum women often means that the medical system (wrongly) assumes that the prison system has procedures in place to ensure that the health needs of women are met, while the prison system also (wrongly) assumes that the medical system is handling all the specialized healthcare of postpartum women, resulting in a situation where neither system does its due diligence to provide for the unique needs of postpartum women. The placement of a woman on the top of a bunkbed after birth is a prime example of how the unique needs of postpartum women are ignored, resulting in health complications.[23] To this day, Angel wonders whether she would have had "nasty scabs all over" if her staples had been removed by medical staff on time.

The absence of postpartum healthcare is not unique to Angel. Others told stories of vaginal tears that went untreated, excessive bleeding, and cesarean stitches that were not removed on time, in addition to painful breast infections, including mastitis. Access to pain medication during the postpartum period is also highly regulated, particularly amid concerns about substance abuse. Though each prison has its own set of rules and regulations that are specific to the facility, many of the women I talked with spoke about blanket rules against narcotic pain medication, even in the wake of research revealing that even postpartum women with a history of drug abuse and those on a methadone treatment regimen can and are encouraged to take pain medication via an individualized treatment plan.[24] Yet the routinized care within both the medical system and the prison system means that few receive an individualized care plan, which means they simply go without.

Lora talked about how she was still in tremendous pain when she returned to prison and was not offered pain medication because of her history of drug abuse. According to Lora, "After I had [my baby], the hospital prescribed me pain killers, but of course they're narcotic, and so once I left the hospital, the prison wasn't going to give me narcotics, even though I had just had a baby."

Those who underwent cesarean sections were especially taken aback about the lack of pain medication following birth, for recovery from a cesarean section is long and difficult.[25] Gloria, who underwent a cesarean section and went without pain medication in the aftermath of her return to prison, said, "When I asked them for some pain killers they were just like, 'Nope,' and I'm just like, 'Dude, I just had a baby.' They say it's because they have some kind of like rule of no narcotics or whatever, but it's like okay, come on now like give me some frickin' something, like I don't think they would understand unless they had a C-section themselves. I mean honestly like when I tell people I had a C-section and had to heal up without pain meds, they just look at me like, 'What?!' I'm like, 'Yep.'" The lack of postpartum care in the aftermath of childbirth was not lost on the women I interviewed. Many of them were confident that their ability to access care would have been much easier if the prison system had national policies mandating quality care in the postpartum period. Still, although prisons are constitutionally obligated to provide healthcare, there are no detailed provisions mandating that prisons must adhere to clear and specific standards, leaving many health needs unmet.[26] As mentioned earlier, doulas are starting to be used more in prisons even during the postpartum period to provide support with some of this work; however, these programs are sparse and should not be considered a cure-all for meeting the medical needs of postpartum women in prison.[27]

Proper postpartum care behind bars is essential because, as Rhonda alluded to in the opening of this chapter, many incarcerated women do not have healthcare providers on the outside whom they can follow up with after their release from prison, especially for those in poverty, who are already more likely to be in poor health with a number of unmet health needs. As with other matters behind bars, there were some I interviewed who were just simply grateful to have any healthcare at all, no matter how poor, because they were accustomed to not having any in the free world—a reality that underscores the glaring disparities of (maternal) healthcare even in communities where, for some, the best care possible may be that which is found in the prison system.

A Dark Cloud of Depression

With respect to the health needs of women after birth, incarcerated women remain especially susceptible to postpartum depression—a unique depression that affects women after birth, characterized by insomnia, mood swings, anxiety, panic attacks, bouts of crying, fear, self-harm, and hopelessness.[28] While postpartum depression can affect one in seven women, the rates of postpartum depression for incarcerated women are arguably higher.[29] Although national data is limited, research shows that a third of incarcerated women may exhibit moderate to severe signs of postpartum depression, a reality further compounded by underlying health conditions, which may include a history of anxiety and mood disorders, and life stressors that may go untreated or exacerbated, as well as the effects from larger social forces, such as institutionalized racism and a global pandemic.[30]

Carceral Consequences of Separation

The forced separation of women from their children almost immediately after birth may be a contributing factor of postpartum depression. The traumatic ways in which the carceral systems separates mothers from their children have lasting consequences. Some women may have weeks, months, years, or even decades left of their sentence until they are released from prison and have an opportunity to reunite with their children. Some may have little to no information about when, if ever, they will see their baby again, especially those in poverty, who experience greater barriers to visitation, an issue I explore in the next chapter. The absence of updates about their baby from a caregiver or relationship tensions with caregivers may further fuel postpartum depression.

Stacy, a first-time mother, explained how being in prison, away from her baby, was not at all how she envisioned new motherhood. In prison, all she had was time—time to think about every milestone she was missing, whether it be her baby's first bath, first coo, or even the first steps. Her mind was constantly at work wondering about the well-being of her baby and whether her baby was sleeping through the night and whether her baby would even remember her after she was released from prison.

Denied Motherhood

Incarcerated women may also miss out on many of the cultural markers that mark new motherhood, including the flood of visitors, gifts, and even meal trains that may come from a support system. As a result, some women I talked with found that sentimental possessions like their baby's hospital bracelet and stamped footprints were considered contraband and therefore not permitted behind bars—a product of the emphasis on rules and control that lace the prison system. Others shared how they were not entirely sure where these items ended up and feared that these special belongings were thrown away in the trash—a thought that haunted them and further exacerbated their postpartum depression.

Through tears, Jada said, "The little bracelet that they put on you in the hospital, that's the only thing that they let me keep and that was just so when I got back out, the doctors could see my tags. I don't even have any photos. I signed the birth certificate, but I have no idea where that ended up. I don't even know if they have my daughter's name spelled right on there." Those like Candy who experienced a stillbirth were especially fraught with tears, as these items were the only physical objects they had by which to remember their baby.

To be sure, saying goodbye at the hospital and grappling with the absence of these sentimental items is often only the beginning of postpartum depression. Alice, a Black mother of three, was twenty-eight when she was behind bars and talked about how she was "completely depressed" and was "so desperate" to see her son that she was willing to do *anything* to be with him again and even pleaded with correctional administrators to release her early. When this did not work, she reached out to her county's district attorney to see if she could provide any additional information about another case that was pending trial in exchange for a reduction in her sentence—an idea that went nowhere.

In some cases, postpartum depression may be so severe that it borders on suicidal ideation, a disturbing reality, especially in the absence of mental healthcare behind bars. Among those in my study, most were not offered any formal counseling, which is startling, given their extensive histories of trauma and punitive encounters with matrices of oppression. As Faye explained, "You get attached to that baby, who was with you for nine months, and it's here physically . . . Every moment of every day that you spend with that baby you get closer. You get that bond, and then once you relinquish your rights to that baby, it's hard. I think there should be some kind of grief counseling, it's like you grieve for your baby, your baby's died and you're grieving until you get to be with that baby again." Those who experienced a miscarriage or stillbirth are also at risk for developing postpartum depression, for the nature of incarceration makes it difficult to cope with grief and in many cases only exacerbates matters. Still sore from giving birth (and in some cases recovering from cesarean surgery, no less), many may struggle to recover from childbirth and adjust to the postpartum period.

While both Rhonda and Faye described their postpartum experiences as akin to death, there are some women, like Latrice, who do experience death. To say that Latrice was depressed after her baby was stillborn would be an understatement. She was also "pissed off" at correctional administrators for not providing her with any counseling in the aftermath of birth—a reality that is not unusual for postpartum women in prison. According to Latrice, "When they returned me back to the facility, there was no 'you need to talk with somebody?' No, 'how you feeling?' No, nothing. I was completely on my own and had to cope with everything." What made Latrice's depression worse, in part, was that she was physically separated from her support system and had no choice but to process her grief alone while conforming to the routinization and control of prison, despite having just experienced tragedy.

As Latrice explained, "Normally you take pain killers, and that pain will go away, but this pain it wouldn't go anywhere, and it was just hurtful. And I just wanted somebody to tell me, 'It's gonna be okay.' But there was nobody there. There was nobody, and mind you, I'm all the way away from my family. That was a horrible, horrible feeling. I wouldn't even wish that on my worst enemy." A lack of care speaks to the larger issue of how prisons are structured to warehouse people, ill equipped to handle the needs of women in the aftermath of childbirth, especially in cases of miscarriage and stillbirth, as they lack the knowledge and expertise to provide any comprehensive care. As with other matters affecting pregnant women in prison, no national data has been collected on the frequency of postpartum depression among incarcerated women nor has any federal legislation been passed to mandate that all correctional institutions make accommodations for the postpartum needs of women.[31] The only women I interviewed who said they received any type of formal counseling or support from their prison after birth were Angel, who had limited access to a doula, and Marissa, who had access to a prison nursery program. Carcerality and the various institutional rules that govern prison contribute to postpartum depression, as prisons are designed with security in mind rather than a trauma-informed approach that centers the specific needs of postpartum women and preserves the maternal-infant bond.

It Takes a Village

In many communities, the postpartum period is revered and viewed as a sacred time for mothers to focus on their recovery and the strengthening of the maternal-infant bond—made possible through the care and support of a community. Research finds that partners and family members, especially other women, are critical in providing support, particularly in impoverished and minority communities where paid support services, such as postpartum doulas and counselors, may be otherwise out of reach and unavailable.[32] Having a strong social support system can provide protection against postpartum depression and can help with many tasks in the aftermath of birth.[33]

Barriers to Support

However, the ability to mobilize a support system and access needed resources behind bars is limited under the maternal web of control, where regulation and order reign. As prisons have been historically designed for men without regard to the unique needs of women, many prisons lack programming tailored to meet the specific needs of postpartum women, including specialized postpartum counseling, postpartum peer support groups, and programs that foster the mother-infant bond. Accordingly, women may be forced to rely on their own support systems, including family, friends, and other incarcerated women, in the days, weeks, and months following childbirth. However, there are many barriers to communication with loved ones on the outside, including but not limited to securing transportation and lodging, and adherence to the institutional rules that govern visitation in prison. The high costs associated with phone calls and even letters may also make it difficult for women to access their support system.[34]

Beyond cost and logistical barriers, women may also find it too painful to seek out support from the person(s) raising their baby. Some of the women I interviewed said they did not want to burden their families with their pain and grief, especially when many of these people may be already overwhelmed from taking care of a newborn and older children. Additionally, some said they were very intentional about the conversations they did have with loved ones, for their families could also be a source of hurt and pain, making them feel judged not only for their criminal offenses but also for leaving caregivers with a weight of responsibility. In some cases, heated conversations over childrearing ensued, as women did their best to parent behind bars and navigate the complexities of relationships with both their baby (and any other children) and the caregivers, making it difficult to rely on loved ones and caregivers for social support in the aftermath of pregnancy—an issue I explore in the next chapter.

Peers as Support

For some, it makes more sense to rely on peers for support, just as they did during pregnancy. Most of the women I talked with said their peers did their best to offer words of encouragement and support and to provide them with a sense of warmth and dignity in an environment designed to strip them of their humanity. Some said that when they returned to prison after giving birth, they were greeted with "homemade" congratulatory gifts and "homecooked" meals prepared by other women in prison.

Gloria described how her peers greeted her with a warm welcome when she came back to prison after giving birth, which was something she remembers fondly still to this day. According to Gloria, "When I came back from the hospital, everybody had like a card and they ran up to me and gave me a hug and said congratulations, and [they] made their own cakes and strudels. I was kinda emotional 'cause it's kinda crazy how much love they have for someone that has just had a baby."

Cherelle said she "never would have made it through" without the support from her peers, and Jeanine said that one of the other women in her prison even crocheted her baby a hat. According to Jeanine, "They were there to comfort me and were more supportive than anyone. They gave me hugs, and one of the older women that I knew in there that I talked to about my pregnancy and stuff, she wanted to be the grandmother of my child."[35]

Women may not only help each other emotionally but also provide support with more practical matters after birth, in some cases, including teaching them about how to make makeshift nursing and postpartum pads and going so far as to offer to switch bunk beds with those assigned to the top who were still recovering from birth to ensure they did not have to climb the stairs. Angel explained how some of the women on her floor also gave her advice about how to relieve engorgement from her clogged milk ducts and showed her techniques to slow vaginal bleeding. Susan shared how her cellmates gave her advice on which social workers and attorneys were the best in navigating the child welfare system, even helping her find the exact location of her baby—an important detail she did not know, as her baby had health issues at birth and required a longer hospital stay.

These cases illustrate the importance of having a strong support network to help navigate the many changes in the aftermath of birth and provide evidence of the ways in which women create systems of support in the absence of institutional support. Indeed, there are protective benefits that come with a support system behind bars, as indicated throughout the book, with those who have strong ties with people both in and out of the prison system having an easier time navigating carceral control. The creation of support systems among incarcerated women and the varied ways in which they navigate new motherhood with a semblance of dignity are yet other ways in which they resist the maternal web of control and the very systems that thwart their humanity and health. Although many of my interviewees were able to find common ground with some of the other women on their floor over the shared pain that comes with separation, not every new mother in prison has this experience, especially those in solitary confinement. Each experience is different and is influenced by the particulars of each prison culture, as well as other factors, such as length of sentence and whether this is a woman's first birth. There were also some I interviewed who said their peers did little to help in the aftermath of birth, with some even insinuating that they should "get over" their grief, for comparisons about how much time one has left to serve may be especially common and a point of tension. The subcultures within prisons are all unique; however, among those I interviewed, there was a sentiment that those with shorter sentences were expected to process their grief much more quickly than those who had years left to serve.

Mining for Liquid Gold

The rise of the carceral state means that even biological matters like lactation are subject to domination and control, making breastfeeding and breast pumping out of reach for many. The lactation needs of women continue to exist even behind bars, yet few prisons have the care and resources in place to foster breastfeeding or to make provisions that would allow women to pump their milk to be sent to their baby, resulting in serious health concerns for both women and babies.[36] Leading health organizations, such as the American College of Obstetricians and Gynecologists, the World Health Organization, and the American Academy of Pediatrics, all recommend that infants be exclusively breastfed for at least the first six months of life because of the health protections breastfeeding provides to both women and babies, including but not limited to protection against disease, a lowered risk of postpartum depression, and a strengthened immune system.[37] But, like other aspects behind bars, much of what incarcerated women are allowed to do is dictated by powerful systems of control, which do not have a vested interest in the care of women and their families, controlling even the most integral and biological of functions.

Regulation of Lactation

While there have been a number of initiatives and resources focused on increasing rates of breastfeeding by providing women with lactation resources and support, including the ability to breastfeed or pump in the workplace, these initiatives have been slow to be implemented behind bars.[38] The most recent research reveals that only six states in the United States have specific laws addressing the lactation needs of the incarcerated.[39] Even then, staff may not be well versed on the particulars of these laws; similarly, prisons may not provide women with the necessary education and resources to support lactation, nor provide them with a private and quiet place in which they can regularly express their milk, nor certified lactation specialists on site who can provide proper education and support.[40] Still, in the absence of formal policies or prison cultures that make provisions for the incarcerated, it is no surprise that the rates of breastfeeding initiation in the hospital, breastfeeding behind bars, and pumping behind bars remain low for those incarcerated. Research finds that even in places that do allow women to pump, few women do, highlighting the disconnect between policies and actual practices, indicating the need for better accommodations and support.[41]

The ways in which both the medical system and the prison system fail lactating mothers begin with pregnancy, as many women are not offered breastfeeding classes and support. In the hospital, women may also be met with several obstacles that hinder breastfeeding and pumping. The emphasis on surveillance and security, even while hospitalized, means that women are unsure about what is permissible. The widespread mistreatment and emphasis on control and surveillance may make women even more uncomfortable and nervous about initiating breastfeeding, making them fearful of punishment. As a result, the absence of an "okay" to breastfeed is perceived as a "no." Even in cases where women are "permitted" to breastfeed, they may not always feel comfortable breastfeeding in front of other people, especially in front of (male) correctional officers. The extensive histories of trauma and abuse among the incarcerated may make women even more apprehensive or uncomfortable about breastfeeding, as it requires yet another state of undress potentially inciting further trauma, especially among those who have experienced sexual abuse.

A Lack of Infrastructure and Support

A lack of communication between the medical system and the prison system also hinders the ability for women to breastfeed and pump both on site at the hospital and behind bars. Both systems may fail to provide women with the education, resources, and support they need to initiate or continue breastfeeding and pumping. Women may not receive essentials such as a breast pump, nipple creams and shields, milk storage bags, a means to refrigerate their milk, or medication to suppress their milk flow if desired, resulting in women being held prisoner both behind bars and in their own body, permitting health problems to flourish with relative ease. In an environment characterized by countless rules and surveillance, accessing resources and support is difficult.

Both hospitals and prisons may fail to provide proper discharge planning that is specific to lactation, as the unfamiliarity, uniqueness, and even the discomfort of having an incarcerated patient may mean that hospitals are unsure about how to properly care for and make provisions for the lactation needs of women, wrongly assuming that because they are incarcerated, they may be forbidden from breastfeeding or pumping. The surveilling watch from correctional officers also acts as a contributing factor, as healthcare staff may assume that conversations about breastfeeding or lactation support will be solely handled by the prison system. The image of a woman in shackles at the ankles, wrists, and belly, accompanied by a correctional officer or even a police officer in a uniform that screams authority, also acts as a powerful, controlling image, making even healthcare staff uncomfortable or uneasy about having extended conversations with women about lactation. Similarly, correctional staff may wrongly assume that all matters of lactation, including infrastructure and support, will be handled by healthcare staff or another correctional staff member or administrator, washing their hands of any responsibility.

As Jada said, "When I had my baby, they did not give me that shot to dry my milk up, they just sent me back to prison, and later I was crying in so much pain because my breasts was so hard. I didn't even have nothing to dull the pain." Jada's narrative highlights the consequences for those caught in the middle of powerful carceral systems that together create a confining web that fails to ensure a continuity of care across institutions. In Jada's case, her hospital assumed that the prison would provide her with medication to suppress her milk after she returned to prison, while the prison assumed that these needs would be met by the medical system during her hospital stay.

Likewise, those working in the prison system, a historically patriarchal system that predominantly employs men, are left unaware, unsure, or even uncomfortable about how to address the lactation needs of women and instead defer to those working in the medical system under the illusion that when women are discharged from the hospital, all their maternal needs are met and they are ready to acclimate back into prison now that the baby, or product, has been successfully produced. The confusion and lack of collaboration regarding who is in charge, combined with a lack of knowledge among correctional staff regarding the specialized postpartum needs of women, means that women are left in a situation where they must advocate for themselves—a scenario that becomes particularly risky for the incarcerated, especially women of color, who are in a state of hypersubjugation, where every interaction they have is expected to adhere to rules of obedience and conformity. The implications for speaking out are especially severe for women of color and Black women, given longstanding cultural narratives that paint Black women as a threat.[42] A few of the women I interviewed were explicitly told by correctional staff and even medical staff that they could not breastfeed during their hospital stay for reasons that remain unclear even to this day. According to Faye, "It really hurt me knowing that I couldn't see him and touch him and hear his cry. I couldn't even frickin' breastfeed him. That's what really scared me. I breastfed both my older boys. You know that's the thing that hurt me the most because he needed that. He needed those nutrients in the breastmilk, and I couldn't even give it to him. I wasn't allowed to breastfeed him while I was in the hospital. They said no. Why? I don't know. But they told me I wasn't allowed to." Looking back, Faye says she wishes she had felt more comfortable inquiring about the particulars of this supposed rule, but at the time, she was fearful that any perceived vocal opposition on her part would be met with punishment. Her narrative illustrates the power dynamics embedded in these interactions, as she found herself at the intersection of two powerful systems that had a hold on her health and life, where the controlling image of her as an incarcerated person only reaffirmed her subjugation and inferiority in relation to these systems, making it impossible to vocalize any opposition.

For many, the problems continue once they return to prison. Given that most women are separated from their baby shortly after birth, they continue to lactate yet have no means to empty the milk from their breasts. Nearly everyone I interviewed said they were not given a breast pump in which to express their milk upon their return to prison, resulting in both physical and emotional pain and a plethora of health problems, including clogged milk ducts and even mastitis, a painful infection of the breast.[43] Jada explained how she was not only in tremendous physical pain, due to clogged milk ducts, but her engorged breasts served as a harsh reminder that she was separated from her baby and unable to provide her baby with important nutrients. According to Jada, "It was rough. After I gave birth to my daughter, my breasts were still sore, full of milk, but she wasn't there. So even though they took my baby, I still had these maternal instincts that I was trying to take care of. So that made it very difficult, emotionally, it was very depressing." The disregard for the lactating needs of women behind bars is a direct consequence of the maternal web of control, in which both the medical system and the prison system fail to provide the necessary infrastructure and support for women to both meet their lactation needs and foster any breastfeeding goals.

Many of the women I interviewed talked about the nutritional benefits of breastmilk, and many (though not all) were eager to breastfeed their baby—both as a means of bonding and to provide their baby with a strong nutritional foundation. In the eyes of the women I interviewed, breastfeeding was "at least something" they could do to help mitigate or right the wrongs of their imprisonment. Additionally, breastfeeding provided at least some semblance of normalcy, if only for a short time at the hospital.

Yet even though many spoke about the desire to breastfeed, only a handful did. Some refrained from breastfeeding because they felt it would cause confusion for their baby to receive breastmilk only to then have to switch to formula upon discharge. Gloria talked about how she breastfed her baby in the hospital but then abruptly stopped just hours after birth, as she found herself becoming too attached and worried that the separation and subsequent switch to formula would create problems at discharge. According to Gloria, "I did breastfeed, but then I kinda like stopped because I was feeling bad because he probably was getting way too attached. I could tell because when he was on my chest he knew where the milk was, and I was gonna feel bad because he ain't gonna get that when he goes home. I didn't want my boyfriend having to go through that change of baby's milk with him. So, I just kinda quit." To be sure, as Jada's narrative illustrates, breastfeeding is a highly personal decision, and some women may never attempt or want to breastfeed, for a variety of reasons, including the emotional pain that may occur from an impending separation—a finding that is consistent with other research.[44] Still, the lack of protections and accommodations for lactating women results in a disturbing carceral environment that threatens the health of both women and children.

Lactation Rooms

Although prisons have been slow to consider the unique needs of lactating women, there are some prisons that recognize the many benefits that come with lactation both for women and for their newborn babies, including strengthened maternal and infant bond, protection against diseases, and a strong nutritional foundation—benefits that may be especially important to incarcerated women who have a number of unmet health needs.[45] For example, the Julia Tutwiler Prison for Women in Alabama provides a private space for women to express their milk, where it is then later packaged and shipped to their baby or picked up by a caregiver.[46] These initiatives may be especially important for women who wish to breastfeed after their release from prison, as continual pumping helps to maintain breastmilk supply, offering important nutrients to newborns.[47]

Still, many incarcerated women are unable to access these resources and this support. There may be a number of logistical barriers that make it difficult for women to express their milk, including lack of funding to create a dedicated quiet space conducive to pumping and a way to keep and store the breastmilk for transport, as well as logistical problems getting the milk to babies, especially if their mothers are incarcerated in rural regions farther away.[48] Therefore the benefits of prison nursery programs that allow infants to remain with their mothers behind bars cannot be overstated, for the premise of these nursery programs is that the maternal-infant bond must be preserved, and therefore women should be allowed and even encouraged to breastfeed their baby.

As mentioned earlier, two thirds of parents never receive an in-person visit from their baby during their incarceration, making it unlikely that women are able to see their baby, an issue I explore in the next chapter.[49] However, even in cases where infants do visit their mothers in prison, women may be unable to breastfeed their baby, due to any number of prison visitation rules that forbid physical touch, even for mothers breastfeeding their baby—yet another example of how the patriarchal prison system fails to consider the unique needs of women. The importance of meeting the needs of women cannot be overstated, for in the absence of accommodations that allow for breastfeeding or pumping, a woman's breastmilk supply will eventually dry up, leaving her unable to initiate breastfeeding or pumping even after her release from prison, threatening her ability to mother with choice and dignity. In this way, the carceral system continues to control women, their bodies, and the ways in which they nurture and bond with their babies long after they are released from prison, ultimately affecting the health and well-being of not only incarcerated women but also their children, who through no fault of their own are caught in the maternal web of control. The carceral state goes beyond the parameters of punishment for a crime and instead causes irrevocable damage to women and their babies, threatening both their health and their well-being for years to come.

Conclusion

The days, weeks, and months following birth are emotionally charged and akin to a roller coaster, as women are separated from their baby and then promptly returned to prison, where they are asked to fall in line as if nothing had happened—despite the many physical, mental, and emotional changes that just occurred. The incarceration of pregnant and postpartum women certainly produces additional forms of pain and trauma that must be processed, yet the nature of the prison system and its various forms of carcerality means that women are placed in an environment where they are unable to fully process their grief. Not only are many denied access to proper counseling, but they are also unable to have open communication with those who could be a source of support amid grief and clinical depression, making for an environment in which mental health struggles proliferate with relative ease.

Postpartum women may also have other health needs that often go unmet, as prisons are far from places that offer care. While there are more progressive efforts in some correctional facilities to accommodate these changes, for the most part, the US prison system does little in the way of addressing the unique needs facing postpartum women behind bars. The lack of policies specifically outlining provisions for the care of postpartum women is yet another way the carceral system continues to exert control over women, for not only are they at the mercy of their respective prisons when it comes to their postpartum care, but in many ways the prison system also regulates the beginnings of motherhood, including the ability to breastfeed and the particulars of the mother-child relationship, with even biological functions and family matters being at the mercy of prison rules and expected to adhere to the particulars of total institutions, threatening both the health and the well-being of women and their babies.

While there are some women who are released from prison prior to giving birth and others who may be enrolled in a nursery program that allows their baby to stay with them, most return to prison in a state of grief, having spent no more than a day or two with their baby at the hospital before being separated. And though this separation is expected, and women may even spend considerable time deciding who will provide care, this often does little to ease the pain of separation. Some women I interviewed were particularly forthright and said they truly wondered how they would survive the rest of their incarceration without their baby at their side.

Postpartum depression is not uncommon for women, and even more so for those behind bars, for giving birth as an incarcerated person is an experience unlike any other. Many are still processing trauma from birth when they return to prison and have anxieties about the well-being of their baby, especially given the many obstacles that limit communication, resulting in the absence of information. While some can find support and comfort in family or peers upon their return to prison following childbirth, others are left alone, especially in the absence of institutional support.

In addition to postpartum depression, postpartum healthcare may be inadequate or absent—despite recommendations from leading medical organizations advocating for care. In some cases, there is an assumption that women will follow up with a care provider after their release from prison, releasing prisons from the responsibility for care, though in a country that lacks universal healthcare, healthcare remains out of reach for many and especially for those who must navigate multiple matrices of oppression and broader social forces that limit access to care. In other cases, women may receive a postpartum appointment, though they may still be forced to contend with inadequate care and the dismissal of pain and their cries for help. Consequently, the postpartum bodies of women are regulated by the state, as women are without the ability to seek alternate care in the wake of abysmal or even nonexistent care.

The regulation of women in the postpartum period extends to other matters, including lactation. Although women return to prison lactating, few are provided with the outlet to breastfeed or even a breast pump to express their breastmilk. The inability to express their breastmilk can result in painful and clogged milk ducts and in some cases infections like mastitis that quite literally act as painful reminders of separation. That is, the carceral system continues to control not only women but also the ways in which babies are fed, as leading medical organizations recommend exclusive breastfeeding in the first six months of life because of the many nutritional benefits and positive health outcomes for both women and their babies. These recommendations make clear that the incarceration of postpartum women is harmful to health.

The maternal web of control continues to affect women even after they are no longer pregnant, as the prison system works in conjunction with the healthcare system and the child welfare system to control the particulars of women's bodies and those of their children. Not only does the web influence the fourth trimester, even after women return to prison following childbirth, but it continues to regulate women and their families even after women are out of the postpartum period and released from prison—an issue I explore in the next chapter.

6

Coming Home

Mothering on the Margins

Even if you do your time, it never goes away.
—Taylor

When Bonnie, a White, thirty-six-year-old mother of three, came to prison, she was "highly addicted" to crystal meth and never gave much thought to the future, taking each day as it came. Prostitution, drugs, and theft were a way of life, and Bonnie was no stranger to the criminal legal system, having been incarcerated multiple times before. With each incarceration, she grew more comfortable with the prison system and found it to be more stable than life on the streets. By the time she was in high school, she had lived in over thirteen different foster homes. Her father died by suicide when she was four, and her mother had her own issues with substance abuse, cycling in and out of jails and prisons throughout much of her childhood. In foster care, life was not much better—she eventually aged out of the system and was forced to make a home in the streets. She became pregnant at seventeen and again at eighteen. A single, young mother on drugs with no way to support herself and her young children, she soon lost custody of both children, pushing her deeper into addiction and a dark depression. Her youngest was just six months old when she was first sent to prison on cocaine charges. Two years later she would be released and placed on parole supervision. Still using while on parole, she was sent back to prison, where she would stay again for another two years. Four years later, she would be back in the same prison again—though, this time while pregnant.

Although she missed her older two children deeply and had not heard from them in years, life behind bars was better than out on the streets, where she was a sex worker. She had been beaten and abused more times than she could count, and some of her clients had even pulled a knife on her. For Bonnie, the emphasis on security and order behind bars was a welcome change. As Bonnie explained, "I learned how to live in prison. I mean I've just done so much time in prison. I can be comfortable in it, and I can live in prison. I know how to do time. I had prayed to God to remove me from the streets and that lifestyle."

Behind bars, she was able to sober up and eventually gave birth to a healthy baby boy. With four months still left to serve after the birth of her son, she was forced to make a caregiver plan, a process that reignited painful memories. Having grown up in the foster care system herself, she was all too familiar with the surveilling web of forces that had promised to keep her safe but instead had failed her, eventually tearing apart both her family of origin and her family of procreation. Although she was vehemently opposed to the thought of placing her own baby in foster care, she had no other options. The father of her baby was also behind bars, and Bonnie had no family left in the picture.

The last four months of her incarceration were the hardest, as she wondered about the whereabouts and well-being of her baby. Her assigned social worker had promised her that she would be able to maintain a relationship and would receive regular updates and even photos, but these turned out to be empty promises. The only contact she would have with her baby during her incarceration was the day she gave birth, channeling her deeper into another dark depression. Bonnie did her best to navigate the child welfare system, searching for any information about her baby, but as with many aspects of the carceral system, all she encountered were red tape and dead ends, which meant that her mind was running wild with fear about all the things that could be happening to her baby.

When Bonnie was released from prison, her baby was four months old. She was excited about the thought of reuniting with him but worried about relapsing and knew that she would have to do things differently this time around to avoid another prison term. On her last day of prison, she received what was left on her commissary account—just fifty-seven dollars and seventeen cents—as well as a set of clothing, a Greyhound bus ticket, and fifty dollars in cash—standard gate fare for those at her prison, though not enough to be able to support herself and her baby.[1] After her release from prison, she went to live at a Christian women's transition center, a place that helps those recently released from prison reintegrate into society.

Though the center did not allow children, they were able to put her in touch with an attorney, who helped her locate her baby. She was overjoyed to learn that her baby was thriving, putting to rest her fears about his well-being. Reassured that her baby was doing well, she leaned into the parenting classes and support groups at the transition center with the goal of one day reuniting more permanently. To do that, she would need to demonstrate to the child welfare system that she was fit to parent and able to provide for the basic needs of both herself and her baby—Bonnie was up for the challenge and more determined than ever. But she soon found that life in the "free world" was not as free or easy as she thought it would be.

Her criminal record followed her, making it difficult to find work and her own place to live, especially since her prison did little in the way of helping with reintegration. She had a couple of interviews but quickly learned that not everyone was willing to see past her criminal record. Without work, it was difficult to find a more permanent place to live. And without a place to live, it was difficult to find work—a vicious symbiotic cycle that made it nearly impossible to reunite. At the time of the interview, Bonnie was sober and still living at the transition center, though her days at the center were numbered, due to institutional rules that limit the number of months women can stay. She eventually found work at a local warehouse company, but the money was still not enough to make ends meet, let alone to regain custody. In the meantime, she clings tight to the updates and photos from the foster care family, hopeful that one day she can be the mom she always dreamed about being. For Bonnie and so many others like her, mothering both behind bars and in the community is anything but easy, for the maternal web of control that marks their pregnancy also follows them after they give birth and are released from prison, ultimately threatening their motherhood.

In this chapter, I focus on how the maternal web of control affects mothering behind bars and in the community after women are released from prison. I show how the prison system works in conjunction with the child welfare system to surveil and control family dynamics, denying women opportunities to parent in a dignified manner—a core tenet of reproductive justice.[2] Whether it is countless prison rules that hinder the ability to see their baby or the physical environment that is off-putting for babies, motherhood is weakened and controlled behind bars. When women are released from prison, the concept of freedom is still limited, for they must secure work and housing before they are able to reunite with their baby. In this way, (formerly) incarcerated pregnant women are haunted by a past that is laced in control and surveillance that keeps them subjugated to a permanent underclass, threatening their ability to mother and to truly move forward.

Throughout this chapter, I argue that the maternal web of control governs not just pregnancy but also motherhood, going beyond criminal punishment by ultimately threatening families. The intensive-motherhood paradigm that permeates society and expects mothers to play a central role in childrearing through the expenditure of large amounts of time, money, and resources is ever present, acting as a carceral force, expecting even incarcerated mothers to endlessly pour resources into their children even from afar without regard to the structural forces that limit motherhood.[3] The maternal web of control that operates both behind bars and in communities undermines motherhood, particularly among more marginalized women without economic supports. The failure to consider the unique structural conditions, tensions, and oppressive forces that constrain motherhood make it difficult to mother newborn babies, ensuring their distance and ultimately threatening the survival of families. I argue that even after women give birth and are released from prison, the maternal web of control never truly ends, forever altering families.

Mothering behind Bars

After women give birth and experience separation, they are sent back to prison, where they stay for the duration of their sentence—anywhere from weeks or months to years or even decades. Once they are discharged from the hospital and return to prison, their mothering does not end. Rather, they are caught in the middle of two different worlds—one behind bars and one in the community—expected to mother as if they are not incarcerated and to adhere to the minutiae of surveilling institutional rules and regulations of prison, as if they are not mothers.

These conflicting forces make it all but impossible for women to mother in the ways they would like—and in the ways that society still expects them to do.

Motherhood Surveilled

The public nature of pregnancy (and motherhood), as described in chapter 1, means that women are highly scrutinized and evaluated on their fitness as mothers, most notably on the amount and intensity of time spent with their children. The surveilling forces that punish women during pregnancy also continue to govern their motherhood, limiting their relationships with their children, while simultaneously expecting them to be ever present. The intensive-mothering paradigm is the gauge through which mothers are evaluated even behind bars, where "good" mothers are highly involved and in constant communication with their baby. "Bad" mothers are those who are not in constant contact with their baby.

The evaluation of incarcerated women on their fitness as mothers occurs across a number of different systems that all work in simultaneity with each other both behind bars and in communities to surveil and control women. The absence of prison visits or phone calls, as monitored and recorded by prisons, may be presented by the prison system as *evidence* to the child welfare system that a woman is uninterested in reunification and custodial care, and therefore should not be granted privileges to see or hear her baby. A fallout with a caregiver over parenting approaches can easily be framed as aggression, hostility, or detachment, or evidence of a nonexistent support system—an important criterion that may be used by the courts to determine whether a woman is authorized to see her child or to one day have custodial care.

This logic ignores the structural conditions that either foster or hinder mothering behind bars, including how poverty and structural racism affect communication and visitation. That is, the presence or absence of a visit has less to do with mothering intentions and instead reflects the ease through which caregivers, who act as important gatekeepers, navigate communication and visitation hurdles. To no surprise, White people and those with more money are more likely to receive an in-person visit from their baby, reaffirming prevailing notions and controlling images from the child welfare system that they are more capable to provide care than their poor, Black counterparts who must navigate the structural racism that makes visitation out of reach.

The many institutional rules found in prisons undermine the ability to have a relationship behind bars, as all forms of communication are surveilled and expected to adhere to a number of rules and regulations that ensure the security of a total institution.[4] While each prison is different, it is not uncommon for all visits to be preapproved, a taxing process on its own that may take weeks or even months but one that becomes further complicated when the visitor is a baby, who may not yet have a birth certificate and Social Security card—essentials needed to clear security. Even then, the punitive nature of prisons means that visits can be taken away at any point for "bad" behavior, including those between new mothers and their babies. The precariousness of visits makes it especially risky for caregivers to travel long distances with a baby in tow, knowing that they could potentially be turned away. The controlling images that paint women of color as threatening also means that they are more likely to experience discipline and to have any visitations stripped from them—reinforcing the notion that they are poor mothers, unfit to retain visitation privileges and unfit to earn custody after their release from prison.

The prison system is not the only carceral system that regulates motherhood behind bars. Under the maternal web of control, the prison system works alongside the child welfare system to control the circumstances through which women can have a relationship with their baby—placing a unique burden on incarcerated mothers to demonstrate their competency and fitness as mothers. Already stigmatized as (now formerly) pregnant inmates, women are expected to convey how their criminality is distinct from their parenthood, through a process that entails involvement from the child welfare system. Yet, for many women in prison, especially women of color, the child welfare system not only does not help them in their attempts to mother behind bars but also actively prevents them from doing so by working with the prison system to limit the means through which they can see their newborn babies, ultimately tearing apart families and hindering the preservation of the maternal-infant bond.

Yet, as recalled in chapter 1, the reasons why women come to prison, pregnant no less, are complex and often have nothing to do with their fitness as a parent. The rise of the carceral state, particularly amid the loss of a social safety net, funnels disadvantaged women into the prison system, as both poverty and racism are criminalized.[5] Some of the women I interviewed intentionally committed a crime that carries prison time because they were pregnant and wanted to ensure the health and survival of their baby. In Jada's case, she was left with no other options but to either commit a crime that carries prison time or risk her children's safety. These decisions are not made lightly and illustrate the gravity of the violence and poverty and the precariousness of living situations that disproportionately affect already marginalized women, illustrating the extreme lengths that some go to for the betterment of their baby.

Yet, it is not just the prison system and child welfare system that surveil mothering behind bars. Caregivers also act as agents of control—extensions of the child welfare system—who evaluate parental fitness and then gatekeep babies accordingly. Shay, a White mother of three, was forty when she came to prison pregnant. The caregivers of Shay's baby cut off all communication with her, withholding her baby, because they felt that Shay would "ghost" her daughter, harming her daughter in the process.[6] Shay was hurt by the insinuation that she would not be involved in her baby's life, just because she was incarcerated. Her case provides insight into how even caregivers have the power to surveil and control, conflating criminality with poor parenting—a finding that is consistent with extant research.[7] As Shay explained, "Ninety percent of the women don't get their kids back when they go to prison, so they were thinking I was one of those women. They wouldn't bring her to visit. They had excuses, so I really had to fight to get her back and show them that I did no wrong or anything."

While some women are able to keep their baby with them in prison in a specialized housing unit, often called prison nursery programs or mother-baby units, effectively bypassing the need for caregivers, most prisons in the United States do not have these programs, leaving the majority with no choice but to leave their baby with a caregiver for the remainder of their imprisonment.[8] To be sure, the nature of relationships with caregivers varies tremendously. Some may have strong relationships and do not have to worry about gatekeeping, while others find themselves at odds with caregivers.

Barriers to Mothering

Structural conditions, such as poverty and institutionalized racism, also act as carceral forces in the maternal web of control that make it difficult for women to stay in contact with their babies, threatening the maternal-infant bond. The economic disparities embedded in communication and visitation practices behind bars are vast, as those with less money may encounter greater communication and visitation hurdles.[9] Moreover, the uniqueness of a newborn baby also makes it difficult to stay in contact, for communication and visitation must be navigated around logistical matters, such as naps and feedings.

Long distances also hinder the maternal-infant bond, as it can be difficult to travel with a baby. Most women are incarcerated in towns one hundred miles or more from their baby, much further away from their homes than incarcerated men, making it hard for those in poverty to visit, especially for families living in rural, remote areas without public transportation. Alice talked about how she did not want her family to travel the long distance to her prison because she felt that being incarcerated was her "responsibility," and she did not want to place the "burden" on her family. According to Alice, "I didn't want to drag them through it. It was a long way to go for a short visit." While many women I interviewed said they wanted to see their baby, they knew the distance would make for a difficult trip and did not want to appear selfish by asking the caregiver to travel a long distance for such a short visit, especially in cases where the caregiver was already taking care of any older children too.

Mothers are placed in impossible situations, where they must assert a strong desire to see their baby as a means of demonstrating love and affection, while at the same time being careful to not ask too much from caregivers or to cause too much disruption or inconvenience. Most of the women I interviewed were very careful not to ask "too much" from their baby's caregiver, as they worried that their requests might come across as too demanding, jeopardizing their relationship with their baby and the ability to receive any updates.

Cherelle's narrative centered on the exhaustion her baby's caregiver experienced over having to carefully pack baby items for a visit only to arrive at prison and learn that these items were not permitted. While each prison has its own set of rules, there may be restrictions regarding the number of diapers and ounces of milk permitted. Cherelle explained the difficulties that come with visitations among newborns: "You have to pack milk, change of clothes, diapers, wipes, load up in car seats. It is quite exhausting, there's security searches." Long security lines can be especially cumbersome with a fussy baby. Inevitably, Cherelle's baby would be asleep only to be awakened by bright fluorescent lighting and loud noises. By the time her baby and caregiver had made it through security, her baby needed to be fed (again), and needed yet another diaper change, making for a stressful visit.

Other women I talked with shared how given the age of their baby, they felt that an in-person visit would really be more for themselves, as their baby would not be old enough to remember the visit, making them feel guilty for even wanting a visit. However, in some ways, they were grateful their baby was too young to remember their visit, as it allowed them to bypass some of the more difficult conversations that come with visitation. According to Cherelle, "Sometimes as parents we're selfish, and we want to see our kids, but we forget about who has to take the kids, and when it's over who has to put the Band-Aids all over these children. They have lots of questions, and they want to know why mommy or daddy can't come home with me."

Her narrative reveals how even the physical environment and structures of prisons are not conducive to families and young children, intentionally designed to be uninviting and surveilling and punitive even to young children, who must navigate a carceral environment, as a prerequisite to being with their mother. Cherelle's narrative also illustrates how children are adversely affected by their mother's incarceration. The research is clear—incarceration harms the children of incarcerated parents, for they too are funneled into punitive environments.[10] Research reveals that children of incarcerated mothers may face psychological, emotional, and developmental challenges resulting from the disruption of the maternal-infant bond, with long-term consequences that funnel these children into social disadvantage and intergenerational poverty.[11] To be sure, the nature of mothering behind bars also depends on a number of factors, including the number of years left of a sentence, with those sentenced to years and even decades having a harder time demonstrating to the child welfare system, to caregivers, and even to their children that they are fit to be parents, further complicating the ability to have a relationship with their child.

While phone calls may appear more practical than an in-person visit, in some cases, even phone calls must adhere to the surveilling rules of prisons that determine when and for how long phone calls can be made, making it hard to navigate around naps and feedings. Even then, communicating with an infant is difficult, as they cannot yet talk—though, they can cry. Gloria explained how phone calls were hard for her because when she called, inevitably all she heard was crying, providing her with little confirmation that her baby was "okay." At other times, her baby would be asleep or in a deep crying spell—also leaving her with little reassurance. Stacy shared how although she was unable to talk with her newborn, she continued to call, so her baby could grow accustomed to her voice. Although she initially talked with her children when she was behind bars, Faye said she had to make the difficult decision to cease all forms of communication because it became too painful to have to say goodbye each time. She was also embarrassed that her children saw her in a prison jumpsuit. In Angel's case, although she longed to hear updates, "[Receiving letters] was kinda discouraging because it was just the postpartum depression, the attachment, the missing her. They [caregivers] mailed me pictures of her, but that made it even worser because I wanted to be there with her, but it made it better because I was able to see her."

In the United States, the intensive-mothering paradigm prevails, as women are expected to be there for their baby twenty-four seven.[12] Yet, the convergence of surveilling forces that comprise the maternal web of control effectively shuts out the means of communication that allow mothers to be there for their babies. Several structural barriers also complicate the ability to be in contact, especially for those in poverty. Continued involvement is important, not only for the maternal-infant bond but also because this is a mechanism through which the child welfare system regulates whether women are fit to be custodial parents. To be sure, mothering behind bars is complicated and deeply personal, influenced by a number of factors. While some have excellent communication with their baby's caregiver and receive detailed updates that support a successful reunification—others do not have these experiences.

Leaving Prison

Nearly all incarcerated women are eventually released from prison. Research reveals that over 95 percent of the incarcerated will one day be released.[13] Some women are released when their baby is just a few months old, while others come home to children who are already toddlers and, in some cases, young teens.[14] Reentry is marked by any number of feelings, including excitement, fear, and worry. With a baby, the stakes are higher than ever, for the child welfare system is yet another carceral force that surveils their parenting even after their release from prison. All the women I interviewed were worried they would "mess up" and eventually return to prison. In discussing her feelings about reentry, Denise said, "I had mixed feelings. I was scared, very scared and excited obviously to be free, but I was scared because I had nowhere to go. I had no one. I had nothing so that was very scary, but I was excited."

Navigating Reentry

In the United States, reentry is often approached with a "sink or swim" mindset, with little in the way of true programming and support. Many women find that their prison does little to help them prepare for the many challenges that accompany both reentry *and* new motherhood. Often, women are released into the very same environment that played a contributing factor in their offending, into a community in which there is little to no safety net, especially for former prisoners in rural areas, only complicating motherhood.

Barbara came home to an environment full of drugs and prostitution and knew that this was no place to raise her baby. In weighing her options, she made the difficult decision to leave her son with his foster care family, where she knew he would be safe. As Barbara explained, "Right outside my door just down the corner of the street, the drugs were being sold, in my apartment building there were people smoking crack, so it was a no-win situation. I knew that it wasn't a place for my son and that he was better off with his foster family. I knew our relationship would be set up to fail in that environment. It would only be a matter of time till he got taken from me." For many mothers, reentry not only entails navigating poverty and drugs and the surveillance that comes from law enforcement, parole officers, and child welfare workers but also sometimes entails making difficult decisions that result in separation. Many of the neighborhoods they come home to are steeped in oppression and control, locking them into a permanent underclass through strict surveillance and regulation that threatens their ability to work and secure housing, among other basic needs.[15] As was the case with Barbara, these carceral forces make it difficult to truly ever reintegrate into society and mother their children with dignity.

Reentry Programming

While each prison has its own way of approaching reintegration, it is not unusual for prisons to fail to provide support and information on how to prepare for life after prison *and* how to raise a baby, particularly amid the smog of systemic poverty, violence, racism, and sexism present in many communities.[16] Information and support related to motherhood, postpartum healthcare, and family reunification may also be absent or without regard to the unique concerns that come with raising a baby in more rural disadvantaged communities.[17]

The absence of gender-responsive supports illustrates how prisons are ill equipped in preparing women for a successful reintegration, consequently increasing the likelihood of reoffending and further involvement from carceral systems that contribute to family separation.[18] A lack of institutional support for new mothers in the wake of their release is especially alarming given the high rates of recidivism, where three quarters of the recently released will be rearrested within five years after their release from prison—startling numbers that illustrate the vast expanse of mass incarceration and the failures (or rather successes) of the criminal legal system to truly invest in rehabilitation and reform.[19] Thus, it is not surprising that worries about "making it" are so prevalent, given the magnitude of what is at stake, as reunification is dependent on having support.

Although the benefits of reentry programming, especially for women, have been well documented, including a lower recidivism rate and a smoother transition back into the community, the prison industry has little financial incentive to assist women with reintegration, let alone to provide for the more specialized needs of new mothers.[20] That is, a direct relationship between the prison system and capitalism exists, wherein the prison system acts as a form of structural violence, locking many families into a perpetual underclass rife with poverty and uncertainty.[21] As Rhonda said, "If you don't have any women here in these beds, these corporations are losing out on some serious money. They don't like it when you know what's going on and that you're knowledgeable and all of that. They don't like it. *They want you to come back.* They have a profit motive. It all comes back to money; they're making profits off the back of prisoners. Yep, we're talking millions of dollars."[22] Though the topic is beyond the scope of this book, Rhonda's narrative brings to light important issues regarding the maternal web of control and the nature of mass incarceration, describing what scholars have termed the "prison-industrial complex," a complex web of relationships among the prison system, government, and other industries in which there is a financial incentive to incarcerate people because of the many businesses that benefit from the incarceration of people.[23] Corrections is a multibillion-dollar industry, and thus, failure to help (former) prisoners reintegrate and address the root causes of crime through evidence-based reentry reform is arguably a strategic financial decision, leaving many scholars to suggest that the prison system is not broken but rather works exactly as intended.[24]

However, the absence of transitional support has profound repercussions, especially for new mothers. Upon their release from prison, women who give birth behind bars are still held accountable to different agencies and systems that govern their motherhood. Being pregnant behind bars results in a unique type of surveillance that emanates not only from the prison system but also from the child welfare system, the medical system, reentry support services, including places of transitional housing, and the courts—entities that all work together to monitor women, collectively creating a network or web of control. As a result, the starry-eyed reunion that many may long anticipate may still be out of reach, even after prison, as women must secure their basic needs first, a prerequisite of having custodial care.

Reentry Centers

Moreover, as part of the surveilling web of control, it is not uncommon for women to be placed on parole supervision following their release from prison, where they may be expected to adhere to a number of conditions that entail heavy regulations that may be counter to motherhood, including paying restitution, attending ongoing meetings with a parole officer, and submitting to random urinalyses, random home inspections, and mandatory attendance at a range of classes.[25] For some, postrelease supervision entails living in community transitional housing with others in a prisonlike environment that is rife with surveillance that effectively disempowers women of their ability to mother their own children, subjugating them to an infantile state.[26]

Lora shared how she was initially ordered to live in a halfway house for three months following her release from prison as part of her parole. By the time the three months had passed, her baby was one week shy of a year old. Through tears, Lora explained how she was sad that she missed out on her baby's first year of life: "I was excited to get out, but I remember being really furious because I had my baby there waiting for me, and as part of the program and part of the parole I was required to go to a halfway house, and I remember being just ripped up in knots because I had already lost so much time with this baby."

While transitional centers may be helpful in navigating the obstacles of reentry, they too "are an extension of the carceral experience, complete with surveillance and intense scrutiny."[27] Those who lived in a residential center shared how they were subjected to many rules, including curfews, that made it difficult to see their children and complicated the ability to demonstrate their fitness as a parent. As was the case with Bonnie, it is not unusual for women's reentry transition centers not to permit children, making it especially hard for women to get the supports they need to be successful in their parenting—a reality that highlights how even transition centers are designed with men in mind, ignoring the unique needs of women. Reentry centers specifically designed for women and the unique needs of mothers may be especially sparse in rural communities, placing them at extreme risk for recidivism in the absence of other support systems.[28]

Rhonda stayed in a residential reentry center and talked about how she would "sneak away" to her children during the day, at a time when she was ordered to be out in the community looking for work. According to Rhonda, "I would just see the kids when I could because at the reentry center, they put you on ankle bracelets and they have to know where you are at all times and all of that stuff, so when they would send me out to look for jobs, I would kinda deviate from the plan and just run home and try to see the kids or whoever was babysitting. I would try to go see them. So, I really didn't get time with him until he was, what, nine months or so." Rhonda's narrative explains how even when women are no longer incarcerated, their lives are still heavily regulated and controlled without regard to their unique needs as new mothers.

Each reentry experience is unique and specific to the particulars. Some of the women I interviewed bypassed transitional housing altogether and came directly home to their baby. It is no surprise that most of these women were White women from a more affluent background, who had more of a support system and family with whom they could live, at least temporarily, which offered some protection from the maternal web of control. Those without a support system encounter many challenges in the reentry period that threaten family reunification.

A Long-Awaited Reunion

Family reunification after prison is a continuous process, dependent upon a number of factors, including length of imprisonment, ties with caregivers, and the frequency and intensity of communication during incarceration, to name but a few.[29] While some are able to quickly resume their roles as mothers and have an otherwise seamless transition, most of my interviewees struggled in their parenting and found that mothering after prison had its own set of challenges, made more difficult by the precariousness of their living situations. Many were appreciative of the caregiver(s) for taking care of their baby during their incarceration, but once they were released, they were eager to exert their authority as mothers, and most planned to provide custodial care. Those who were able to maintain contact through in-person visits and phone calls during their incarceration were more likely to experience a smoother transition when it came to parenting. However, research reveals that two thirds of incarcerated parents never receive even a single in-person visit from their children during their incarceration, making the transition difficult for many.[30]

Alice's case illustrates the importance of strong bonds during incarceration and the difference they made during her reentry period. Although she never received in-person visits, due to geographical barriers, her baby's caregiver kept her up to date and informed through phone calls, so Alice felt as though she "never lost real contact." According to Alice, "They sent me letters and cards and pictures and stuff of my baby, so we just picked up where we left off in the hospital. They [the caregivers] were happy for me to come back and get my baby." Although Alice had a smooth transition, some find that life had gone on while they were in prison.

Perhaps one of the biggest fears among women after they go home is that their baby will reject them or be more attached to their caregiver, forever viewing them as outsiders looking in through the window of someone else's world. Although many of the women I talked with were thankful for the caregiver(s) for taking care of their baby at a time when they could not, most were eager to exert their authority as mothers and had a goal of one day providing custodial care.

While some women, like Bonnie, have experienced the trials of reintegration before, coming home to a baby or young child whom they had only had a brief opportunity to know is uncharted territory. In the wake of their release, some may wish to get acclimated and back on their feet first, while others seek family reunification right away. The particulars of the period immediately following prison are all unique and dependent on the status of parole supervision, an issue I explore later in the chapter.

In some cases, women may find that their baby and any other older siblings had already forged strong bonds with their caregiver(s) and showed some degree of hesitation or even resistance to their mother, and it was not uncommon for their baby or (in some cases, now toddler) to cry when they tried to hold them. This rejection was hard. As Destiny explained, "Could you imagine you get your child back and you have no clue who they are? They don't connect with you. I mean, it's devastating." Many shared how they struggled to take on the title of "mom" because they felt like imposters intruding on the lives of their children, especially since, in many cases, their baby had already solidified strong bonds with their caregiver(s). According to Lora, even though her daughter was still very much a baby when she was released, her daughter had already come to call her caregiver "mom." As Lora explained, "She still doesn't call me mom. I catch her all the time calling me by my first name, and I'm like, 'No, I'm your mom!'"

For many, the move into custodial parenthood is gradual, for they must not only secure their basic needs but also strengthen their relationship with their baby first. As eager as many were to have their child(ren) live with them, they were careful to avoid stepping on any toes and did not want to disrupt any existing relationships. Taylor shared how she discussed the move to custodial parenthood with her parents, who served as caregivers, during her incarceration, making for an easier transition. According to Taylor, "We decided that when I had got released, I just couldn't take [my daughter] out of her home of what she had known it would be. I stayed four months at my parents', so we were parenting together and trying to adjust in that regard. It was subtle. It wasn't something that we just jerked her out."

In some cases, like Taylor's, especially where family was involved, caregivers allowed the mothers to move in with them, at least until they could get on their feet, giving them some time to bond with their baby and learn all their baby's routines, with the goal of one day living together in their own place. Moving in with a caregiver(s) also helped to ease some of the pressures associated with reentry, such as finding work and a place to live, a point I return to later in the chapter. However, this is not the norm for everyone, for some do not have the financial means or support system to be able to move in with the caregiver following their release from prison.

Mothering in the "Free World"

It is not just women who are impacted by a pregnancy behind bars; the children born to these women are also affected by the maternal web of control, for they too are caught in the middle of punitive, carceral forces that have lasting effects on their health and well-being. The research is clear—the separation of women from their babies hinders families and has hidden consequences, including trauma, delinquency, depression and anxiety, antisocial behavior, psychological problems, low educational attainment, and more.[31] In many ways, the babies (and older children) of incarcerated mothers also pay for their mother's crimes, making the need for family reunification even more important.[32]

Motherhood Challenges

Yet, the stigma attached to a pregnancy in prison never seems to quite go away. As much as women tried to move past their incarceration, carcerality is ubiquitous. Gloria described a time when she was at a routine doctor's appointment for her baby and was asked to account for the circumstances surrounding her child's birth. In doing so, she revealed that she had been pregnant in prison, and one of the nurses made a condescending remark to her about her time behind bars. Gloria explained:

> I was judged at the doctor's appointment. The nurse was like, "I can't believe you had him in prison. Don't you feel bad for having him in prison?" I'm like, "No. It wasn't my choice," and she's just like, "Oh man if that were me, I just couldn't live with myself," and I'm like, "Oh my God, really, lady? [laughs] Like who are you?" Like it got me mad, and then I told my doctor that I don't like her nurse, so she gives me a different nurse. And then like she was talking to my son like, "Geez you poor baby, you was just locked up when you was just a baby and you don't even know," and I was just like, "I don't appreciate you talking to my son like that."

Those with longer sentences who came home not to a baby but to an older child may find it harder to connect or to exert their authority as a mother, making discipline especially difficult given their own criminal transgressions. As Taylor explained,

> It was really hard with my daughter because here I am, mom, but I'm not really the mom, so who's in this role, right? So, I tried to let my mom kinda stay in the position of authority, but at the same time, I didn't want my daughter to think I didn't want to be her mom or that I didn't care about her, so it was really hard. It hurt my daughter and was very hard on her. There were times when I would try to tell her something, to do something or not to do something, and I'd get, "Well you weren't here, you didn't raise me."

In their struggles to reintegrate, some also found that they were prohibited from stepping foot on their children's school grounds because of the nature of their charges, making it difficult to reintegrate and be a present and involved parent.[33] Amanda said, "I had so much shame and guilt that I couldn't even take my daughter to school or attend her events. It's so embarrassing because like her friends always ask her, 'Why isn't your mom here?'" Others told similar stories about their struggles to be known as mom. Some of the other women I talked with were quite hurt after hearing their child address another person as "mom," yet another painful reminder of their incarceration and subsequent separation. At times, jealousy surfaced, worsening their depression, while others were just relieved that their baby had forged a strong bond with someone while they were away.

Whether it was disciplining an older child or staying calm in the middle of a colicky crying baby spell, those I interviewed talked about the challenges that came with raising their children in the wake of their release. In some ways, they felt as though they were constantly being judged on their parenting abilities, and to some degree, they were, for motherhood under the carceral state is highly regulated, requiring mothers to demonstrate their competency to many people, including to their own children and caregivers, as families also act as surveilling forces, in addition to child welfare agencies, parole officers, and, in some ways, themselves. As Jeanine said, "It's not fair to some of those pregnant women 'cause whenever they get out, they're gonna have to prove to the judge that they're fit to be a mother and all this and that, and I don't know, I think it's just a messed-up situation honestly."

For some women, the pressures of taking care of a child under these surveilling circumstances, on top of issues like the baby blues or postpartum depression, were simply too much and caused some to reconsider their plans of seeking custodial care. According to Susan,

> When I came home, I was very excited of course. I cried. You know we all cried and said hi, and then I got anxiety really bad. I mean like with all the baby crying and at first, I was like, "I can handle it." I mean I've had kids before; I know what to expect, but you know as soon as my daughter was running around and the baby was crying at the same time, I felt like

I didn't know what to do. So, I went and saw a specialist, and she's like, "You probably have post-traumatic anxiety," and I was like, "I think I do."

Jeanine told a similar story. Although she had initially planned on reuniting with her daughter and raising her full-time, she soon realized that it was too much and asked her grandmother to serve as her daughter's legal guardian. As Jeanine explained, "Whenever I got out, I was depressed. I had the baby blues. I didn't know how to deal with all the depression I was going through. Emotionally and financially, I couldn't take care of her because I just got out of prison. I didn't have nothing, so I couldn't take care of her at the time, so I gave her grandma legal guardianship over her because I saw that they had a bond, so I didn't want to take that from her."

Managing the Stigma of Incarceration

These narratives illustrate how incarceration has a hold on family relationships, altering the ways in which women interact with their children, making it difficult to even wear the title of "mom" in the face of surveilling forces that disrupt their motherhood. Some of the women I interviewed said their baby's caregiver(s) did not want to be associated with them because they had been to prison, revealing the deep-seated stigma attached to maternal incarceration, especially in rural communities, where there are fewer opportunities for anonymity.[34] Crystal, for example, said that her older son's caregiver, who happened to be her own father, did not want her to contact her son when she came home from prison because he was too embarrassed to be associated with someone, including his own daughter, who had been to prison. According to Crystal, "The last thing [my dad] wanted was my son going to school and saying, 'My mommy was in prison, my mommy was in prison!'" Crystal's experience illustrates how experiences with family reunification are also dependent on the degree to which incarceration is accepted in families.

Custodial care arrangements are all different and particular to the circumstances. While some women are able to retain custody of their baby while they remain in prison, those with a longer sentence typically lost custody, for under the federal Adoption and Safe Families Act, termination of parental rights may occur if a parent has been separated from their child for fifteen of the previous twenty-two months.[35] For those looking to regain custody, the stigma attached to maternal incarceration and in particular to a pregnancy behind bars makes it hard to demonstrate competency as a mother—a point that was especially true among women of color, who also had to navigate the systemic racism that comprises the child welfare system.[36]

Some of the women I interviewed were forthright in acknowledging that they would not make a good mother and had no plans of seeking custodial care. There were others who had originally planned on seeking custodial care after their release but could now see for themselves that their child was happy in their current environment and in some cases the home that they were in was much nicer than any home they could ever hope to provide, making them reconsider their decision to pursue custodial care.

To be sure, the carceral system transforms the mother-child relationship in the most profound of ways. Even though every single one of the women I interviewed was eventually released from prison, the fear that they would one day return to prison haunted them, for the stakes were higher than ever now that they had caught a glimpse of freedom and had reunited with their child(ren)—at least to some degree. Jasmine shared how her daughter was deeply affected by her absence while in prison and had severe separation anxiety nearly every time she left the house. According to Jasmine, "Even now my little girl, she holds on to the stuff, even now like I go out, and she's like, 'But mommy, are you really going to come back?' You see, you see? She thinks I'm gonna leave her and not come back, but I've been back plenty of times. I want my kids to know that they can depend on me." As Jasmine's remarks indicate, not only does incarceration affect those who serve time behind bars; it also affects their children, even long after they are born. The threat of coming back to prison is always in the background, particularly amid a carceral environment that regulates women. Many (formerly) incarcerated pregnant women must continuously demonstrate their fitness as mothers—a task that is hard to do given that for many, their life is constantly on the margins.

Makin' It in the "Free World"

Much has been written about the struggles of reintegration and how incarceration adversely affects the ability to secure work and housing, among other basic needs. What is not discussed as often is how these struggles are gendered, posing a unique threat to mothers in their attempts to reunite with their children.[37] While reentry may be a struggle to some degree for all those who spend time in prison, new mothers face unique obstacles during reentry, hindering their ability to parent with dignity under the maternal web of control.

Securing Basic Needs

As mentioned, many of the women I interviewed had nothing more than a bus ticket and fifty dollars in gate money when they left prison and had to start completely over, forcing some to live in shelters or to rely on transitional housing, while others rely on support from friends and family.[38] The ability to secure these basic needs is a prerequisite to motherhood, for in the United States, poverty is criminalized, and failure to secure essentials is a marker of poor parenting, an individual problem, rather than a consequence of deep-seated inequities.[39] Nearly all the women I interviewed were keenly aware that gaining custodial care of their child(ren) was dependent on their ability to secure these essentials, making the need to find work and housing of utmost importance—arduous tasks for anyone but especially those already living on the margins in rural areas with few to no prospects.[40]

There were some, like Tiana, who had to spend several nights on the streets finding shelter underneath park gazebos and bridges because they were unsuccessful in their search for housing and did not have a social network. Those who planned on having custodial care also had to stretch what little money they had to provide for their children and were open about the steep costs of diapers, wipes, formula, and daycare, and about their financial insecurities.

When Gloria was released, her baby was just three months old, and she did not have any family nearby to help with her transition into the community and the many challenges that come with parenting an infant. As Gloria explained, "My sister's boyfriend was in prison for a long time and when he came out, he couldn't take care of his kids 'cause he didn't know how, and we used to always be like, 'It's not hard to take care of kids, like come on now.' And now I understand what he means 'cause it's hard, it really is, and especially coming home to a new baby. It was really hard."

It did not help that Gloria, like so many others, lived in a "childcare desert," a term that has come to mark communities that do not have enough childcare options—a phenomenon that is especially profound in rural places, where 60 percent of rural families live in a childcare desert.[41] In Gloria's case, the few options that were available in town had lengthy wait lists and were very expensive, which meant that the caregiving work fell on Gloria. Taking care of an infant, in addition to her other child, made it difficult for Gloria to take care of herself and prioritize her sobriety. Still more, a lack of childcare hurt her ability to find work—a condition of her parole order.

Gloria's situation is hardly unique. Amid soaring childcare costs, women are hurt the most. Failure to secure work not only hurts women and their families economically, but it also increases the likelihood of recidivism and family separation.[42] The importance of affordable childcare was evidenced during the pandemic, when over one million women left the workplace, due to both the scarcity of childcare options and soaring childcare costs among what few options were available.[43] Affording these essentials is especially cumbersome for women with a history of incarceration, for their income tends to be substantially lower than that of both nonincarcerated women and even men who have been incarcerated.[44] Yet, it is not just the costs of childcare that make it difficult for women to successfully reintegrate. They must also contend with sex and race discrimination amid a labor market built for men.[45]

Many of the industries that allow those with a criminal record to work are male-dominated industries like construction and waste-management services.[46] As Amber explained, "Men who have been to prison can walk onto a construction site and get a job, just walk up there and say, 'Hey I need a job,' and they'll hire them. Women can't do that; women need more help getting jobs because for one they do have kids." Formerly incarcerated men are also better positioned to obtain work upon their release because they are more likely to have opportunities for hands-on vocational training programs behind bars, like welding, and there are more reentry services for men in communities.[47] Many female-dominated industries, like nursing and childcare, prohibit those with a criminal record from work in these fields, making it hard for women to find employment, especially in rural areas where there are even fewer opportunities for women recently released from prison.[48]

In addition to gender discrimination in the labor market, women of color also face racial discrimination and must also contend with the unique intersection of these forms of oppression, which hinder their ability to successfully reintegrate and reunite with their children. Rhonda, a Black woman, was keenly aware of the discrimination and surveillance that formerly incarcerated Black women experience, especially those who give birth behind bars. She knew that her reentry journey would be more difficult than that of her White peers because of the intersection of her identities, which made her especially vulnerable to surveillance and control. For a Black woman from a smaller, rural community, where social support services and employment prospects were already scarce, racial and gender discrimination was also thick. Rhonda faced immense scrutiny, for she was one of only a few Black women in her small town, making reintegration especially difficult.[49] According to Rhonda, "When I was released, I was beyond excited, I was happy, but it's like I had to do a reality check to myself. I had to do a self-check, like okay, 'Now I have a felony, so things are different, some things that you used to do, some things that you used to get away with, you can't get away [with] anymore,' so it's like I kept telling myself that."

To be sure, though, finding work is a challenge even for White women. Melody talked about how she had "White privilege" and was offered a paid internship in the months following her imprisonment; however, when the company changed ownership and ran a background check on all employees just a few weeks into her new role, the offer was rescinded.[50] While being White may have helped her secure an internship, it was not enough to override some of the newer policies at the company that prohibited those with a criminal record from work. Yet, as Kimberlé Crenshaw notes, the oppression and discrimination that women face are not experienced separately but rather operate in simultaneity, intersecting with each other to create a web that further confines women and hinders their ability to successfully reintegrate. The research is clear; many of the challenges concerning reentry disproportionately affect women of color, for they must contend with both racial discrimination *and* gender discrimination, as well as the unique type of oppression that results from the convergence of these oppressions, where forces, such as poverty, neighborhood violence, and the maternal web of control, all converge, making a seamless transition out of reach for many.[51]

Perhaps nothing illustrates the power of the simultaneity of oppression during the reentry period more clearly than differences in unemployment rates, with unemployment rates among the formerly incarcerated being highest for Black women.[52] The most recent numbers indicate that 43.6 percent of Black formerly incarcerated women are unemployed, while 23.2 percent of White formerly incarcerated women are unemployed.[53] These findings shed light on the consequences incarceration has on employment, for the rates of unemployment are significantly lower among both Black women and White women who have *not* been incarcerated (6.4 percent for Black women and 4.3 percent for White women).[54]

Motherhood under the Carceral State

For many, life after prison means a near-constant state of insecurity that threatens motherhood. Although those with strong social bonds have an easier time securing necessities, even they are not immune to poverty and uncertainty, living life on the margins.[55] Even though Taylor found work, she lived in constant fear that she would lose her job because she had been to prison. As Taylor said, "My charges will follow me for the rest of my life, so even though I've changed and I spent my entire incarceration learning and bettering myself to help other people and doing that since I've been home too, it doesn't matter. It still follows you. Even if you do your time, it never goes away." The power of the carceral system means that for many, they are just one background check or event away from losing their job, home, and everything that matters most, including their children.

Several of the women I interviewed did lose custody of their baby because they were unable to find work and a place to live. Tiana was unemployed when I met her. Although she initially found work and a place to live and even had custodial care of her baby, it was not long before she lost her job and then her apartment, forcing her to panhandle as a result. While panhandling worked for a short period, eventually the child welfare system found out and she lost custody of her baby. According to Tiana, "I lost both of my jobs and couldn't get rehired, so I lost my apartment and ended up homeless because of it, so I went through the whole winter sleeping outside and sleeping at a church and stuff like that because I was homeless, so they had to take my daughter. It was hard for me to find jobs and find people 'cause they look at my background and they think, 'oh, she has these charges,' so sleeping outside and sleeping at a church, it was the terrible, most horrible experience I've ever had. It was worse than prison." At the time of the interview, Tiana was still looking for work and remained focused on regaining custody of her daughter. Tiana's postprison experience was worse for her than prison because her basic needs were not met, making it impossible to survive. As related earlier, Tiana was one of the women I interviewed who intentionally committed a crime so she could be sent to jail and, later, prison to have her basic needs met—a decision that, while far from easy, provides insight into the precariousness that was Tiana's world and the matrices of oppression she experienced.[56]

Yet, it is not just the inability to secure basic needs that complicates reintegration and the ability to parent; the environment women come home to makes it difficult to stay out of prison. Many have concerns about relapsing. While some may quit using or at least switch to a "softer" drug during pregnancy, the challenges of reentry and parenthood, along with postpartum depression, make the pressures to use that much stronger. When Lacey was released from prison, she was eager to demonstrate to her family that she was independent and could make it on her own, especially since her family had looked down upon her for being pregnant in prison. However, Lacey was out of prison just a couple of days before she knew that she would need support and accountability to stay away from drugs. As Lacey explained, "I was back on the street. I didn't want to go home to my mom, again pride. I really didn't want to be judged or follow any rules or hear any drama, so I stayed out on the street a couple of nights and then I was like, 'Okay, if you don't go home to mom, then you're gonna start using,' so I went ahead and went, and I managed to stay clean."

While some participants like Lacey had family or friends who could help them stay clean by providing a safe and stable place to live away from the more tantalizing calls of the streets, others shared how their family and friends were drug users themselves, making the urge to resist using even more difficult. As much as they wanted to stay away from drugs, some were without a place to stay and growing hungrier by the day, leaving little to no choice but to return to the closest support system they had, even if that meant drugs were present.

Preserving Motherhood

Even amid threats to motherhood, I found that women do their best to preserve their motherhood because they value it so much, as indicated in chapter 1—even if it may look different than the way they had envisioned. Although Barbara had to place her baby in the foster care system after her neighborhood became too unsafe, her decision came out of a place of love and care. Additionally, when Jeanine was released from prison, she was eager to move in with her boyfriend, her baby's father, hoping to be together as a family, but she knew it would be unfair to their daughter to be raised around the drugs her father used, forcing Jeanine to end the relationship—even though the ending of the relationship pushed her further into poverty. As Jeanine explained, "I kinda cut off ties with him. I kinda snapped out of it like I can't be doing this shit. I need to get my kids together. I mean, I need to get my life together, so I can get my kids back. I need to get out of this town because this town is going to get me into nothing but trouble and stuff like that."

Knowing the struggles of addiction and the fears of relapsing, Lacey had candid conversations with her son about her drug use and "trained" him on how to respond if he sensed she started using again. Lacey explained that "[my son] knows certain things to look for if I relapse, what things are gonna look like. Like don't go by what I say, go by what you see. If there's no food in the refrigerator or I got all these excuses about what happened to my check, or if I don't go into work for a few days, you *need* to call grandma because something's going on." Amid her fears of relapsing, the response plan was a way to ensure there were procedures in place to preserve her family. To be sure, no two reentry stories are the same, and the degree to which women experience challenges during the reentry period that risks their motherhood is shaped by a myriad of factors, including race and class, extent of social support, and length of imprisonment, among other issues.

Conclusion

Although women are separated from their baby in the aftermath of birth, their mothering continues, even behind bars. For many, mothering from a distance is far from easy, made more difficult by controlling forces that hinder the ability of women to stay in contact with their baby, funneling many more deeply into a dark depression. Yet, incarcerated mothers are still expected to mother and be present for their children, even though maintaining contact with a newborn is complicated for a number of reasons. While some caregivers go out of their way to provide women with detailed updates, keeping them in the loop, others do not maintain contact, leaving women in the dark about the well-being and whereabouts of their baby. Caregivers have tremendous power in fostering the maternal-infant relationship, for they act as gatekeepers to the baby. Correctional facilities are far from ideal places to have visits, for they are often loud, cold, and uncomfortable places that are often located in remote areas far from home, making visitation difficult, especially for those without the means to travel. For as difficult as it is to mother behind bars, there are some who can find solace in the company of other women and understand the unique pain that comes from incarceration and the separation from their children.

The amount of time women have left to serve after they give birth depends on their sentence length, with some serving months or even years. Regardless of the length of time, the release from prison is a long-awaited period, particularly for new mothers who are ready to reunite with their baby. Reentry is marked by a range of emotions, including excitement about a long-awaited reunion with their baby, fear in the wake of the many challenges that lie ahead, and even sadness as women say goodbye to those they had grown close with behind bars. While everyone I interviewed had hoped for a seamless transition, the period that immediately followed their release from prison was marked with many challenges—both expected and unexpected.

While some can come straight home to their baby, many find themselves still under some form of correctional supervision that sometimes delays reunification. Parole orders and residential reentry centers also act as extensions of the carceral state, as women are subjected to further surveillance and control through the expectation to submit to additional rules and procedures that are unique to parole and residential reentry centers. Some of the women I interviewed said they felt as though they were in a never-ending place of having to demonstrate their competency and fitness as a mother to a number of entities, including caregivers, parole officers, and child welfare workers, who acted as gatekeepers to their baby.

Even with meticulous planning, parenthood is not without its challenges. Even though some plan on providing custodial care, parenting under the surveillance of the carceral state is taxing, leaving some to forgo their plans for custodial care. Those who continued with their plans for custodial care shared how they were careful to navigate relationships with caregivers to avoid stepping on anyone's toes or disrupting their baby's routines. From having to acquire basic needs like diapers and dealing with crying to discipline issues among older children, many shared stories about their struggles to mother amid the adjustment back into society, inciting a constant fear of relapsing and returning to prison.

In addition to navigating motherhood, reintegration meant finding essentials like work and housing—difficult tasks, as incarceration and the maternal web of control continued to follow these women. Those who come home to a support system are more likely to have a safety net in their search to acquire these basic needs—essentials for their children to stay with them. Women of color in poverty encounter more barriers in the search for these essentials, for they must also contend with gendered racism and the maternal web of control that threatens their motherhood even after they are no longer behind bars.

Conclusion

Beyond the Prison Gates

Homelessness, unemployment, drug addiction, mental illness, and illiteracy are only a few of the problems that disappear from public view when the human beings contending with them are relegated to cages. . . . Prisons do not disappear social problems, they disappear human beings.
—Angela Davis, *Masked Racism: Reflections on the Prison Industrial Complex*

The general public has this sense that the people that are in jail and prison are the people that belong there.
—Angel

Although pregnancy is a biological issue, reproduction has also become a social and political issue bathed in patriarchal control that emanates from powerful, carceral systems. The commodification and control of maternal bodies is not new but rather is a practice that predates slavery, as pregnant women have been bought and sold and then bred, have been subjected to forced medical experimentation, and have been unlawfully sterilized.[1] The overturning of *Roe v. Wade* is yet another event in a long history of practices that have focused on the regulation and control of reproduction.[2] The disembodiment of women, the widespread use of surveillance and technology, and the sweeping extent of fetal-protection legislation that has been passed across the United States makes it easier than ever to exert control on women.[3]

The criminal legal system is just one of many carceral systems that supports the control of reproduction, for the criminal legal system engages in a number of practices that work to subjugate women and criminalize reproduction, including through fetal-protection laws, the criminalization of those who seek abortion, and the difficulty of accessing contraceptives. The incarceration of women during pregnancy is yet another example among a long list of regulation practices. It is no surprise that most women are incarcerated during their prime reproductive years, shedding light on how incarceration itself ensures that only certain women are allowed to reproduce.

While much of the contemporary conversation around reproductive injustices amid the overruling of *Roe v. Wade* is centered on the right not to have children—an important issue, to be sure—what is often missing is the right to parent with a sense of dignity—a core tenet of reproductive freedom.[4] Although all women experience some degree of surveillance and control during pregnancy, the experiences of women at the periphery of society have long been excluded from these conversations, making them especially vulnerable to domination and control as interlocking systems of oppression subjugate them even further. The narratives contained within this book illustrate how those who are pregnant behind bars experience a hyper form of control, impeding the ability to be pregnant and to give birth and mother in a dignified manner.

Behind bars, pregnant women are regulated by powerful carceral systems that produce a type of control that is specific to pregnancy among the incarcerated, yet the prison state is hardly the only institution that acts as a weapon of control for incarcerated pregnant women. Rather, as the narratives in this book have showed, carcerality infiltrates into other systems, for the medical system and the child welfare system both regulate and control women during pregnancy, especially those who are marginalized and perceived to be a "threat" to the existing social order.[5] While these systems each produce their own forms of control that surveil and regulate pregnant women behind bars, they also work in simultaneity with each other to produce a more powerful type of control that is specific to the experiences of incarcerated pregnant women, collectively regulating all aspects of pregnancy, birth, and motherhood through a process that I call the "maternal web of control."

To be sure, there are consequences to this web of control, for the means through which incarcerated women are controlled during pregnancy go beyond any criminal punishment. Even though arguably all pregnant women in prison experience the trappings of the maternal web of control that leave them powerless and subject to harm, poor women and women of color remain especially vulnerable to domination and oppression. That is, racism, sexism, and classism all operate within these powerful social systems, tightening the control on pregnant women, reinforcing the maternal web of control and threatening the health and families of thousands of women.

Among the women in this study, nearly all said they never planned to be pregnant in prison, for they grew up with plans to be teachers, nurses, and social workers, complete with big backyards and shady front porches. They grew up wanting to be mothers with trips to the park and the zoo. Prison, and all the trappings of the carceral system, were never a part of their plan, let alone to be pregnant in prison, and yet, through the rise of the carceral state and the buildup of a prison nation, barbed wires replaced white picket fences, for prison was their new reality.

Although most of the women profiled in this book were sentenced to a couple of years in prison, their incarceration affected them long after they were released. And it is not just the incarcerated whose lives are shaped by a prison sentence—children and families serve a sentence of their own. This is the power of the carceral state, a state where not only the incarcerated are forever subject to surveillance, regulation, and control but entire families and communities are punished, illuminating the ways in which carcerality is not confined to prison doors.

The ways in which reproduction and pregnant women are penalized is uniquely American, providing insight into how carcerality has infiltrated nearly every aspect of society, including in the most intimate spaces of women. The control and policing of women's bodies is not new and by all accounts is not going away any time soon, for the overuse of imprisonment as a form of punishment, even among pregnant women, is a product of the institutionalized legacy of slavery and the emphasis on capitalism, for even in other countries with high rates of crime and incarceration, pregnant women are not locked up and routinely separated from their children.[6]

The Framing of Stories

The power of the maternal web of control and the rise of carcerality are evident even in the ways that women tell their incarceration stories. Most, though not all, of the women I interviewed framed their time behind bars within the context of individualism, ignoring the more structural forces that contributed to their incarceration, such as poverty, gendered racism, and the buildup of the carceral state, which leave many neighborhoods and communities disadvantaged. Many framed their story about their crime(s) and subsequent incarceration around a poor *decision* that they made, ignoring the structural forces at work. The absence of discussion about the structural forces that produce incarceration, especially among pregnant women, is not terribly surprising given the strong sense of individualism in the United States that centers the importance of individual responsibility and choice.[7] To engage in conversations about structural forces would mean to acknowledge the continued expansion of punitive policies and practices in the United States that have effectively created an environment in which surveillance and regulation have become normalized, especially for poor Black and Brown women.[8]

As discussed, women are the fastest-growing segment of the correctional population—a phenomenon that did not occur overnight but rather one that has been at work for some time through aggressive policies and investments in law enforcement and surveillance technology that creates a surveilling, panopticon-like environment that may actually produce "crime."[9] Thus it comes as no surprise that the United States has more people under correctional control than any other country.[10]

As other scholars have pointed out, the term "mass incarceration" is not entirely accurate, implying an indiscriminate incarceration of the masses rather than recognizing the targeted and disproportionate use of punishment and incarceration among racial and ethnic minorities.[11] With certainty, incarceration is an intentional and deliberate weapon used to control "unruly" populations, including the bodies of maternal women, through state-sanctioned violence.[12] Its targeted approach is by design and grounded in a historical legacy of slavery, with those who pose a "threat" to society being incarcerated, locked up and warehoused behind barbed wires, in shackles, with maternal and fetal technology, such as wireless monitors and ultrasound, together creating the ultimate cage.[13] To be sure, the issue of who constitutes a threat is one that is socially constructed, rooted in gendered racism, with Black women being more likely to be framed as threatening.[14]

Central to the incarceration of pregnant women is distrust and control—a distrust in women, in their bodies, and in their ability to give birth and to mother—resulting in the view that pregnancy among incarcerated women must be managed and controlled, not only through the strict surveillance found in prison but also through families, the medical system, and the child welfare system. The image of shackled, out-of-control, dangerous, and unruly drug-addicted mothers acts as a controlling image, reaffirming the "need" for protection and surveillance from the very carceral forces that regulate women even after they give birth and return to their communities.

However, perhaps what is most ironic about the maternal web of control is that it is disguised as protection and concern. In Lacey's case, the judge framed her prison sentence as coming from a place of care by saying something to the effect of "I'm going to sentence you [to prison], so *we* can make sure that baby gets prenatal care." For Lacey, her incarceration was perceived as justified and even beneficial because it provided a means to access prenatal care, food, shelter, and healthcare—all of which she needed during pregnancy—illustrating how both paternalism and the already-subjugated state of women keeps them locked in an underclass.

Lessons Learned

Certainly, some of the narratives in this book reveal how some marginalized women may view their incarceration as a blessing rather than punishment, expressing gratitude for their imprisonment. In the United States, a country that is far from being a social welfare state, incarceration provides an opening for marginalized women to access resources that are otherwise unavailable in their rural communities, such as prenatal care, housing, food, and drug-treatment programs. And to that end, the narratives in this book call to mind important issues regarding imprisonment as a form of both protection and punishment.

In some ways, the framework some of my participants used to tell their story almost resembled infantilism, as women leaned into their subjugated status as both prisoner and patient, reinforcing the paternalistic nature of these carceral forces, where personal responsibility is expected and encouraged. Many were candid about *their* wrongdoings and shared with me their promises to "never do *it*" again, sharing stories of how they had since changed following their imprisonment, referring to their time behind bars as a "time out" or a "lesson." These narratives reflect the powerful scripts that are instilled in them through the convergence of these carceral complex forces behind bars, almost as if their framing was a way to convey to the prison system and to other carceral systems, such as the child welfare system, that they were indeed reformed, had learned their lesson, and were ready to live among others again in the "free world."

Gloria, for example, shared how she wanted to be a "living testimony" to other women caught in the crossfires of the criminal legal system by informing others of how "bad" her incarceration was, hoping to scare would-be "delinquents" onto the "straight path" away from prison. According to Gloria, "Yeah, I hear a lot of 'oh my God, you were the girl who was in prison with the baby,' and I'm like, 'oh my God, yep, that was me.' I mean, so there's people that want to hear my story too, and it's pretty good. It feels good telling people my story because . . . maybe they could tell someone, 'Hey I talked to this girl that had a baby in prison, and she had it hard in there, so *don't do it.*'"

The last line of Gloria's narrative suggests that there is an element of personal choice involved in incarceration, as she shared the hardships she had endured in prison and advised her peer to simply "don't do it" in order to avoid the carceral control of incarceration, without consideration to the social environment that allows mass incarceration to take place. And while I acknowledge that there is an element of agency and choice when it comes to offending, the systematic incarceration of marginalized women during pregnancy provides evidence of the carcerality that permeates society and encourages policing, surveillance, regulation, and control. In this way, incarceration flourishes with ease, making it easier than ever to limit the autonomy of women, trapping many into a state of permanent subjugation and regulation. In this environment, poverty, race, and pregnancy are criminalized, and families are subject to these oppressive forces.

Though the maternal web of control is certainly powerful beyond measure, the narratives contained within this book illustrate how women are not simply passive actors in this web, for they, along with their peers, engage in resistance, ingenuity, and innovation as a means of overriding, at least where possible, the domination and control that mark their lives. While the stories in this book are those of struggles laced with tears and dashed dreams, they are also stories of strength, courage, change, and growth, highlighting the ways in which women find hope in an otherwise hopeless place. In the end, these are also stories of strength and hope.

Implications

As activist Angela Davis argues, prisons should be made obsolete and abolished, for prisons do little more than relieve society of having to consider and seriously address the problems that it hides—problems that disproportionately affect disadvantaged communities by simply reproducing or perpetuating the existing harms and conditions that contribute to mass incarceration.[15] As the narratives in this book illustrate, the incarceration of pregnant women is harmful. It is harmful to women. It is harmful to babies. It is harmful to families, and it is harmful to communities. In the wake of this harm, this reckless practice should be ended immediately. Yet, the prison industrial complex is a multibillion-dollar industry, offering corporations financial incentives to incarcerate, making it unlikely that incarceration as a form of punishment is going away any time soon.[16]

Maternal Web of Support

In the meantime, I advocate for a buildup of a support nation that emphasizes the importance and expansion of schools, community centers, health services, social service agencies, libraries, parks, and places of recreation that collectively become prevalent enough to overshadow the prison nation, making the incarceration of pregnant women less and less frequent, weakening the carceral regime, and moving toward a robust support network. These elements are critical to the creation of a maternal web of support, and thus, any conversation about criminal legal reform and the incarceration of pregnant women must include the structural conditions that contribute to a carceral, punitive environment—it is then that conversation can begin about how these systems can become places of support.

I advocate for an approach that is analogous to that advocated by Victor Rios with his concept of a "youth support complex" that provides a support network for Black and Latino boys experiencing hyper forms of surveillance and punishment and caught in a "youth control complex."[17] As Rios argues, a youth support complex must involve participation across a number of different entities, including schools, community support centers, politicians, and criminal justice institutions that collectively come together to meet youth where they are, giving them the institutional supports they need to thrive, dismantling punitive forces of surveillance and control.[18] Rather than a maternal web of control that controls and surveils incarcerated women during pregnancy and beyond, I advocate for a *maternal web of support*, marking a shift away from a punitive approach to one that centers the health and preservation of families, with consideration to the unique needs of pregnancy, especially among marginalized women in rural communities without the necessary supports.

I offer practical considerations to better support pregnant women both behind bars and in communities, for the harms facing pregnant women behind bars are an outgrowth of the inequities occurring in communities. I caution readers that to decarcerate and create systemic change both behind bars and in birth spaces everywhere requires the participation of *all*, for the incarceration of women and the consequences of the maternal web of control are adaptive problems entailing many parts and have no easy or simple solution. That is, to create change, doctors, correctional officers, social workers, families, parole officers, politicians, doulas, friends, and neighbors must all be involved.

Thankfully, there are efforts already underway both in the United States and abroad that provide insight into what decarceration and a maternal web of support system could look like for pregnant women trapped in the prison nation. The release of incarcerated pregnant women across ten states during the COVID-19 pandemic amid growing concerns about health provides insight into how the prioritization of health can supersede the need for imprisonment.[19] There is much variation in the treatment of pregnant women in prison; while some states and facilities have made considerable gains to provide a more dignified approach to pregnant women, complete with detailed provisions to ensure their care and the well-being of their baby, these conditions are not in place everywhere. As mentioned earlier, the turn to the criminal legal system in times of crises and scarcity does not mean that prisons are equipped to handle the unique needs of women during pregnancy, including their more specialized nutritional and health needs. While some may find some short-term benefits behind bars, such as the presence of community, healthcare, food, and drug treatment, the prison system has not kept pace with calls for reform, lagging significantly behind the already poor maternal care in the United States that threatens the health and well-being of women and babies both in and outside the prison system.[20] The effects of incarceration, particularly during pregnancy, are vast, with lasting consequences for families, making any conversations about decarceration and criminal legal reform difficult and ongoing work that takes time. Given this reality, my recommendations are only a starting point. It is my sincere hope that the needs of incarcerated pregnant women are lifted out of the periphery in conversations about reproductive injustices and oppression and become central to conversations about reform.

Social Equity and Inclusion

The strength of the maternal web of control lies in its relation to systemic poverty and institutionalized racism, where the ability to incarcerate, control, and regulate women is tied to subjugation and oppression. There is a unique form of oppression that stems from the *intersection* of these systems of control that may never be fully measured or realized. These multiple, interlocking systems of control each produces its own forms of carcerality that regulate and disrupt pregnancy behind bars. In that regard, any calls for criminal legal reform must also address these social environments that contribute to carcerality and the maternal web of control. Communities would do well to dismantle systemic barriers and consider policy approaches that address the underlying roots of inequalities, including sexism, poverty, and racism, for these powerful forces work to criminalize and incarcerate women. True reform entails expanding safeguards and institutional resources of support to ensure that those experiencing pregnancy have the essentials needed to have a safe and optimal pregnancy and the ability to parent with dignity. Keeping families together necessitates a safe and stable place to live, a guaranteed family income, proper nutrition, affordable and accessible drug treatment, childcare, counseling and therapy services, and healthcare, including care that addresses mental and physical health and the tenets of reproductive justice, including the right to have an abortion. Efforts to ensure that these essentials are met would mark a significant move away from the punitive forces that govern women and a shift toward systemic equality.

When I asked the participants their thoughts on more progressive responses to the incarceration of pregnant women, such as prison nursery programs, nearly all were in favor of them. However, one narrative stood out the most. While Leslie was an advocate of prison nursery programs, she cautioned that an expanded use of these programs is not the silver bullet to the incarceration of pregnant women. Rather, as Leslie said,

> That's great that they're letting them keep them with them in the prison, but that's a whole new game for women coming out of prison. Because when we leave prison, we're lucky if they give you a hundred dollars. When your child is in prison, yeah, they give you your little bed and diapers and what not, but once you're released, that changes the whole thing. They're not doing anything physically, mentally, financially to help you take care of that child. Where are you going to go when you walk out of those gates with a baby? They're not focusing on what happens when you don't got the cell, and the crib, and the formula, and the mental attention that you need to have a child after birth. I don't think that's being addressed, so it's an incarceration problem, but it's not, you know what I mean?

Leslie went on to share her ideas for better supporting pregnant justice-involved women, and her ideas centered on a need to "fix" the many issues affecting incarcerated women, such as housing, childcare, poverty, mental illness, physical and sexual abuse, trauma, HIV, drugs, education—and the list continues. She cautioned that a failure to address the many issues plaguing incarcerated women would surely mean a wave of recidivism. As she said, "You have to address where society is—if there is no work, there's no food. There will be robbery and rape and mayhem, drug addiction, homelessness, and anger. I can't say how my life would have turned out had I not been pregnant in prison, but I also have that gut feeling that if my child would have been born to me under those current conditions of my lifestyle, where I couldn't even make ten dollars, there's no telling what I would have done." A condemnation of all forms of isms, including sexism, racism, and classism, is central to achieving racial and socioeconomic equity, and actions tied to antiracism would go a long way in addressing the inequities that foster incarceration. Voting for officials who advocate for the expansion of policies that support historically marginalized women experiencing pregnancy, and the incorporation of implicit bias trainings across all workplaces and institutions, are all starting places. A commitment to social and reproductive justice entails requiring people to become educated about the carceral forces that work to land women in prison, and efforts to advance reproductive justice should consider the unique issues affecting all women, not just those living in the community. The undoing of the prison nation and the maternal web of control cannot be addressed until these underlying issues are confronted.

Data Collection

Behind bars, the need for reform continues. As mentioned throughout the text, prisons have not been required to collect data about the nature and extent of pregnant women in their prisons. The problems that emanate from a lack of national data are harmful in more ways than one. As the Advocacy and Research on Reproductive Wellness of Incarcerated People argues, "Women who don't count don't get counted, and women who don't get counted don't count."[21] In the absence of national data, Carolyn Sufrin and her team have led a landmark research study to collect the most comprehensive national data to date to better understand the scope of pregnant women in prisons (and jails) and the problems they face.[22] Under the First Step Act of 2018, the Bureau of Justice Statistics is now required to gather data on maternal health and pregnancy outcomes for those pregnant in federal prisons.[23] The more data is collected about pregnant women behind bars, the easier it becomes to enact change and introduce policy reform.

Healthcare

Leading organizations, such as the American College of Obstetricians and Gynecologists, the World Health Organization, and the American

Academy of Pediatrics, have already outlined health standards for pregnant women, including but not limited to the need for quality availability of prenatal and postnatal care, the right to have an abortion, assessment and treatment for mental health disorders, and lab work. They have emphasized the importance of having robust accessible and affordable healthcare that meets the specific needs of women during pregnancy to ensure optimal maternal and fetal health outcomes. It is time for all correctional institutions to listen to them and to ensure that incarceration does not hinder the ability to adhere to these provisions. The practice of drug testing women during pregnancy and at birth should not be used to criminalize or punish women, including the threat of family separation, but rather should only be used to better meet the needs of women and their (unborn) babies.[24] The practice of drug testing women during pregnancy and birth incites fear, increases stress, and deters women from seeking care.[25] Central to quality healthcare behind bars is the importance of continuity of care after women are released from prison, ensuring they have access to healthcare on the outside, especially in rural areas where services are scarce and maternity care deserts are aplenty.[26]

The medical complex in the United States is fraught with problems, particularly as it pertains to maternal care, even for nonincarcerated women. The medical complex would do well to dismantle care from capitalism with a focus on evidenced-based practices that support healthy and empowered pregnancies and births. Expanded care and the dismantling of barriers to access to healthcare are essential. Women should have greater options for care during birth, including those away from a hospital setting, such as freestanding birth clinics that are more focused on a holistic, woman-centered approach. There is a greater need for maternal care, especially in rural areas that are marked as maternity care deserts. Central to any health procedures, including inductions, cervical checks, and cesarean sections, among others, is the need for informed consent, where all pregnancy and birth decisions are made between a woman and her provider, and women are presented with options that outline the risks and benefits of each procedure—a move away from the more routinized and assembly-line approach. Practices that thwart the health of women and their children should end immediately. Shackling women at any point during pregnancy and labor goes against evidence-based practices and should not be done.[27] Fortunately, grassroots organizers are already forming across a number of states, lobbying to their state legislature to ban the use of restraints on pregnant women and expand access to care.[28] Placing women on the top of a bunk bed threatens health. Assigning a lower bunk bed to pregnant and postpartum women is just one way prisons can support the health of women. Correctional facilities should have the necessary tools and appropriate and specific staffing on hand at all times for easy transport in the event of birth or any other medical emergency. When a woman is confined on an operating table or in the vulnerable state of childbirth, she does not pose a security risk, negating the need for shackles and the intrusive presence of a correctional officer. Greater communication and collaboration, as well as cross-training among the medical and correctional complexes, would also ensure that incarcerated women have the proper health needs in place and that women are treated with care and dignity in medical settings. Culturally competent care both behind bars and in birth settings everywhere is critical. Above all, listening to women, especially women of color, and validating their concerns are central to bringing down maternal morbidity and mortality rates and obstetric violence.

Support

Pregnancy should be treated as a transformational period that requires support across a variety of entities, with special consideration to the preservation of families and support systems. Behind bars, prisons can dismantle cost from practices such as visitation and phone calls, ensuring that there are no cost-prohibitive barriers for women to communicate with their support system throughout pregnancy.[29] A support system should be viewed as critical to the health and well-being of women. The inability to communicate with a support network threatens health and places women deeper into a state of depression and addiction.[30] Incarcerated pregnant women should be given the proper time and space to have important conversations with loved ones, caregivers, and birth fathers to discuss pressing issues, such as a baby name and caregiver arrangements. These conversations should not be viewed as a privilege but as a right and a key factor in the ability to parent with dignity. Central to the issue of support is the need for women to be housed with other pregnant women or at least other mothers in prison. The practice of solitary confinement is threatening to maternal health.[31] Behind bars, prisons can offer much in the way of education and support, including employing doulas and other childbirth educators who can provide classes, organize peer support groups, and provide education and information so women have the tools needed to optimize health outcomes and to parent with dignity. Not only is a support network helpful and vital during pregnancy, but women should also have the ability to give birth with a support person present if desired, including a doula. Being incarcerated should not mean the presence of a surveilling correctional officer and the absence of a support person during the transformative period of childbirth. Support should also be viewed as essential to the postpartum period and recovery. A support network is also vital after birth and can help improve the physical, mental, and emotional recovery from childbirth.[32]

Family Preservation

The forced separation of mothers from their children has lasting effects that are damaging to health and communities. Efforts should be made as much as possible to preserve the family unit, and in cases of separation, visitation and communication should be supported to the fullest extent possible. Conversations around family reunification should begin on day one. The participants mentioned the need for alternative forms of punishment that would allow incarcerated women to both serve their time and remain with their baby. As Lora explained,

> I remember when I was pregnant, and I was just thinking there's got to be a way that I don't have to just leave this baby and go to prison for God's sake. I mean I was absolutely doing drugs, and I was absolutely doin' the dirt, but there should have been another way where I didn't have to leave my brand-new baby. Thank God I had my aunt, but I always wonder about the women who don't have someone who will step up and take that baby—then what? The system is just creating more problems for it to consume later.

Lora's narrative brings to light an important point regarding the lasting effects of maternal incarceration, for even though all the women profiled in this book have since been released from prison, their incarceration will affect them and their children for years to come. In talking with the participants, I found that nearly all shared their worries regarding how their time behind bars would adversely affect their children, especially as they grew older and were forced to make difficult decisions regarding what, if anything, to tell them about their birth story and their incarceration. Some states, like Minnesota, are leading efforts to create change, for Minnesota became the first state to stop the practice of separating newborn babies from their incarcerated mothers and instead has plans to place pregnant women in a community transitional center and equip them with counseling, drug-treatment programs, and parenting resources.[33] Prison nursery programs should be expanded, available at all prisons, as well as dedicated lactation spaces that allow women to express their milk and send it home to their babies and to breastfeed them during visitation. Correctional facilities that have prison nursery programs report relatively low rates of recidivism and improved maternal-infant bonds.[34] Visitation rooms should be redesigned to be family friendly for children, complete with bright colors and toys, marking a move away from the cold and dreary, punitive and sterile environments found in prisons. Security protocols should be revisited to meet the needs of children and newborns, allowing visitors to bring in additional diapers, wipes, milk, and other essentials needed for infants. Barriers to family visitation should be removed as much as possible. In California, an annual event called Get On the Bus offers free transportation for children to visit their mothers in prison.[35] In Kansas, the Women's Activity and Learning Center has a series of parenting classes that permit women to stay with their children away from the facility on a three-day retreat.[36] In partnership with the Kansas Children's Discovery Center, women are also able to visit a children's museum together through a new program called Play Free that is focused on strengthening family ties, allowing even children of incarcerated mothers to have enriching play experiences, recognizing the importance of physical touch and affection, especially among young children who are not yet able to bond through conversations—these are the very types of programs that need to be expanded across the country.[37]

Reintegration

Support for reintegration should begin on day one of incarceration. The high recidivism rates in the United States make it painfully obvious that incarceration is not working and that efforts to curb criminal offending must take a different approach.[38] Although the participants in my study were incarcerated across different prisons in the Midwest, nearly all said that their prison did little to help them prepare for the world outside, as most left prison with nothing more than a bus pass, a change of clothing, and no more than fifty or a hundred dollars to their name, which makes the likelihood of a successful reintegration low. Reintegration for women looks different than it does for men. It looks different for mothers than it does for nonmothers, and accordingly, any reentry reform attempts must include specific consideration of the unique needs of mothers with young children, providing women with the classes, resources, employment opportunities, and housing opportunities that allow them to meet their parole conditions *and* to be a present mother and parent with dignity. The sexism, racism, and classism that permeate society and the intersections of these forms of oppression, among others, often make it extremely difficult for women to fully reintegrate into society, especially those who live in rural areas, away from many support networks, placing them at risk for family separation. There is a greater need for transition centers for women that permit children to stay on site with them. Churches, schools, parole officers, landlords, employers, and social service agencies all have work to do in accepting women and their children back into society. Gloria mentioned that her parole officer was especially proud of her, which empowered her to keep going, equipping her with the encouragement and support she needed to thrive beyond bars—a conversation that she remembers still to this day. According to Gloria, "He [my parole officer] was just like, 'I'm really proud of you.' You know how they say the majority of the girls go back to prison? He's like, 'I believe you're one of those girls that won't go back,' and I'm like, 'Well thank you, that means a lot because I'm not gonna go back.'" Gloria's narrative illustrates how those in the criminal legal system can be a part of the solution. These are the encouraging conversations that need to be happening across all institutions to create a web of support for women.

The creation of a web of support from these services would go a long way toward ensuring that mothers are able to parent with dignity and provide for their children in a way that removes the threat of the child welfare system. Child welfare services should focus on their helping missions, providing resources and supports to parents rather than their current carceral approach, which threatens families and mimics the practices of the criminal legal system. Child welfare services should focus on meeting women where they are and addressing the underlying issues that contribute to maltreatment, which often stem from poverty and institutionalized racism. Families play a critical role in the reintegration process as well and can be of tremendous support as women reintegrate into society. Even iconic shows like *Sesame Street* are changing the narrative around parental incarceration: the show has introduced the first Muppet, Alex, who has a parent who is incarcerated, and its resource program, Sesame Workshop, provides concrete tools and resources to help parents and caregivers navigate parental incarceration.[39] These are the types of conversations that need to be happening in communities across the country to help reintegrate women and their children into society.

Through the implementation of these practices and more, the maternal web of control can become weakened and slowly transformed into a maternal web of support. Each of the entities that women encounter throughout their pregnancy has the potential to be a tremendous source of support, helping to improve maternal-infant health, reduce recidivism, and strengthen families. Any provisions of reproductive care in communities must include the most marginalized in society, including incarcerated women. The tough-on-crime ideologies remain strong, but there is hope for the future. As Angel said,

> The general public has this sense that the people that are in jail and prison are the people that belong there. They're a bunch of bad people, they're the violent people that we shouldn't care about . . . so, it's not until you're in that place or know somebody close to you that's been through that where you're horrified about the things in there that are happening to good people. This is a huge topic. The world needs to know what really goes on inside and maybe it will change a heart for certain things. You're the first person I shared this with, and it's been on my heart for a long

time, and I never even let it out, so I think I was more excited to talk to you than you were to me.

Although incarcerated pregnant women may not be viewed as part of the mothering mainstream, their stories matter. The women in this study are but a few of those whose lives and families have been forever affected by mass incarceration and its systematic separation of mothers from their babies. And their stories demonstrate how policies and practices—correctional and otherwise—reverberate through entire families and communities. Families and communities hold tremendous collective power to provide mothers with a support system. One does not need to work in a prison or a hospital to create change. These examples of change highlight how even bus drivers and children's museums can be on the front lines of criminal legal reform and real change.

AFTERWORD

It must surely be a tribute to the resilience of the human spirit that even a small number of those men and women in the hell of the prison system survive it and hold on to their humanity.
—Howard Zinn, *You Can't Be Neutral on a Moving Train: A Personal History of Our Times*

I'm in a place where I don't necessarily know what's next, but I've come to the realization that that's okay. I'm just going to keep moving forward.
—Jasmine

Like many formerly incarcerated women, most of the women I interviewed were still struggling to some degree at the time of this writing. While some had since become homeowners, even earning college degrees, the majority were still looking for something more. Despite encountering struggles in the aftermath of their release from prison, all those I interviewed said they were relatively satisfied with their life and had more freedom to embark on a new chapter.

Many had big plans. Some were focused on "staying clean," while others were determined to make up for lost time with their children or to restore broken relationships with family members. Some even talked about how they were starting on an entirely new path like returning to school and starting a career. Most were tired of living paycheck to paycheck and wanted to break the cycle of poverty and become financially stable with dreams of one day buying a vehicle and owning their own home.

Although the threat of relapse and recidivism was still a common worry, everyone shared their determination to refrain from drugs and crime. At the time of this writing, only Serena had returned to prison, on a parole violation. All shared that they wanted to be seen as more than the sum of their offenses, and there was a consensus that they were not going to let their past define them. They were determined to show to others and to themselves that they were not just former inmates, criminals, and offenders but rather women who had made mistakes, telling varying tales of how they had learned from their mistakes, using their time behind bars to help other women stay out of prison—a framing that again reflects how criminality is often framed as an individual issue without regard to the structural inequalities that contribute to offending.

Since her incarceration, Latrice had become a criminal legal reform advocate, inspired by her own journey, and felt it was her "personal mission" to humanize the incarcerated. As Latrice explained, "I can't leave all the other women behind, they're beautiful. They need help, and if I'm out here, and I'm able to help, I feel like that's my responsibility to do so and help humanize us 'cause you're dehumanized when you're there. So that's my focus, you know, restoring humanization to people that have been incarcerated."[1] The true magnitude of their time behind bars and the effects of incarceration and the maternal web of control remain to be seen. Maternal incarceration, especially while pregnant, is a unique pain that cannot be quantified.

Most said they planned on being an "open book" with their children, and many said they planned on telling their children *everything* about their time behind bars—when they are older, and the timing is more appropriate. As Crystal said, "I will tell them when they're older, but I'm not exactly sure *how*. I mean with age comes wisdom and so hopefully in ten years I can think of another way to explain to tell them." There were a few who said they planned to tell no one, including their children, about their incarceration in order to remain removed as much as possible from this period, referencing the stigma attached to maternal incarceration, particularly during pregnancy. Taylor and Cherelle mentioned a return to prison at some point—to thank their peers and even a correctional officer or two. As Cherelle explained, "I would have never made it without the support from the women in that room," a sentiment that illustrates the importance of social support behind bars.

Even though they were now in the "free world," they were not as entirely free as they wanted to be—realities that illustrate the power of the carceral state and the permanent subjugation of the formerly incarcerated to the status of second-class citizens. Whether it entailed worries about what to tell their children about their time behind bars or the lingering threat of the child welfare system coming into their home and removing their child(ren), or even a demeaning encounter at a pediatrician's office, as was the case with Gloria, their incarceration follows them. Their biggest fear of all, even more than incarceration, was losing their children. As Rhonda explained, "I think about constantly that when my son gets older, I have to explain to him how he ended up with a birth certificate [from a different state], so you have these long-lasting effects, these long-lasting consequences."

Despite the many challenges facing formerly incarcerated pregnant women, nearly all the women I interviewed said they were relatively happy with where they were in life. While the carceral state and the threat of the prison system and the child welfare system remained ever present, for most of them, simply being out of prison was evidence enough that the present was better than the past. Taylor said, "When I compare where I was, I'm 100 percent satisfied. I have a house. I have a car. I have my family. I have my daughter. What more can you ask for? If you look at it like that, you know, I had nothing when I was locked up. You have to be happy with where you are, whether you're living in a tent or a palace, otherwise you'll never do anything. You'll never get anywhere." Central to Taylor's narrative and those of many of the others was how proud they were of their children. As they rattled off a long list of their children's accomplishments, they were beaming with pride, for in many ways their children's accomplishments were just as much their own and further proof that they had "made it."

Even though the participants were all headed in different directions and had endured way too much struggle and trauma, there was a unique sense of optimism about the future. While none of them had ever planned to be pregnant in prison and had no wish to return, their pregnancy behind bars fueled them. In a carceral environment both within and beyond bars meant to tear down women and strip them of their humanity, creating a unique pain and struggle that is specific to a pregnancy behind bars, there is also a unique strength among (formerly) incarcerated pregnant women.

Destiny's words provide hope to us all:

Society looks at us as if we are useless and don't amount to anything because we had a kid in prison, and they think, How are they going to make it with their record? Their kid must already be screwed. How are they going to get a job? And how are they going to afford this and that.... But I've shown everybody wrong. Ha! Yeah, it's been rough, but I'm starting to see the light. I'm a true believer in whatever won't kill me will only make me stronger. So, my heart may hurt a tiny bit, but I learned to pick myself back up and dust myself off from evil. Yep, that's what I do. My past doesn't define me. It's only my future that I'm going toward.

ACKNOWLEDGMENTS

They say it takes a village to raise a child, but the same can be said for writing a book. The process of transforming ideas onto paper is nothing short of a collaborative effort, and I am grateful to have had a number of people in my corner who helped me along the way. First and foremost, I would be remiss not to thank the participants of this study. They shared their lives with me—their biggest hopes and fears. In a time of potential vulnerability, they trusted me with their stories, and the magnitude of that is not lost on me. Without them, this book would not exist. Eileen Avery took me under her wings from day one. She has challenged me to think critically, and she saw the potential in me and in this work long before I saw it in myself. She has been a steady source of support, compassion, and understanding and taught me the importance of having high standards. My training as a sociologist and criminologist is because of her. Joan Hermsen taught me to always ask the tough questions and to be mindful of how and where social inequalities exist. Her intersectional insights allowed me to dig deeper and take this project to the next level. David Mitchell has challenged me to view my work from different perspectives and shown me that learning does not have to end after school. His understanding of the criminal legal system has made this book that much stronger. Thank you for always taking the time to meet with me and serving as a sounding board for my ideas. Jay Gubrium taught me how to dig deeper and showed me that everyone has a story to tell. Thank you for teaching me the art of storytelling. I credit my training as a qualitative scholar to you.

Ron Matson, Marché Fleming-Randle, Kathy Perez, and John Burchill, thank you for introducing me to the discipline, and thank you for believing in me. I will always look back on our time together with fond memories. My love and passion for sociology and criminology is because of you. Thank you. Thank you also to Shukura Bakari-Cozart and Lawanda Holt-Fields and the Wichita State University McNair Scholars

Program for being the first to introduce me to research and for instilling in me the importance of having big, big dreams. It's true, "TRIO WORKS." Financial support for this work was made possible through the Ronald E. McNair Scholars Program Fellowship, the James S. Rollins Slavery Atonement Endowment, and the Irma D. Mathes Dissertation Support Award at the University of Missouri.

My colleagues at Emporia State University have been fantastic throughout this process. I could not ask for better colleagues. Thanks especially to Alfredo Montalvo, Shelly Rowley, Jan Todd, Evandro Camara, Susan Zuber-Chall, David Westfall, Kristin Rindom, Michael Smith, and Amy Sage Webb-Baza for all your support. The students at ESU have also been incredible, and my countless conversations with them have informed this book in more ways than one. Many thanks especially to Tori Compton and Paige Kring for their help with earlier drafts of this manuscript. Their attention to detail is second to none. My editor, Ilene Kalish, her assistant, Priyanka Ray, and their dedicated team at New York University Press have been nothing short of incredible. Ilene saw the vision for this book early on and her enthusiasm for the project has been unwavering. Her comments, along with Emily Wright's, have been spot on and made this book that much stronger. Their patience with me has been everything. Thank you to the anonymous reviewers for their detailed comments; this book is undoubtedly stronger because of their feedback.

Finding time to write with three littles is far from easy—a huge shoutout and countless thanks to my daughters' teachers for providing such excellent care so I could focus on writing. Many thanks to my community of working parents and those who just "get it," providing an endless wave of encouragement and support, especially Katelynn Towne, Robyn Swink, Don Willis, Sarah Lirley, Faiza Rais, Rachel Shannon, Jasmine Linabary, Rachel Kohman, Samantha Estrada, Stephanie Williams, and Darla Mallein—what would I do without you? Thank you for showing me the power of my voice and knowing exactly what to say exactly when I need to hear it. Thanks for bouncing ideas back with me and for sending me texts with a simple yet powerful phrase: GO WRITE. It has been an honor and a privilege to learn both beside you and from you. I am so thankful for our friendship. Denise Franklin and Jonathan Scrafford both showed me the power of women in the birth space and what a maternal web of support looks like. I will forever be thankful to you both.

My family has been there for me since day one. Thank you especially to my mom and dad for their countless sacrifices and perpetual encouragement that made it possible for me to achieve this dream. It is because of you two that the girl with all the books became the girl who wrote a book. Thanks especially to my grandparents—both living and deceased, thank you for always loving me and being there for me. I understand this assignment, and I hope I do you proud.

Cecilia, Julianna, and Leticia Rodriguez Carey, my mighty girls—what can I say? While I may have started this project well before any of you were born, my pregnancy with each of you helped inform this project, and much of it was written with you on my lap as infants. Each of you helped me finish it in your own unique ways. Celia, I can still recall the time before I had an important meeting for this project and you told me, "You can do it, mom. I know you can." It was then that I knew I could. Jules, I still think of your words "brave, brave, brave" as you boarded the train, a moment that instantly ignites bravery and courage in myself. And Leti, thanks for giving me all the reasons in the world to just go for it and to do what seemed impossible. Thank you all for your understanding and support as mommy pursued her dreams. I pray that each of you do the same one day. When you do, I will always be your biggest fan. We did it, girls.

And to Jason Carey, it is an understatement to say that this book would not have been written without you. Your love, support, and friendship are incredible. You are my greatest source of encouragement, always putting to rest my doubts and insecurities and understanding and loving me as only you know how to do. You truly outdo yourself as a life partner, husband, and best friend. Thank you for your endless sacrifices—you are the fuel that has made this book possible. I am forever grateful for you. There is no one else I would rather take this crazy ride called life with than you. I love you the mostest, mostest, mostest times infinity.

NOTES

PREFACE

1. Center for Reproductive Rights (n.d.); Higgins (2022).
2. Center for Reproductive Rights (n.d.); Higgins (2022).
3. Aswad (2022); Goodman and McPhillips (2023).
4. See Margaret Atwood's *Handmaid's Tale* (1985); O'Hara (2017).
5. Roberts (1997); Solinger (2005).
6. Chappell (2013); Haley (2016); Roberts (1997); Solinger (2005).
7. Chappell (2013); Haley (2016); Roberts (1997); Solinger (2005).
8. Alexander (2010); Graff (2015).
9. Wagner and Rabuy (2017).
10. Wagner and Rabuy (2017). "Corrections" refers to both the incarceration of people in prisons and jails and the supervision of people in the community, such as those under probation or parole supervision. See Wagner and Rabuy (2017).
11. Clarke et al. (2006); Wang et al. (2022b).
12. Sufrin et al. (2019). More live births take place in prisons, but there are more pregnant people entering jails. See Advocacy and Research on Reproductive Wellness of Incarcerated People (n.d.).
13. "Postpartum" refers to the recovery period after pregnancy and may last up to six months.
14. See Cook (2014) for a history. HCF was originally named the Kansas State Industrial Reformatory, modeled after the first reformatory in the United States in Elmira, New York.
15. Hill (2019). See Lévesque and Ferron-Parayre (2021). Though the term "obstetric violence" is one that is contested in academic circles, I use the term "obstetric violence" to refer to mistreatment, abuse, and/or neglect during or surrounding the period of childbirth. Lévesque and Ferron-Parayre (2021).
16. Garcia (2023).
17. Hill (2019).
18. Hill (2019).
19. I introduce the concept of reproductive justice in the introduction. Some scholars use the term "criminal legal system" instead of "criminal justice system" to denote that for many, justice does not exist. See Bryant (2021) for a discussion.
20. All names are pseudonyms to provide confidentiality to participants.

INTRODUCTION

1 Sutton and Carvalho (2017).
2 Stillbirth is a pregnancy loss after twenty weeks of pregnancy. See Sufrin et al. (2019).
3 "Coming home" is a phrase many of the participants used to refer to their release from prison and reintegration into society.
4 Graff (2015).
5 Graff (2015).
6 Solinger (2005).
7 Solinger (2005).
8 Sutherland (1997).
9 "Carcerality" generally refers to the ways in which behaviors are regulated through methods of surveillance. See Lerman and Weaver (2014).
10 On October 2, 2024, the Government Accountability Office (GAO) issued a reported titled "Pregnant Women in State Prisons and Local Jails: Federal Assistance to Support Their Care," indicating that the Department of Justice has plans to collect data on the extent of incarcerated pregnant women. See GAO (2024).
11 Advocacy and Research on Reproductive Wellness of Incarcerated People (n.d.); Baunach (1985); Chesney-Lind and Pasko (2004); Haney (2010); McCorkel (2013); Richie (2012).
12 Kajstura and Sawyer (2024); Sufrin et al. (2019).
13 See McCarthy (2013–2019). The Netflix series *Orange Is the New Black*, written by Jenji Kohan, is based on the book by Piper Kerman with the same title. Paltrow and Flavin (2014); Quinn (2014). Among the research and depictions that do exist, many are focused on the context of mothering, ignoring the unique needs of incarcerated women who are not mothers. See Michalsen and Flavin (2009); Southall (2019).
14 Burgess-Proctor (2006).
15 Burgess-Proctor (2006).
16 Baunach (1985); Burgess-Proctor (2006); Chesney-Lind and Pasko (2004); Flavin (2009); Haney (2010); McCorkel (2013); Richie (2012).
17 Abbott and Scott (2017); Hutchinson et al. (2008); Hotelling (2008); Howard et al. (2011); Huang, Atlas, and Parvez (2012); Ocen (2012); Schroeder and Bell (2005); Shlafer et al. (2018); Sufrin et al. (2019); Kring Villanueva, From, and Lerner (2009).
18 Morgan and Roberts (2012).
19 Morgan and Roberts (2012:243).
20 Roberts (1997).
21 Morgan and Roberts (2012); Solinger (2005).
22 Sutherland (1997:9).
23 Roberts (1997); Solinger (2005).
24 Roberts (1997); Solinger (2005).

25 Haley (2016).
26 Haley (2016).
27 It is recognized that there are varying forms of stigma around pregnancy that change across time and place. See Dodworth (2014); Kendall and Tamura (2010); McClelland and Newell (2008); Sharpe (2015) as examples.
28 Collins (1990).
29 Dodworth (2014); Knight (2015); McClelland and Newell (2008).
30 Flavin (2009); Paltrow and Flavin (2014).
31 Rich (1976).
32 Foucault (1975).
33 Foucault (1975).
34 Burgess-Proctor (2006).
35 Asian Communities for Reproductive Justice (2005:3).
36 Hayes, Sufrin, and Perritt (2020:S21); Sufrin (2017).
37 Price (2010).
38 Price (2010); Shlafer, Hardeman, and Carlson (2019).
39 Hayes et al. (2020).
40 French, Goodman, and Carlson (2020). French, Goodman, and Carlson's work relies on research from the Carceral State Project's 2018–2019 symposium.
41 French et al. (2020).
42 Lerman and Weaver (2014).
43 Roberts (2002; 2022).
44 Rios (2011).
45 Davis-Floyd (2003).
46 Roberts (2022).
47 Sufrin (2017).
48 Richie (2012).
49 Frye (1983:4–5).
50 Crenshaw (1991).
51 Crenshaw (1991).
52 "Staying clean" is a phrase that most of the participants used to refer to the avoidance of drugs and/or alcohol.
53 "Marginalization" was not a term the participants used but rather one that sociologists may use to describe those who are on the fringes of society and relegated to a lower social position devoid of much power. See Varghese and Kumar (2022).
54 Lerman and Weaver (2014).
55 Crenshaw (2012:1427).
56 Collins (1990).
57 Widra (2023).
58 Richie (2012); Simon (2007).
59 Brayne (2014); Graff (2015).
60 Crandall (2020).
61 Crandall (2020); Reid (2018).

62 Crandall (2020).
63 Alexander (2010).
64 "Smart on crime" refers to an approach in criminal justice policies aimed at comprehensive criminal justice reform driven by data. It is often grounded in alternative approaches to incarceration and viewed as a contrast to "tough on crime" approaches. See Altheide and Coyle (2006). See Hamer (2021) for a discussion on terminology.
65 "Correctional supervision" refers to those under the control and supervision of the criminal justice system. It is used in reference to those either on probation, on parole, in jail, or in prison. Maruschak and Minton (2020).
66 Walmsley (2018).
67 Maruschak and Minton (2020); Walmsley (2018).
68 "Tough on crime" refers to an approach in criminal justice policies aimed at "law and order" with an emphasis on stiff punishments and long prison sentences. It is viewed as a contrast to "smart on crime" approaches. See Altheide and Coyle (2006) for a discussion.
69 West and Sabol (2009).
70 Carson and Kluckow (2023).
71 Crenshaw (2012:1428).
72 Alexander (2010).
73 The "free world" is a term the participants used to describe the world outside of prison. Flavin (2009); Richie (2012).
74 National Resource Center on Justice Involved Women (2016).
75 National Resource Center on Justice Involved Women (2016).
76 Maruschak and Minton (2020).
77 Rabuy and Kopf (2015).
78 National Resource Center on Justice Involved Women (2016).
79 DeHart (2008); National Resource Center on Justice Involved Women (2016).
80 Bronson et al. (2020).
81 Maruschak, Bronson, and Alper (2021).
82 Glaze and Maruschak (2010).
83 Cramer et al. (2017).
84 Travis, Cincotta McBride, and Solomon (2005).
85 Thulstrup and Eklund Karlsson (2017).
86 Riessman (2008).
87 Presser and Sandberg (2015).
88 Sandberg and Ugelvik (2016:129).
89 Holstein and Gubrium (1995).
90 In the United States, prisons are classified into different categories. Examples of such categories include sex and custody or security level. It was an intentional decision not to release the names of the states the participants were incarcerated in to provide further protection.

91 Beichner and Rabe-Hemp (2014); Kang-Brown and Subramanian (2017). While different entities have varying definitions of what constitutes rural, factors typically include housing and population density, where rural is in contrast to urban and even suburban areas.
92 Beichner and Rabe-Hemp (2014); Kang-Brown and Subramanian (2017).
93 See Greer (2000) for a discussion of the unique subcultures and relationships women build in prisons.
94 Penney (2019).
95 Holstein and Gubrium (1995); Presser and Sandberg (2015); Riessman (2008).
96 Holstein and Gubrium (1995); Presser and Sandberg (2015); Riessman (2008); Scott and Lyman (1968).
97 Ashby (2011).
98 Bonilla-Silva (2021).
99 Participants used various terms to refer to their race, including White or Caucasian, Black or African American, Hispanic, Asian, biracial, etc.
100 The women in this study were more educated than the national population of incarcerated people in the United States. See Couloute (2018). Over half have acquired at least some college experience, though at the time of their incarceration, this was not the case.
101 All the participants identified as cisgender, meaning that their biological sex at birth was female and they identify as a woman. Therefore, I use the term "pregnant women" or "mothers" throughout the text but acknowledge the multiple forms of gender identity among pregnant people.
102 I asked the participants what their socioeconomic status was—the terms "middle-class" and "White trash" are their terms, not mine.
103 Newport (2017).
104 To provide further protection to the participants, I categorized their crimes as "violent" or "nonviolent."
105 "Parole" refers to community supervision following a release from prison. See Carson and Kluckow (2023) for more information.
106 Daniel (2019).
107 Council of Europe (2021); Warner (2015).
108 Goffman (1961).
109 I acknowledge that there is a wide variation in cultural responses to pregnancy. For example, baby showers, gender-reveal parties, and baby registries may be more of a middle-class phenomenon. See Mwase-Musicha et al. (2022).

CHAPTER 1. WELCOME TO PRISON
1 Wodahl (2006).
2 "Probation" refers to supervision in the community and is typically reserved for those found guilty of lesser crimes. See Carson and Kluckow (2023) for more information.

3. "HIV" stands for "human immunodeficiency virus"—a virus that affects the body's immune system. See World Health Organization (2024).
4. Quinn (2014); Thomas and Lanterman (2019).
5. Gustafson (2009); Ortiz and Jackey (2019).
6. Wang (2021: n.p.).
7. Under the First Step Act, federal prisons are now required to collect data on pregnancy outcomes—state prisons are still not required to capture this data.
8. Hatters Friedman, Kaempf, and Kauffman (2020).
9. American Civil Liberties Union (2015); Egelko (2015).
10. Sufrin et al. (2019).
11. Hatters Friedman et al. (2020).
12. Liauw et al. (2016).
13. Cherot (2023).
14. Clarke et al. (2006).
15. Lopes et al. (2024).
16. Centers for Disease Control and Prevention (2024). Okwori et al. (2022); Troutman, Rafique, and Comeaux Plowden (2020).
17. Troutman et al. (2020).
18. Wang (2022b).
19. Haney (2010); McCorkel (2013).
20. Aizer, Hoynes, and Lleras-Muney (2022); Beichner and Rabe-Hemp (2014).
21. Reeve (2011).
22. Sufrin (2017).
23. Sufrin (2017).
24. See Elliott, Powell, and Brenton (2013); Manoogian (2015); Romagnoli and Wall (2012) for examples of how *good* mothering exists across different social contexts.
25. Froggé (2019); Sufrin (2017).
26. "The underground economy" refers to illegal economic work, including but not limited to drug dealing, prostitution, and gambling. In Jasmine's case, she engaged in prostitution and drug dealing.
27. This is not to say that the US prison system is a showcase of quality care; however, for those facing extreme poverty and hardship, the structure and stability of a total institution may be a welcome change.
28. Kajstura and Sawyer (2024).
29. Collins (1990); Kajstura and Sawyer (2024).
30. Collins (1990).
31. Collins (1990).
32. O'Neill Hayes and Barnhorst (2020).
33. Kajstura and Sawyer (2024).
34. Roberts (2022).
35. Roberts (2022).
36. Roberts (2022).
37. Roberts (1997; 2019).

38   Aiello and McQueeney (2016); Edin and Kefalas (2005).
39   Aiello and McQueeney (2016); Edin and Kefalas (2005).
40   Edin and Kefalas (2005).
41   Aiello and McQueeney (2016:38).
42   Aiello and McQueeney (2016); Edin and Kefalas (2005).
43   Kasdan (2009); Sufrin (2019).
44   Sufrin et al. (2021).
45   Kelsey et al. (2017).
46   Price (2010).
47   Cartwright et al. (2018).
48   Kelly (2022).
49   Kelly (2022).
50   Cartwright et al. (2018); Kasdan (2009); Sufrin et al. (2021).
51   Cartwright et al. (2018).
52   It is acknowledged that each state and prison has its own policies regarding abortion. See Sufrin et al. (2021) for examples of such policies. Cartwright et al. (2018); Kasdan (2009).
53   Carrión, Hasselbacher, and Thompson (2023).
54   Gornall (2007). See Center for Reproductive Rights (n.d.) for a discussion of terminology and map of hostile states.
55   Cartwright et al. (2018); Kasdan (2009); Sufrin et al. (2021).
56   Paltrow (2013).
57   Chan (2021); Pew Research Center (2014).
58   Chan (2021); Hallett and Johnson (2014).
59   Glaze and Maruschak (2010).
60   Thompson (2023).
61   Glaze and Maruschak (2010).
62   Arditti (2012); Beichner and Rabe-Hemp (2014).
63   Aiello and McQueeney (2016).
64   The intensive-mothering paradigm centers on a complete focus on the child, above the needs of a mother, where mothers are expected to be physically present with their children and to spend a great deal of money on them. See Hays (1998); Aielllo and McQueeney (2019).
65   See Aiello and McQueeney (2016) for a discussion of how incarcerated mothers in a jail setting resisted the stigma of maternal incarceration.
66   Edin and Kefalas (2005).
67   See Federal Bureau of Prisons (n.d.).

CHAPTER 2. THE UNRULY MATERNAL BODY

1   The red tape or obstacles that hinder an abortion in a correctional setting include but are not limited to self-pay, transportation needs, restrictive policies, attitudinal barriers, etc.
2   Kajstura and Sawyer (2024).

3   Kajstura and Sawyer (2024).
4   Kajstura and Sawyer (2024).
5   Becker and Newsom (2003); Cherot (2023).
6   Edin and Kefalas (2005).
7   Edin and Kefalas (2005:53).
8   Han (2013).
9   "CPS" was a term participants used to refer to child protective services.
10 Paltrow (2013).
11 Edin and Kefalas (2005); Paltrow (2013).
12 Davis-Floyd (2003).
13 Davis-Floyd (1987).
14 Davis-Floyd (2003).
15 Paltrow (2013).
16 Miranda, Dixon, and Reyes (2015); Paltrow and Flavin (2014).
17 Paltrow and Flavin (2014; 2013).
18 Paltrow and Flavin (2013).
19 Paltrow (2013).
20 Hanssens et al. (2018); Wang and Geng (2019).
21 Wang (2022b).
22 Sufrin (2017).
23 Equal Justice Initiative (2021).
24 Wildeman and Wang (2017).
25 Metcalf (2018).
26 Herring (2020).
27 Contraband includes anything that is not permitted inside prisons, including but not limited to drugs, weapons, and cell phones. Peterson et al. (2021).
28 Sufrin et al. (2020).
29 Sufrin et al. (2020).
30 Eggertson (2013); Murphy and Rosenbaum (1998).
31 Aiello and McQueeney (2016); French, Popovici, and Tapsell (2008); Kolind and Duke (2016); Peeler et al. (2019); Redko, Rapp, and Carlson (2008).
32 "Lowest" refers to being at the lowest point in life, i.e., experiencing rock bottom.
33 Eggertson (2013).
34 Aiello and McQueeney (2016).
35 Harp and Bunting (2020); Knight (2015).
36 McCabe (2022).
37 Farst, Valentine, and Hall (2011).
38 Knight (2015); Paltrow and Flavin (2014).
39 Knight (2015); Murphy and Rosenbaum (1998).
40 Paltrow and Flavin (2013).
41 Blocher (2022); Walsh (2016).
42 Blocher (2022).
43 Byrn et al. (2023); Schoneich et al. (2023).

44 Harp and Bunting (2020:258).
45 Leading organizations like the American College of Obstetricians and Gynecologists (ACOG), Centers for Disease Control and Prevention (CDC), and the American Academy of Pediatrics (AAP) recommend that pregnant women consume a balanced diet of fresh fruits and vegetables, protein, dairy, and grains, as well as consume additional calories in the second and third trimester, in addition to high levels of iron and folic acid, among other vitamins and minerals. See Daniel (2019); Murkoff (2016).
46 Collins and Thompson (2012); Shlafer et al. (2019).
47 Collins and Thompson (2012); Shlafer et al. (2019).
48 Davis (1998).
49 Paltrow and Flavin (2013).
50 Timmermans et al. (2009).
51 Daniel (2019).
52 Daniel (2019).
53 Daniel (2019).
54 Daniel (2019); Kramer et al. (2023).
55 Collins and Thompson (2012).
56 Collins and Thompson (2012).
57 Weill-Greenberg and Corey (2024).
58 Callahan, Jason, and Robinson (2016); Sawyer (2017).
59 Daniel (2019).
60 Hotelling (2008).
61 Maruschak (2008); Sufrin (2017).
62 Ferszt and Clarke (2012).
63 A missed miscarriage is a miscarriage that is absent physical signs or symptoms.
64 Sufrin et al. (2019).
65 Britton (2003).
66 Chappell (2013); Rivas (2013).
67 Njoku et al. (2023).
68 Hoffman et al. (2016); FitzGerald and Hurst (2017); Roberts (1997).
69 Candy and others used the term "hole" to describe solitary confinement.
70 These searches may also be performed due to suspicions about security breaches and can range from pat-downs to strip searches and cavity searches. See World Medical Association (2023).
71 World Medical Association (2023).
72 Port City Daily Staff (2021).
73 Daniel (2019).

CHAPTER 3. PREGNANCY 101

1 Han (2013).
2 Balin (1988); Garbes (2018); Han (2013); Oakley (1980).
3 Han (2013).

4 Garfinkel (1956).
5 Garfinkel (1956).
6 Hotelling (2008).
7 Han (2013).
8 Aiello and McQueeney (2019); Bute and Jensen (2010).
9 Aiello and McQueeney (2019); Bute and Jensen (2010).
10 Namey and Drapkin Lyerly (2010).
11 McCorkel (2013).
12 Hotelling (2008).
13 Jewkes and Johnston (2009); Shlafer et al. (2019).
14 Declercq et al. (2014).
15 Kuhlik and Sufrin (2020).
16 Kuhlik and Sufrin (2020).
17 Namey and Drapkin Lyerly (2010).
18 National Resource Center on Justice Involved Women (2016).
19 Each prison and unit has its own subculture, and this may not hold true across all correctional facilities and even across units within the same correctional facility.
20 Lieser (2019); Schroeder and Bell (2005).
21 Examples of prison doula programs include the Alabama Prison Birth Project, the Michigan Prison Doula Initiative, and the Minnesota Prison Doula Project. Lieser (2019); Schroeder and Bell (2005).
22 Lieser (2019); Schroeder and Bell (2005).
23 Lieser (2019); Schroeder and Bell (2005).
24 Casey-Acevedo and Bakken (2002).
25 Halter (2018); Mulligan (2019).
26 Rodriguez Carey (2019).
27 Craig (2009).
28 Craig (2009).
29 Goshin and Woods Byrne (2009).
30 Caniglia (2018).
31 Caniglia (2018).
32 Mipro (2024).
33 Rodriguez Carey (2019)
34 Rodriguez Carey (2019).
35 Rodriguez Carey (2019).
36 Rodriguez Carey (2019).
37 Rodriguez Carey (2019).
38 Lin and Harris (2009).
39 Hotelling (2008); Rodriguez Carey (2019).
40 Roberts (2019; 2022).
41 Casey-Acevedo and Bakken (2002); Rodriguez Carey (2019).
42 Casey-Acevedo and Bakken (2002).
43 Enos (2001).

44 Borelli et al. (2010); Kring Villanueva et al. (2009).
45 Any costs or fees associated with nursery programs vary widely across correctional facilities.
46 Mallon (2020).
47 Annie E. Casey Foundation (2020).
48 Roberts (2019: n.p.).
49 Child Welfare Information Gateway (2021).
50 Enos (2001).

CHAPTER 4. THE ULTIMATE CAGE
1 See Mukamal (2023); Richie (1996).
2 Hoyert (2021).
3 Ellis (2023).
4 Campbell (2021).
5 Bridges (2008); Davis-Floyd (2003).
6 Davis-Floyd (2003).
7 Davis-Floyd (2003).
8 Davis-Floyd (2003); Hill (2019).
9 Davis-Floyd (2003); Hill (2019).
10 Ahrens (2015).
11 Ahrens (2015).
12 Davis-Floyd (2003); Hill (2019).
13 Obstetrics and Gynecology Risk Research Group et al. (2009).
14 Kelly et al. (2024).
15 Hill (2019).
16 Hill (2019).
17 Kelly et al. (2024).
18 Davis (2019).
19 "Count" refers to the practice of counting the incarcerated to ensure everyone is present; see Metcalf (2018).
20 Martin et al. (2012).
21 Froggé (2019).
22 Ahrens (2015).
23 Cherot (2023).
24 Cherot (2023).
25 Mortazavi and Akaberi (2016).
26 Davis-Floyd (1987).
27 Campbell (2021); Perrotte, Chaudhary, and Goodman (2020).
28 Davis-Floyd (1987:485–86).
29 Campbell (2021); Perrotte et al. (2020).
30 Campbell (2021); Lévesque and Ferron-Parayre (2021).
31 Perrotte et al. (2020).
32 Campbell (2021).

33 Campbell (2021); Perrotte et al. (2020).
34 Davis-Floyd (1987).
35 Ellis (2023).
36 National Institutes of Health (2010).
37 Rosenstein et al. (2019).
38 Bridges (2008); Davis (2019).
39 Bridges (2008); Davis (2019).
40 Ahrens (2015); Louis-Jacques (2024).
41 Anderson (2021).
42 Anderson (2021); Ocen (2012); Sichel (2008).
43 Anderson (2021); Ocen (2012); Sichel (2008).
44 Anderson (2021); Ocen (2012); Sichel (2008).
45 Ocen (2012); Sichel (2008).
46 Nelson (2006); Ocen (2012); Sichel (2008).
47 Nelson (2006); Ocen (2012); Sichel (2008).
48 Anderson (2021).
49 Anderson (2021).
50 Anderson (2021); Thomas et al. (2024).
51 Kramer et al. (2023).
52 Anderson (2021); Ocen (2012).
53 "CO" is a term that refers to correctional officers.
54 Ferszt, Palmer, and McGrane (2018); Hotelling (2008); Nelson (2006); Ondeck (2014).
55 Collins (1990).
56 Buckley (2015).
57 Saxena and Messina (2021).
58 Gjerdingen, Froberg, and Fontaine (1991); Fry-McComish, Groh, and Moldenhauer (2013).
59 Casey-Acevedo and Bakken (2002).
60 Hayes et al. (2020).
61 Hutchinson et al. (2008).
62 Hotelling (2008); Lieser (2019); Schroeder and Bell (2005).
63 Hotelling (2008); Schroeder and Bell (2005).
64 Hotelling (2008); Lieser (2019); Schroeder and Bell (2005).
65 Examples of prison doula programs include the Alabama Prison Birth Project, the Michigan Prison Doula Initiative, and the Minnesota Prison Doula Project. Lieser (2019); Schroeder and Bell (2005).
66 Sufrin et al. (2019).
67 The extent of miscarriages among incarcerated women in the United States is difficult to calculate, with wide variation across states, some states having as high as 20 percent, whereas other states have about 6 percent. Sufrin et al. (2019).
68 See Foucault (1975).
69 Tully, Stuebe, and Verbiest (2017).

CHAPTER 5. SILENCED CRIES
1. Hoffman et al. (2016).
2. Piejko (2006).
3. Davis (2019); Hill (2019).
4. Kramer et al. (2023).
5. Lopez-Gonzales and Kopparapu (2022).
6. Lopez-Gonzales and Kopparapu (2022).
7. Schroeder and Bell (2005).
8. Lopez-Gonzalez and Kopparapu (2022).
9. Lopez-Gonzalez and Kopparapu (2022); Patient-Centered Outcomes Research Institute (2023).
10. Lopez-Gonzalez and Kopparapu (2022); Patient-Centered Outcomes Research Institute (2023).
11. Cheng, Fowles, and Walker (2006); Daniel (2019).
12. World Health Organization (2023).
13. Patient-Centered Outcomes Research Institute (2023).
14. Patient-Centered Outcomes Research Institute (2023).
15. Ellis (2023).
16. Cheng et al. (2006); Daniel (2019).
17. Pendleton, Saunders, and Shlafer (2020).
18. FitzGerald and Hurst (2017); Hoffman et al. (2016).
19. Pendleton et al. (2020).
20. US Department of Justice (2016).
21. Although Angel had a doula during childbirth, she did not have access to a doula during the postpartum period. While doulas can be a critical resource, they are not a silver bullet against the power of the carceral state.
22. Fahey (2017).
23. It is acknowledged that rules and practices regarding sleeping arrangements vary greatly across correctional facilities and some prisons may make accommodations to ensure pregnant women have a bottom bunk.
24. Jones et al. (2009).
25. Kealy, Small, and Liammputong (2010).
26. Kramer et al. (2023).
27. Shlafer et al. (2015).
28. Hutchinson et al. (2008).
29. Mughal, Azhar, and Siddiqui (2021).
30. Hutchinson et al. (2008); Njoroge, White, and Waller et al. (2022); Mughal et al. (2021).
31. Howland et al. (2021).
32. Howland et al. (2021); Hutchinson et al. (2008).
33. Negron et al. (2014).
34. Wagner and Jones (2019).

35 It is not uncommon for the incarcerated to make pseudo-families in prison. See Kolb and Palys (2018).
36 Asiodu, Beal, and Sufrin (2021).
37 Stuebe (2009).
38 Abbott and Scott (2017). The Fair Labor Standards Act offers workplace protections for those in the United States.
39 Justice-Involved Women & Children–Center for Leadership Education in Maternal & Child Public Health (2023).
40 Abbott and Scott (2017).
41 Asiodu et al. (2021).
42 Collins (1990); Davis (2019).
43 Amir (2014).
44 Abbott and Scott (2017); Shlafer et al. (2018).
45 Asiodu et al. (2021).
46 Shelburne (2018).
47 Carey (2020).
48 This practice varies widely across facilities, and its use often depends on funding, storage space, and the availability of staff and volunteers. Abbott and Scott (2017).
49 Wang (2022a).

CHAPTER 6. COMING HOME

1 Gate fare varies across facilities. See John Biewen, "Hard Time: Life after Prison," American Public Media, March 2003, https://americanradioworks.publicradio.org for more information on these differences.
2 Price (2010).
3 Hays (1998).
4 Mignon and Ransford (2012).
5 Brown (2010).
6 "Ghosting" was a phrase participants used to refer to the sudden cut-off of communication without warning from caregivers.
7 Mignon and Ransford (2012).
8 Caniglia (2018); Kring Villanueva et al. (2009).
9 Arditti (2012).
10 Martin (2017).
11 Arditti (2012).
12 Hays (1998).
13 James (2015).
14 The age of the child upon a woman's release from prison depends on the length of her sentence.
15 Beichner and Rabe-Hemp (2014); Haney (2010); McCorkel (2013).
16 Braman (2007).
17 Beichner and Rabe-Hemp (2014).
18 James (2015); Petersilia (2003); Price (2015); Richie (2012).

19 Alper, Durose, and Markman (2018). "Recidivism" refers to reoffending.
20 Bowman and Travis (2012); Ortiz and Jackey (2019).
21 Ortiz and Jackey (2019); Price (2015); Richie (2012).
22 The incarceration industry is thought to be an $80 billion industry. See Wagner and Rabuy (2017).
23 Davis (1998).
24 Ortiz and Jackey (2019).
25 "Making it" was a term several participants used to describe being "successful" in the aftermath of their imprisonment. It usually meant an avoidance of drugs/crime and prosocial behaviors, such as employment or success in securing housing. See Petersilia (2003) or Travis (2005).
26 Haney (2010); McCorkel (2013).
27 Daniel and Sawyer (2020).
28 Beichner and Rabe-Hemp (2014).
29 Poehlmann-Tynan (2020).
30 Wang (2022b).
31 Poehlmann-Tynan (2020).
32 Arditti (2012); Brown and Bloom (2009); Poehlmann-Tynan (2020); Siegel (2011).
33 Each case is unique and particular to the circumstances. Those charged with sex offenses or drug offenses may be more likely to have these types of restrictions as a required element of their parole order or of an offender registry that necessitates distance from school grounds.
34 Aiello and McQueeney (2016).
35 Walsh (2016).
36 Roberts (2002).
37 Braman (2007).
38 Armstrong and Lewis (2019).
39 Roberts (2022).
40 See Arditti and Few (2006).
41 See Center for American Progress (2020) for a listing of childcare deserts; Schochet (2019).
42 Arditti (2012); Brown and Bloom (2009).
43 Ferguson and Lucy (2024).
44 Arditti and Few (2006).
45 Brown (2010).
46 Wang and Bertram (2022).
47 Brown (2010).
48 Beichner and Rabe-Hemp (2014); Brown (2010).
49 Beichner and Rabe-Hemp (2014).
50 At its most basic level, "White privilege" refers to the invisible benefits that come with being White. See McIntosh (1989).
51 There have been efforts to encourage industries to "ban the box," in reference to the box on employment applications that asks prospective employees about their

criminal history, to remove some of the stigma associated with incarceration and provide those with a record more opportunities for employment. See Price (2015).
52 Couloute and Kopf (2018); Crenshaw (1991).
53 Couloute and Kopf (2018).
54 Couloute and Kopf (2018).
55 Barrick, Lattimore, and Visher (2014).
56 Collins (1990); Crenshaw (1991).

CONCLUSION
1 Roberts (1997); Solinger (2005).
2 Center for Reproductive Rights (n.d.); Higgins (2022); Roberts (1997); Solinger (2005).
3 Brayne (2014); Paltrow and Flavin (2014); Roberts (1997).
4 Center for Reproductive Rights (n.d.); Higgins (2022); Price (2010).
5 Roberts (1997; 2002).
6 Warner (2015).
7 Ortiz and Jackey (2019).
8 The rise of incarceration is distinct from actual crime data/trends. See Stemen (2017).
9 Brayne (2014).
10 Bentham (1995); Foucault (1975); Richie and Martensen (2020); Walmsley (2018).
11 Graff (2015); Richie (2012).
12 Richie and Martensen (2020); Wacquant (2010).
13 Richie and Martensen (2020); Wacquant (2010).
14 Collins (1990).
15 Davis (1998).
16 Davis (1998).
17 Rios (2011).
18 Rios (2011).
19 Villarreal (2020).
20 Advocacy and Research on Reproductive Wellness of Incarcerated People (n.d.).
21 Advocacy and Research on Reproductive Wellness of Incarcerated People (n.d.).
22 Advocacy and Research on Reproductive Wellness of Incarcerated People (n.d.).
23 Advocacy and Research on Reproductive Wellness of Incarcerated People (n.d.).
24 McCabe (2022).
25 McCabe (2022).
26 Cherot (2023).
27 Kramer et al. (2023).
28 Walters (2012).
29 Wagner and Jones (2019).
30 Hutchinson et al. (2008).
31 American Civil Liberties Union (2019).
32 Lopez-Gonzales and Kopparapu (2022).

33 State of Minnesota (2021).
34 Goshin, Byrne, and Henninger (2014).
35 Center for Restorative Justice Works (n.d.).
36 Logan (1992).
37 Kansas Children's Discovery Center (n.d.).
38 Alper et al. (2018).
39 Sesame Workshop (n.d.).

AFTERWORD
1 Several participants planned to get involved in criminal justice reform advocacy to bring awareness to the problem of mass incarceration and to humanize the incarcerated.

BIBLIOGRAPHY

Abbott, Laura, and Tricia Scott. 2017. "Women's Experiences of Breastfeeding in Prison." *MIDIRS Midwifery Digest* 27(2):217–23.
Advocacy and Research on Reproductive Wellness of Incarcerated People. N.d. "Pregnancy in Prison Statistics PIPS Project." Advocacy and Research on Reproductive Wellness of Incarcerated People. Accessed November 12, 2024. https://arrwip.org.
Ahrens, Deborah. 2015. "Incarcerated Childbirth and 'Broader Birth Control': Autonomy, Regulation, and the State." *Missouri Law Review* 80(1):1–51.
Aiello, Brittnie, and Krista McQueeney. 2016. "'How Can You Live without Your Kids?': Distancing from and Embracing the Stigma of 'Incarcerated Mother.'" *Journal of Prison Education and Reentry* 3(1):32–49.
———. 2019. "'I Always Thought I Was a Good Mother': Intensive Mothering in a Women's Jail." *Sociological Imagination* 54(2):26–43.
Aizer, Anna, Hilary Hoynes, and Adriana Lleras-Muney. 2022. "Children and the US Social Safety Net: Balancing Disincentives for Adults and Benefits for Children." *Journal of Economic Perspectives* 36(2):149–74.
Alexander, Michelle. 2010. *The New Jim Crow: Mass Incarceration in the Age of Colorblindness*. New York: New Press.
Alper, Mariel, Matthew R. Durose, and Joshua Markman. 2018. "2018 Update on Prisoner Recidivism: A 9-Year Follow-up Period (2005–2014)." Bureau of Justice Statistics, May 23. https://bjs.ojp.gov.
Altheide, David L., and Michael J. Coyle. 2006. "Smart on Crime: The New Language for Prisoner Release." *Crime Media Culture: An International Journal* 2(3):286–303.
American Civil Liberties Union. 2015. "Harmen v. Ahern (Pregnancy Testing in Alameda County Jails)." American Civil Liberties Union, October 28. www.aclunc.org.
———. 2019. "Still Worse Than Second-Class: Solitary Confinement of Women in the United States." American Civil Liberties Union, January 1. www.aclu.org.
Amir, Lisa H. 2014. "Managing Common Breastfeeding Problems in the Community." *British Medical Journal* 348(g2954):1–9.
Anderson, Erica. 2021. "Childbirth in Chains: Why the Shackling of Incarcerated Pregnant Women Is Unconstitutional." *University of Cincinnati Law Review*, April 23. https://uclawreview.org.
Annie E. Casey Foundation. 2020. "Black Children Continue to Be Disproportionately Represented in Foster Care." Annie E. Casey Foundation, April 13. https://datacenter.kidscount.org.

Arditti, Joyce A. 2012. *Parental Incarceration and the Family: Psychological and Social Effects of Imprisonment on Children, Parents, and Caregivers*. New York: New York University Press.

Arditti, Joyce A., and April L. Few. 2006. "Mothers' Reentry into Family Life Following Incarceration." *Criminal Justice Policy Review* 17(1):103–23.

Armstrong, Mia, and Nicole Lewis. 2019. "What Gate Money Can (and Cannot) Buy." The Marshall Project, September 10. www.themarshallproject.org.

Ashby, Christine. 2011. "Whose 'Voice' Is It Anyway? Giving Voice and Qualitative Research Involving Individuals That Type to Communicate." *Disabilities Study Quarterly* 31(4).

Asian Communities for Reproductive Justice. 2005. "A New Vision for Advancing Our Movement for Reproductive Health, Reproductive Rights, and Reproductive Justice." Asian Communities for Reproductive Justice, accessed July 31, 2024. https://forwardtogether.org.

Asiodu, Ifeyinwa, Lauren Beal, and Carolyn Sufrin. 2021. "Breastfeeding in Incarcerated Settings in the United States: A National Survey of Frequency and Policies." *Breastfeeding Medicine* 16(9):710–16.

Aswad, Jem. 2022. "'Guns Have More Rights Than Women,' Says Taraji P. Henson at BET Awards.'" *Variety*, June 26. https://variety.com.

Atwood, Margaret. 1985. *The Handmaid's Tale*. Boston: Houghton Mifflin.

Balin, Jane. 1988. "The Sacred Dimensions of Pregnancy and Birth." *Qualitative Sociology* 11(4):275–301.

Barrick, Kelle, Pamela K. Lattimore, and Christy A. Visher. 2014. "Reentering Women: The Impact of Social Ties on Long-Term Recidivism." *Prison Journal* 94(3):279–304.

Baunach, Phyllis Jo. 1985. *Mothers in Prison*. New Brunswick, NJ: Transaction.

Becker, Gary, and Edwina Newsom. 2003. "Socioeconomic Status and Dissatisfaction with Health Care among Chronically Ill African Americans." *American Journal of Public Health* 93(5):742–48.

Beichner, Dawn, and Cara Rabe-Hemp. 2014. "'I Don't Want to Go Back to That Town': Incarcerated Mothers and Their Return Home to Rural Communities." *Critical Criminology* 22(4):527–43.

Bentham, Jeremy. 1995. *The Panopticon Writings*. London: Verso.

Blocher, Jenna. 2022. "'The Family Separation Crisis That No One Knows About': How Our Flawed Legal and Prison Systems Work to Keep Incarcerated Parents from Their Children." *Brandeis University Law Journal* 10(1):53–71.

Bonilla-Silva, Eduardo. 2021. *Racism without Racists: Color-Blind Racism and the Persistence of Racial Inequality in America*. 6th ed. Plymouth, UK: Rowman & Littlefield.

Borelli, Jessica L., Lorie Goshin, Sarah Joestl, Juliette Clark, and Mary W. Byrne. 2010. "Attachment Organization in a Sample of Incarcerated Mothers: Distribution of Classifications and Associations with Substance Abuse History, Depressive Symptoms, Perceptions of Parenting Competency, and Social Support." *Attachment & Human Development* 12(4):355–74.

Bowman, Scott W., and Raphael Travis Jr. 2012. "Prisoner Reentry and Recidivism according to the Formerly Incarcerated and Reentry Service Providers: A Verbal Behavior Approach." *Behavior Analyst Today* 13(3–4):9–19.

Braman, Donald. 2007. *Doing Time on the Outside: Incarceration and Family Life in Urban America*. Ann Arbor: University of Michigan Press.

Brayne, Sarah. 2014. "Surveillance and System Avoidance: Criminal Justice Contact and Institutional Attachment." *American Sociological Review* 79(3):367–91.

Bridges, Khiara M. 2008. *Reproducing Race: An Ethnography of Pregnancy as a Site of Racialization*. Berkeley: University of California Press.

Britton, Dana M. 2003. *At Work in the Iron Cage: The Prison as Gendered Organization*. New York: New York University Press.

Bronson, Jennifer, Jessica Stroop, Stephanie Zimmer, and Marcus Berzofsky. 2020. "Drug Use, Dependence, and Abuse among State Prisoners and Jail Inmates, 2007–2009." Bureau of Justice Statistics, August 10. https://bjs.ojp.gov.

Brown, Geneva. 2010. "The Intersectionality of Race, Gender, and Reentry: Challenges for African-American Women." American Constitution Society, November 10. www.acslaw.org.

Brown, Marilyn, and Barbara Bloom. 2009. "Reentry and Renegotiating Motherhood: Maternal Identity and Success on Parole." *Crime & Delinquency* 55(2):313–36.

Bryant, Erica. 2021. "Why We Say 'Criminal Legal System,' Not 'Criminal Justice System.'" Vera Institute of Justice, December 1. www.vera.org.

Buckley, Sarah J. 2015. "Executive Summary of *Hormonal Physiology of Childbearing: Evidence and Implications for Women, Babies, and Maternity Care*." *Journal of Perinatal Education* 24(3):145–53.

Burgess-Proctor, Amanda. 2006. "Intersections of Race, Class, Gender, and Crime: Future Directions for Feminist Criminology." *Feminist Criminology* 1(1):27–47.

Bute, Jennifer J., and Robin E. Jensen. 2010. "Low-Income Women Describe Fertility-Related Expectations: Descriptive Norms, Injunctive Norms, and Behavior." *Health Communication* 25(8):681–91.

Byrn, Mary A., Elizabeth A. Buys, Mahasin Mujahid, and Kristine Madsen. 2023. "Disparities in the Provision of Perinatal Care Based on Patient Race in the United States." *Birth: Issues in Perinatal Care* 50(3):1–9.

Callahan, Sarah, Leonard A. Jason, and LaVome Robinson. 2016. "Reducing Economic Disparities for Female Offenders: The Oxford House Model." *Alcohol Treatment Quarterly* 34(3):292–302.

Campbell, Colleen. 2021. "Medical Violence, Obstetric Racism, and the Limits of Informed Consent for Black Women." *Michigan Journal of Race & Law* 26:47–75.

Caniglia, John. 2018. "Growing Up behind Bars: How 11 States Handle Prison Nurseries." *Cleveland.Com*, March 4. www.cleveland.com.

Carey, Teresa. 2020. "Fighting to Get Breast Pumps to Mothers in Prison." *Freethink*, May 30. www.freethink.com.

Carrión, Fabiola, Lee Hasselbacher, and Terri-Ann Thompson. 2023. "Leveraging the Tools Available: Using the Hyde Amendment to Preserve Minimum Abortion Ac-

cess and Mitigate Harms in Restrictive States." *Journal of Law, Medicine & Ethics* 51(3):544–48.
Carson, E. Ann, and Rich Kluckow. 2023. "Prisoners in 2022—Statistical Tables." Bureau of Justice Statistics, November 30. https://bjs.ojp.gov.
Cartwright, Alice F., Mihiri Karunaratne, Jill Barr-Walker, Nicole E. Johns, and Ushma D. Upadhyay. 2018. "Identifying National Availability of Abortion Care and Distance from Major US Cities: Systematic Online Search." *Journal of Medical Internet Research* 20(5):186.
Casey-Acevedo, Karen, and Tim Bakken. 2002. "Visiting Women in Prison: Who Visits and Who Cares?" *Journal of Prisoner Rehabilitation* 34(3):67–83.
Center for American Progress. 2020. "Do You Live in a Childcare Desert?" Center for American Progress. https://childcaredeserts.org/2018.
Center for Reproductive Rights. N.d. "After *Roe* Fell: Abortion Laws by State." Center for Reproductive Rights, accessed July 31, 2024. https://reproductiverights.org.
Center for Restorative Justice Works. N.d. "Get on the Bus." Center for Restorative Justice Works, accessed July 31, 2024. https://crjw.org.
Centers for Disease Control and Prevention. 2024. "Unintended Pregnancy." Centers for Disease Control and Prevention. www.cdc.gov.
Chan, Stephanie T. 2021. "'Part of God's Plan for My Life': How Conservative Protestant Students Make Sense of Social Forces and Social Inequality." *Religion & Education* 49(1):23–41.
Chappell, Bill. 2013. "California's Prison Sterilizations Reportedly Echo Eugenics Era." *National Public Radio*, July 9. www.npr.org.
Cheng, Ching-Yu, Eileen R. Fowles, and Lorraine O. Walker. 2006. "Continuing Education Module: Postpartum Maternal Health Care in the United States; A Critical Review." *Journal of Perinatal Education* 15(3):34–42.
Cherot, Elizabeth. 2023. "March of Dimes Maternity Care Deserts 2023 Executive Summary." March of Dimes, accessed July 31, 2024. www.marchofdimes.org.
Chesney-Lind, Meda, and Lisa Pasko. 2004. *The Female Offender: Girls, Women, and Crime*. 2nd ed. Thousand Oaks, CA: Sage Publications.
Child Welfare Information Gateway. 2021. "Child Welfare Practice to Address Racial Disproportionality and Disparity." Child Welfare Information Gateway, accessed July 31, 2024. www.childwelfare.gov.
Clarke, Jennifer G., Megan R. Hebert, Cynthia Rosengard, Jennifer S. Rose, Kirsten M. DaSilva, and Michael D. Stein. 2006. "Reproductive Health Care and Family Planning Needs among Incarcerated Women." *American Journal of Public Health* 96(5):834–39.
Collins, Patricia Hill. 1990. *Black Feminist Thought: Knowledge, Consciousness, and the Politics of Empowerment*. Boston, MA: Unwin Hyman.
Collins, Shayda A., and Sharon H. Thompson. 2012. "What Are We Feeding Our Inmates?" *Journal of Correctional Health Care* 18(3):210–18.
Cook, David. 2014. "HCF History." Kansas Department of Corrections, January 10. www.doc.ks.gov.

Couloute, Lucius. 2018. "Getting Back on Course: Educational Exclusion and Attainment among Formerly Incarcerated People." Prison Policy Initiative, October. www.prisonpolicy.org.

Couloute, Lucius, and Daniel Kopf. 2018. "Out of Prison and out of Work: Unemployment among Formerly Incarcerated People." Prison Policy Initiative, July. www.prisonpolicy.org.

Council of Europe. 2021. "Imprisonment Rates Continue to Fall in Europe according to the Council of Europe's Annual Penal Statistics on Prison Populations for 2020." Council of Europe, August 4. www.coe.int.

Craig, Susan C. 2009. "A Historical Review of Mother and Child Programs for Incarcerated Women." *Prison Journal* 89(1):35S–53S.

Cramer, Lindsey, Margaret Goff, Bryce Peterson, and Heather Sandstrom. 2017. "Parent-Child Visiting Practices in Prisons and Jails: A Synthesis of Research and Practice." Urban Institute. www.urban.org.

Crandall, Russell C. 2020. *Drugs and Thugs: The History and Future of America's War on Drugs*. New Haven, CT: Yale University Press.

Crenshaw, Kimberle. 1991. "Mapping the Margins: Intersectionality, Identity Politics, and Violence against Women of Color." *Stanford Law Review* 43(6):1241–99.

———. 2012. "From Private Violence to Mass Incarceration: Thinking Intersectionally about Women, Race, and Social Control." *UCLA Law Review* 59:1418–72.

Daniel, Roxanne. 2019. "Prisons Neglect Pregnant Women in Their Healthcare Policies." Prison Policy Initiative, December 5. www.prisonpolicy.org.

Daniel, Roxanne, and Wendy Sawyer. 2020. "What You Should Know about Halfway Houses." Prison Policy Initiative, September 3. www.prisonpolicy.org.

Davis, Angela. 1998. "Masked Racism: Reflections on the Prison Industrial Complex." *Colorlines*, September 10. https://colorlines.com.

Davis, Dána-Ain. 2019. *Reproductive Injustice: Racism, Pregnancy, and Premature Birth*. New York: New York University Press.

Davis-Floyd, Robbie. 1987. "The Technological Model of Birth." *Journal of American Folklore* 100(398):479–95.

———. 2003. *Birth as an American Rite of Passage*. 2nd ed. Berkeley: University of California Press.

Declercq, Eugene R., Carol Sakala, Maureen P. Corry, Sandra Applebaum, and Ariel Herrlich. 2014. "Major Survey Findings of Listening to Mothers (SM) III: Pregnancy and Birth; Report of the Third National U.S. Survey of Women's Childbearing Experiences." *Journal of Perinatal Education* 23(1):9–16.

DeHart, Dana D. 2008. "Pathways to Prison: Impact of Victimization in the Lives of Incarcerated Women." *Violence Against Women* 14(12):1362–81.

Dodworth, Jane. 2014. "Sex Worker and Mother: Managing Dual and Threatened Identities." *Child & Family Social Work* 19(1):99–108.

Dyer, Lauren, Rachel Hardeman, Dovile Vilda, Katherine Theall, and Maeve Wallace. 2019. "Mass Incarceration and Public Health: The Association between Black Jail Incarceration and Adverse Birth Outcomes among Black Women in Louisiana." *BMC Pregnancy and Childbirth* 19(525).

Edin, Kathryn, and Maria Kefalas. 2005. *Promises I Can Keep: Why Poor Women Put Motherhood before Marriage*. Berkeley: University of California Press.

Egelko, Bob. 2015. "Alameda County Ends Mandatory Pregnancy Tests for Female Inmates." SFGATE, October 29. www.sfgate.com.

Eggertson, Laura. 2013. "Stigma a Major Barrier to Treatment for Pregnant Women with Addictions." *Canadian Medical Association Journal* 185(18):1562.

Elliott, Sinikka, Rachel Powell, and Joslyn Brenton. 2013. "Being a Good Mom: Low-Income, Black Single Mothers Negotiate Intensive Mothering." *Journal of Family Issues* 36(3):351–70.

Ellis, Nicquel Terry. 2023. "As the Nation Battles a Maternal Health Crisis, More Women of Color Are Choosing Birth Centers over Hospitals." *CNN*, December 9. www.cnn.com.

Enos, Sandra. 2001. *Mothering from the Inside: Parenting in a Women's Prison*. Albany: State University of New York Press.

Equal Justice Initiative. 2021. "COVID-19's Impact on People in Prison." Equal Justice Initiative, April 16. https://eji.org.

Fahey, Jenifer O. 2017. "Best Practices in Management of Postpartum Pain." *Journal of Perinatal & Neonatal Nursing* 31(2):126–36.

Farst, Karen J., Jimmie L. Valentine, and R. Whit Hall. 2011. "Drug Testing for Newborn Exposure to Illicit Substances in Pregnancy: Pitfalls and Pearls." *International Journal of Pediatrics* 951616.

Federal Bureau of Prisons. N.d. "Community Ties." Federal Bureau of Prisons, accessed July 31, 2024. www.bop.gov.

Ferguson, Stephanie, and Isabella Lucy. 2024. "Data Deep Dive: A Decline of Women in the Workforce." US Chamber of Commerce. www.uschamber.com.

Ferszt, Ginette G., and Jennifer G. Clarke. 2012. "Health Care of Pregnant Women in U.S. State Prisons." *Journal of Health Care for the Poor and Underserved* 23(2):557–69.

Ferszt, Ginette G., Michelle Palmer, and Christine McGrane. 2018. "Where Does Your State Stand on Shackling Pregnant Incarcerated Women?" *Nursing for Women's Health* 22(1):17–23.

FitzGerald, Chloë, and Samia Hurst. 2017. "Implicit Bias in Healthcare Professionals: A Systematic Review." *BMC Medical Ethics* 18(1):19.

Flavin, Jeanne. 2009. *Our Bodies, Our Crimes: The Policing of Women's Reproduction in America*. New York: New York University Press.

Foucault, Michel. 1975. *Discipline and Punish: The Birth of the Prison*. New York: Pantheon Books.

French, Gabrielle, Allie Goodman, and Chloe Carlson. 2020. "What Is the Carceral State?" Carceral State Project. https://storymaps.arcgis.com.

French, Michael T., Ioana Popovici, and Lauren Tapsell. 2008. "The Economic Costs of Substance Abuse Treatment: Updated Estimates and Cost Bands for Program Assessment and Reimbursement." *Journal of Substance Abuse Treatment* 35(4):462–69.

Froggé, George M. 2019. "Supporting Pregnant Incarcerated Women through Childbirth: Educational Perspectives." *International Journal of Childbirth Education* 34(2):51–54.
Frye, Marilyn. 1983. *The Politics of Reality: Essays in Feminist Theory*. Berkeley, CA: Crossing Press.
Fry-McComish, Judith, Carla J. Groh, and Judith A. Moldenhauer. 2013. "Development of a Doula Intervention for Postpartum Depressive Symptoms: Participants' Recommendations." *Journal of Child Adolescent Psychiatric Nursing* 26(1):3–15.
Garbes, Imania. 2018. *Like a Mother: A Feminist Journey through the Science and Culture of Pregnancy*. New York: Harper Wave.
Garcia, Lorraine M. 2023. "Obstetric Violence in the United States and Other High-Income Countries: An Integrative Review." *Sexual and Reproductive Health Matters* 31(1):2322194.
Garfinkel, Harold. 1956. "Conditions of Successful Degradation Ceremonies." *American Journal of Sociology* 61(5):420–24.
Gjerdingen, Dwenda K., D. G. Froberg, and Patricia Fontaine. 1991. "The Effects of Social Support on Women's Health during Pregnancy, Labor, and Delivery, and the Postpartum Period." *Family Medicine* 23(5):370–75.
Glaze, Lauren E., and Laura M. Maruschak. 2010. "Parents in Prison and their Minor Children." Bureau of Justice Statistics, March 30. https://bjs.ojp.gov.
Goffman, Erving. 1961. *Asylums: Essays on the Social Situations of Mental Patients and Other Inmates*. New York: Doubleday/Anchor.
Goodman, Brenda, and Deidre McPhillips. 2023. "Bacterial Infection Linked to Recent Baby Formula Shortage May Join Federal Disease Watchlist." *CNN*, May 9. www.cnn.com.
Gornall, Jonathan. 2007. "Where Do We Draw the Line?" *British Medical Journal* 334(7588):285–89.
Goshin, Lorie Smith, and Mary Woods Byrne. 2009. "Converging Streams of Opportunity for Prison Nursery Programs in the United States." *Journal of Offender Rehabilitation* 48(4):271–95.
Goshin, Lorie Smith, Mary W. Byrne, and Alana M. Henninger. 2014. "Recidivism after Release from a Prison Nursery Program." *Public Health Nursing* 31(2):109–17.
Goshin, Lorie S., D. R. Gina Sissoko, Grace Neumann, Carolyn Sufrin, and Lorraine Byrnes. 2018. "Perinatal Nurses' Experiences with and Knowledge of the Care of Incarcerated Women during Pregnancy and the Postpartum Period." *Journal of Obstetric, Gynecologic, and Neonatal Nursing* 48(1):27–36.
Government Accountability Office. 2024. "Pregnant Women in State Prisons and Local Jails: Federal Assistance to Support Their Care." Government Accountability Office, October. www.gao.gov.
Graff, Gilda. 2015. "Redesigning Racial Caste in America via Mass Incarceration." *Journal of Psychohistory* 43(2):120–33.
Greer, Kimberly R. 2000. "The Changing Nature of Interpersonal Relationships in a Women's Prison." *Prison Journal* 80(4):442–68.

Gustafson, Kaaryn. 2009. "The Criminalization of Poverty." *Journal of Criminal Law & Criminology* 99(3):643–716.
Haley, Sarah. 2016. *No Mercy Here: Gender, Punishment, and the Making of Jim Crow Modernity*. Chapel Hill: University of North Carolina Press.
Hallett, Michael, and Byron Johnson. 2014. "The Resurgence of Religion in America's Prisons." *Religions* 5(3):663–83.
Halter, Emily. 2018. "Parental Prisoners: The Incarcerated Mother's Constitutional Right to Parent." *Journal of Criminal Law & Criminology* 108(3):539–68.
Hamer, Emily. 2021. "Wis. Jail to Stop Calling Incarcerated People 'Inmates.'" *Wisconsin State Journal*, August 17.
Han, Sallie. 2013. *Pregnancy in Practice: Expectation and Experience in the Contemporary US*. New York: Berghahn Books.
Haney, Lynne A. 2010. *Offending Women: Power, Punishment, and the Regulation of Desire*. Berkeley: University of California Press.
Hanssens, Lisa G. M., Veerie Vyncke, Eva Steenberghs, and Sara J. T. Willems. 2018. "The Role of Socioeconomic Status in the Relationship between Detention and Self-Rated Health among Prison Detainees in Belgium." *Health & Social Care in the Community* 26(4):547–55.
Harp, Kathi L., and Amanda M. Bunting. 2020. "The Racialized Nature of Child Welfare Policies and the Social Control of Black Bodies." *Social Politics* 27(2):258–81.
Hatters-Friedman, Susan, Aimee Kaempf, and Sarah Kauffman. 2020. "The Realities of Pregnancy and Mothering While Incarcerated." *Journal of the American Academy of Psychiatry and the Law* 48(3):1–11.
Hayes, Crystal M., Carolyn Sufrin, and Jamila B. Perritt. 2020. "Reproductive Justice Disrupted: Mass Incarceration as a Driver of Reproductive Oppression." *American Journal of Public Health* 110(S1): S21–S24.
Hays, Sharon. 1998. *The Cultural Contradictions of Motherhood*. New Haven, CT: Yale University Press.
Herring, Tiana. 2020. "Since You Asked: What Role Does Drug Enforcement Play in the Rising Incarceration of Women?" Prison Policy Initiative, November 10. www.prisonpolicy.org.
Higgins, Abigail. 2022. "Abortion Rights Advocates Fear Access to Birth Control Could Be Curtailed." *Washington Post*, June 24. www.washingtonpost.com.
Hill, Milli. 2019. *Give Birth like a Feminist: Your Body, Your Baby, Your Choices*. Huntington, WV: HQ.
Hoffman, Kelly M., Sophie Trawalter, Jordan R. Axt, and M. Norman Oliver. 2016. "Racial Bias in Pain Assessment and Treatment Recommendations, and False Beliefs about Biological Differences between Blacks and Whites." *Proceedings of the National Academy of Sciences of the United States of America* 113(16):4296–4301.
Holstein, James. A., and Jaber F. Gubrium. 1995. *The Active Interview*. Thousand Oaks, CA: Sage Publications.
Hotelling, Barbara A. 2008. "Perinatal Needs of Pregnant, Incarcerated Women." *Journal of Perinatal Education* 17(2):37–44.

Howard, David L., Donna Strobino, Susan G. Sherman, and Rosa M. Crum. 2011. "Maternal Incarceration during Pregnancy and Infant Birthweight." *Maternal and Child Health Journal* 15(4):478–86.
Howland, Mariann A., Bethany Kotlar, Laurel Davis, and Rebecca J. Shlafer. 2021. "Depressive Symptoms among Pregnant and Postpartum Women in Prison." *Journal of Midwifery & Women's Health* 66(4):494–502.
Hoyert, Donna L. 2021. "Maternal Mortality Rates in the United States, 2019." National Center for Health Statistics, May 3. www.cdc.gov.
Huang, Katy, Rebecca Atlas, and Farah Parvez. 2012. "The Significance of Breastfeeding to Incarcerated Pregnant Women: An Exploratory Study." *Birth: Issues in Perinatal Care* 39(2):145–55.
Hutchinson, Katherine Conlon, Ginger A. Moore, Cathi B. Propper, and Amy Mariaskin. 2008. "Incarcerated Women's Psychological Functioning during Pregnancy." *Psychology of Women Quarterly* 32(4):440–53.
James, Nathan. 2015. "Offender Reentry: Correctional Statistics, Reintegration into the Community, and Recidivism." Congressional Research Service, January 12. https://sgp.fas.org.
Jewkes, Yvonne, and Helen Johnston. 2009. "'Cavemen in an Era of Speed-of-Light Technology': Historical and Contemporary Perspectives on Communication within Prisons." *Howard Journal of Criminal Justice* 48(2):132–43.
Jones, Hendree E., Kevin O'Grady, Jennifer Dahne, Rolley Johnson, Laetitia Lemoine, Lorriane Milio, Alice Ordean, and Peter Selby. 2009. "Management of Acute Postpartum Pain in Patients Maintained on Methadone or Buprenorphine during Pregnancy." *American Journal of Drug and Alcohol Abuse* 35(3):151–56.
Justice-Involved Women & Children–Center for Leadership Education in Maternal & Child Public Health. 2023. "Breastfeeding and Lactation Support for Incarcerated People in the U.S." Justice-Involved Women & Children–Center for Leadership Education in Maternal & Child Public Health, April 11. https://mch.umn.edu.
Kajstura, Aleks, and Wendy Sawyer. 2024. "Women's Mass Incarceration: The Whole Pie 2024." Prison Policy Initiative, March 14. www.prisonpolicy.org.
Kang-Brown, Jacob, and Ram Subramanian. 2017. "Out of Sight: The Growth of Jails in Rural America." Vera Institute of Justice, June. www.vera.org.
Kansas Children's Discovery Center. N.d. "Play Free." Kansas Children's Discovery Center, accessed July 31, 2024. https://kansasdiscovery.org.
Kasdan, Diana. 2009. "Abortion Access for Incarcerated Women: Are Correctional Health Practices in Conflict with Constitutional Standards?" *Perspectives on Sexual and Reproductive Health* 41(1):59–62.
Kealy, Michelle A., Rhonda E. Small, and Pranee Liamputtong. 2010. "Recovery after Caesarean Birth: A Qualitative Study of Women's Accounts in Victoria, Australia." *BMC Pregnancy and Childbirth* 10:47.
Kelly, Clodagh, Melissa Whitten, Sophie Kennedy, Anne Lanceley, and Jacqueline Nicholls. 2024. "Women's Experiences of Consent to Induction of Labour: A Qualitative Study." *Sexual & Reproductive Healthcare* 39:100928.

Kelly, Matthew. 2022. "After Summer of Mercy: More Protests, Violence, and the Murder of a Doctor." *Wichita Eagle*, July 28. www.kansas.com.

Kelsey, C. M., Nickole Medel, Carson Mullins, Danielle Dallaire, and Catherine Forestell. 2017. "An Examination of Care Practices of Pregnant Women Incarcerated in Jail Facilities in the United States." *Maternal and Child Health Journal* 21(6):1260–66.

Kendall, Todd D., and Robert Tamura. 2010. "Unmarried Fertility, Crime, and Social Stigma." *Journal of Law & Economics* 53(1):185–221.

Klein, Elizabeth G., Joseph Macisco, Allison Lazard, Audrey Busho, Austin Oslock, and Brett Worly. 2020. "Framing Pregnancy-Related Smoking Cessation Messages for Women of Reproductive Age." *Addictive Behaviors Report* 12(2):100290.

Knight, Kelly Ray. 2015. addicted.pregnant.poor. Durham, NC: Duke University Press.

Kolb, Abigail, and Ted Palys. 2018. "Playing the Part: Pseudo-Families, Wives, and the Politics of Relationships in Women's Prisons in California." *Prison Journal* 98(6):678–99.

Kolind, Torsten, and Karen Duke. 2016. "Drugs in Prisons: Exploring Use, Control, Treatment, and Policy." *Drugs: Education, Prevention and Policy* 23(2):89–92.

Kramer, Camille, Karenna Thomas, Ankita Patil, Crystal M. Hayes, Carolyn B. Sufrin. 2023. "Shackling and Pregnancy Care Policies in US Prisons and Jails." *Maternal and Child Health Journal* 27(1):186–96.

Kring Villanueva, Chandra, Sarah B. From, and Georgia Lerner for the Women's Prison Association. 2009. "Mothers, Infants, and Imprisonment: A National Look at Prison Nurseries and Community-Based Alternatives." *Prison Legal News*, May. www.prisonlegalnews.org.

Kuhlik, Lauren, and Carolyn Sufrin. 2020. "Pregnancy, Systematic Disregard and Degradation, and Carceral Institutions." *Harvard Law & Policy Review* 14(2):417–66.

Lerman, Amy E., and Vesla M. Weaver. 2014. *Arresting Citizenship: The Democratic Consequences of American Crime Control*. Chicago: University of Chicago Press.

Lévesque, Sylvie, and Audrey Ferron-Parayre. 2021. "To Use or Not to Use the Term 'Obstetric Violence': Commentary on the Article by Swartz and Lappeman." *Violence Against Women* 27(8):1009–18.

Liauw, Jessica, Jessica Foran, Brigid Dineley, Dustin Costescu, and Fiona G. Kouyoumdjian. 2016. "The Unmet Contraceptive Need of Incarcerated Women in Ontario." *Journal of Obstetrics and Gynaecology Canada* 38(9):820–26.

Lieser, Mary A. 2019. "Birth behind Bars: The Difference Trauma-Informed Doula Care Can Make." *Midwifery Today* (130):34–36.

Lin, Ann C., and David R. Harris, eds. 2009. "The Colors of Poverty: Why Racial and Ethnic Disparities Exist." Policy Brief 16. National Poverty Center. www.npc.umich.edu.

Logan, Gloria. 1992. "Family Ties Take Top Priority in Women's Visiting Program." *Corrections Today* 54(6):160–61.

Lopes, Lunna, Alex Montero, Marley Presiado, and Liz Hamel. 2024. "Americans' Challenges with Health Care Costs." Kaiser Family Foundation, March 1. www.kff.org.

Lopez-Gonzales, Diorella M., and Anil K. Kopparapu. 2022. "Postpartum Care of the New Mother." Treasure Island, FL: StatPearls Publishing.

Lorde, Audre. 1984. *Sister Outsider: Essays and Speeches*. New York: Crossing Press.

Louis-Jacques, Adetola. 2024. "What I'd Like Everyone to Know about Racism in Pregnancy Care." American College of Obstetricians and Gynecologists, accessed July 31, 2024. www.acog.org.

Mallon, Gary P. 2020. "Black and Brown Children's and Families' Lives Matter: Addressing Racial Bias and Oppressive Policies and Practices in the U.S. Child Welfare System." *Child Welfare* 98(3):5–9.

Manoogian, Margaret, Joan Jurich, Yoshie Sano, and Ju-Lien Ko. 2015. "'My Kids Are More Important Than Money': Parenting Expectations and Commitment among Appalachian Low-Income Mothers." *Journal of Family Issues* 36(3):326–50.

Martin, Eric. 2017. "Hidden Consequences: The Impact of Incarceration on Dependent Children." *National Institute of Justice Journal* 278:1–7.

Martin, Joseph L., Bronwen Lichtenstein, Robert B. Jenkot, and David R. Forde. 2012. "'They Can Take Us Over Any Time They Want': Correctional Officers' Responses to Prison Crowding." *Prison Journal* 92(1):88–105.

Maruschak, Laura M. 2008. "Medical Problems of Prisoners." Bureau of Justice Statistics, April 1. https://bjs.ojp.gov.

Maruschak, Laura M., Jennifer Bronson, and Mariel Alper. 2021. "Parents in Prison and Their Minor Children, Survey of Prison Inmates, 2016." Bureau of Justice Statistics, March 30. https://bjs.ojp.gov.

Maruschak, Laura M., and Todd D. Minton. 2020. "Correctional Populations in the United States, 2017–2018." Bureau of Justice Statistics, August 27. https://bjs.ojp.gov.

McCabe, Katharine. 2022. "Criminalization of Care: Drug Testing Pregnant Patients." *Journal of Health and Social Behavior* 63(2):162–76.

McCarthy, Andrew, et al., dirs. 2013–2019. *Orange Is the New Black*, by Jenji Kohan. Tilted Productions/Lionsgate Television. Netflix.

McClelland, Gabrielle, and Robert Newell. 2008. "A Qualitative Study of the Experiences of Mothers Involved in Street-Based Prostitution and Problematic Substance Use." *Journal of Research in Nursing* 13(5):437–47.

McCorkel, Jill A. 2013. *Breaking Women: Gender, Race, and the New Politics of Imprisonment*. New York: New York University Press.

McIntosh, Peggy. 1989. "White Privilege: Unpacking the Invisible Knapsack." *Peace and Freedom*, July/August: 10–12.

Metcalf, Jerry. 2018. "A Day in the Life of a Prisoner." The Marshall Project, July 12. www.themarshallproject.org.

Michalsen, Venezia, and Jeanne Flavin. 2014. "Not All Women Are Mothers: Addressing the Invisibility of Women under the Control of the Criminal Justice System Who Do Not Have Children." *Prison Journal* 94(3):328–46.

Mignon, Sylvia I., and Paige Ransford. 2012. "Mothers in Prison: Maintaining Connections with Children." *Social Work in Public Health* 27(1–2):69–88.

Mipro, Rachel. 2024. "Kansas Women's Prison Could Build Nursery under New Legislation." *Kansas Reflector*, February 19. https://kansasreflector.com.

Miranda, Leticia, Vince Dixon, and Cecilia Reyes. 2015. "How States Handle Drug Use during Pregnancy." *Pro Publica*, September 30. https://projects.propublica.org.

Morgan, Lynn M., and Elizabeth F. S. Roberts. 2012. "Reproductive Governance in Latin America." *Anthropology & Medicine* 19(2):241–54.

Mortazavi, Forough, and Arash Akaberi. 2016. "Worries of Pregnant Women: Testing the Farsi Cambridge Worry Scale." *Scientifica* 4:1–10.

Mughal, Saba, Yusra Azhar, and Waquar Siddiqui. 2021. *Postpartum Depression*. Treasure Island, FL: StatPearls Publishing.

Mukamal, Debbie. 2023. "SLS Report Analyzes How Women Incarcerated for Killing Their Abusers Fare in the Criminal Legal System." *Stanford Lawyer Magazine*, July 17. https://law.stanford.edu.

Mulligan, Carly. 2019. "Staying Together: Mothers and Babies in Prison." *British Journal of Midwifery* 27(7):436–41.

Murkoff, Heidi. 2016. *What to Expect When You're Expecting*. 5th ed. New York: Workman Publishing.

Murphy, Sheigla, and Marsha Rosenbaum. 1998. *Pregnant Women on Drugs: Combating Stereotypes and Stigma*. New Brunswick, NJ: Rutgers University Press.

Mwase-Musicha, Loveness, Michael G. Chipeta, Judith Stephenson, and Jennifer A. Hall. 2022. "How Do Women Prepare for Pregnancy in a Low-Income Setting? Prevalence and Associated Factors." *PLoS One* 17(3):1–11.

Namey, Emily E., and Anne Drapkin Lyerly. 2010. "The Meaning of 'Control' for Childbearing Women in the US." *Social Science & Medicine* 71(4):769–76.

National Institutes of Health. 2010. "Panel Questions 'VBAC Bans,' Advocates Expanded Delivery Options for Women." National Institutes of Health, March 10. www.nih.gov.

National Resource Center on Justice Involved Women. 2016. "Fact Sheet on Justice Involved Women in 2016." National Resource Center on Justice Involved Women, accessed July 31, 2024. https://cjinvolvedwomen.org.

Negron, Rennie, Anika Martin, Meital Almog, Amy Balbierz, and Elizabeth A. Howell. 2014. "Social Support during the Postpartum Period: Mothers' Views on Needs, Expectations, and Mobilization of Support." *Maternal and Child Health Journal* 17(4):616–23.

Nelson, Roxanne. 2006. "Laboring in Chains: Shackling Pregnant Inmates, Even during Childbirth, Still Happens." *American Journal of Nursing* 106(10):25–26.

Newport, Frank. 2017. "Middle-Class Identification in U.S. at Pre-Recession Levels." *Gallup News*, June 21. http://news.gallup.com.

Njoku, Anuli, Marian Evans, Lillian Nimo-Sefah, and Jonell Bailey. 2023. "Listen to the Whispers before They Become Screams: Addressing Black Maternal Morbidity and Mortality in the United States." *Healthcare* 11(3):438.

Njoroge, Wanjikũ, Lauren K. White, and Rebecca Waller, et al. 2022. "Association of COVID-19 and Endemic Systemic Racism with Postpartum Anxiety and Depression among Black Birthing Individuals." *JAMA Psychiatry* 79(6):600–609.

Oakley, Ann. 1980. *Becoming a Mother.* New York: Schocken Books.
Obstetrics and Gynecology Risk Research Group, Rebecca Kukla, Miriam Kuppermann, Margaret Little, Anne Drapkin Lyerly, Lisa M. Mitchell, Elizabeth M. Armstrong, and Lisa Harris. 2009. "Finding Autonomy in Birth." *Bioethics* 23(1):1–8.
Ocen, Priscilla A. 2012. "Punishing Pregnancy: Race, Incarceration, and the Shackling of Pregnant Prisoners." *California Law Review* 100(5):1239–1312.
O'Hara, Mary Emily. 2017. "Here's Why Women Keep Dressing like 'Handmaids' at Statehouses." *NBC News*, June 21. www.nbcnews.com.
Okwori, Glory, Michael G. Smith, Kate Beatty, Amal Khoury, Liane Ventura, and Nathan Hale. 2022. "Geographic Differences in Contraception Provision and Utilization among Federally Funded Family Planning Clinics in South Carolina and Alabama." *Journal of Rural Health* 38(3):639–49.
Ondeck, Michele. 2014. "Healthy Birth Practice #2: Walk, Move Around, and Change Positions throughout Labor." *Journal of Perinatal Education* 23(4):188–93.
O'Neill Hayes, Tara, and Margaret Barnhorst. 2020. "Incarceration and Poverty in the United States." American Action Forum, June 30. www.americanactionforum.org.
Ortiz, Jennifer M., and Hayley Jackey. 2019. "The System Is Not Broken, It Is Intentional: The Prisoner Reentry Industry as Deliberate Structural Violence." *Prison Journal* 99(4):484–503.
Paltrow, Lynn M. 2013. "*Roe v Wade* and the New Jane Crow: Reproductive Rights in the Age of Mass Incarceration." *American Journal of Public Health* 103(1):17–21.
Paltrow, Lynn M., and Jeanne Flavin. 2013. "Arrests of and Forced Interventions on Pregnant Women in the United States, 1973–2005: Implications for Women's Legal Status and Public Health." *Journal of Health Politics, Policy, and Law* 38(2):299–343.
———. 2014. "Pregnant, and No Civil Rights." *New York Times*, November 7. www.nytimes.com.
Patient-Centered Outcomes Research Institute. 2023. "Postpartum Care for Women up to One Year after Birth (a Systematic Review)." Patient-Centered Outcomes Research Institute, accessed July 31, 2024. www.pcori.org.
Peeler, Mary, Kevin Fiscella, Mishka Terplan, and Carolyn Sufrin. 2019. "Best Practices for Pregnant Incarcerated Women with Opioid Use Disorder." *Journal of Correctional Health Care* 25(1):4–14.
Pendleton, Virginia, Jennifer B. Saunders, and Rebecca Shlafer. 2020. "Corrections Officers' Knowledge and Perspectives of Maternal and Child Health Policies and Programs for Pregnant Women in Prison." *Health and Justice* 8(1):1–12.
Penney, Veronica. 2019. "An Inmate Was Raped, Impregnated by a Guard. He was Busted. His Coworkers Blame, Harass Her." *Miami Herald*, September 27. www.miamiherald.com.
Perrotte, Violette, Arun Chaudhary, and Annekathryn Goodman. 2020. "'At Least Your Baby Is Healthy': Obstetric Violence or Disrespect and Abuse in Childbirth Occurrence Worldwide; A Literature Review." *Open Journal of Obstetrics and Gynecology* 10(11):1544–62.

Petersilia, Joan. 2003. *When Prisoners Come Home: Parole and Prisoner Reentry*. New York: Oxford University Press.

Peterson, Bryce, Megan Kizzort, Kim KiDeuk, and Rochisha Shukla. 2021. "Prison Contraband: Prevalence, Impacts, and Interdiction Strategies." *Corrections* 8(5):428–45.

Pew Research Center. 2014. "Religious Landscape Study: Adults in the Midwest." Pew Research Center, accessed July 31, 2024. www.pewresearch.org.

Piejko, Ewa. 2006. "The Postpartum Visit: Why Wait 6 Weeks?" *Australian Family Physician* 35(9):674–78.

Poehlmann-Tynan, Julie. 2020. "Reuniting Young Children with Their Incarcerated Parents." *Zero to Three* 40(4):30–39.

Port City Daily Staff. 2021. "Cooper Signs Pregnant Prisoner Protection Bill into Law, Supported by Unlikely Coalition." *Port City Daily*, September 12. https://portcitydaily.com.

Presser, Lois, and Sveinung Sandberg, eds. 2015. *Narrative Criminology: Understanding Stories of Crime*. New York: New York University Press.

Price, Joshua M. 2015. *Prison and Social Death*. New Brunswick, NJ: Rutgers University Press.

Price, Kimala. 2010. "What Is Reproductive Justice? How Women of Color Activists Are Redefining the Pro-Choice Paradigm." *Meridians: Feminism, Race, Transnationalism* 10(2):42–65.

Quinn, Audrey. 2014. "In Labor, in Chains." *New York Times*, July 26. www.nytimes.com.

Rabuy, Bernadette, and Daniel Kopf. 2015. "Prisons of Poverty: Uncovering the Preincarceration Incomes of the Imprisoned." Prison Policy Initiative, July 9. www.prisonpolicy.org.

Rasheed, Parveen, and Latifa S. Al-Sowielem. 2003. "Health Education Needs for Pregnancy: A Study among Women Attending Primary Health Centers." *Journal of Family & Community Medicine* 10(1):31–38.

Redko, Cristina, Richard C. Rapp, and Robert G. Carlson. 2008. "Waiting Time as a Barrier to Treatment Entry: Perceptions of Substance Users." *Journal of Drug Issues* 36(4):831–52.

Reeve, Kesia. 2011. "The Hidden Truth about Homelessness: Experiences of Single Homelessness in England." Centre for Regional and Economic Research, accessed July 31, 2024. www.crisis.org.

Reid, John Nicholas. 2018. "The Birth of the Prison: The Functions of Imprisonment in Early Mesopotamia." *Journal of Ancient Near Eastern History* 3(2):81–115.

Rich, Adrienne. 1976. *Of Woman Born: Motherhood as Experience and Institution*. New York: Norton.

Richie, Beth E. 1996. *Compelled to Crime: The Gender Entrapment of Battered Black Women*. New York: Routledge.

———. 2012. *Arrested Justice: Black Women, Violence, and America's Prison Nation*. New York: New York University Press.

Richie, Beth E., and Kayla M. Martensen. 2020. "Resisting Carcerality, Embracing Abolition: Implications for Social Work Practice." *Affilia: Journal of Women and Social Work* 35(1):12–16.

Riessman, Catherine Kohler. 2008. *Narrative Methods for the Human Sciences*. Thousand Oaks, CA: Sage Publications.

Rios, Victor. 2011. *Punished: Policing the Lives of Black and Latino Boys*. New York: New York University Press.

Rivas, Jorge. 2013. "California Prisons Caught Sterilizing Female Inmates without Approval." *ABC News*, July 8. https://abcnews.go.com.

Roberts, Dorothy. 1997. *Killing the Black Body: Race, Reproduction, and the Meaning of Liberty*. New York: Random House/Pantheon.

———. 2002. *Shattered Bonds: The Color of Child Welfare*. New York: Basic Books/Civitas.

———. 2019. "How the Child Welfare System Polices Black Mothers." *Scholar & Feminist Online* 15(3).

———. 2022. *Torn Apart: How the Child Welfare System Destroys Black Families—and How Abolition Can Build a Safer World*. New York: Basic Books.

Roberts, Kennedy, Bernice Roberts, Christopher Clomus Mathis, and Angela K. Woods. 2007. "African Americans and Their Distrust of the Health Care System: Healthcare for Diverse Populations." *Journal of Cultural Diversity* 14(2):56–60.

Rodriguez Carey, Rebecca. 2019. "'Who's Gonna Take My Baby?': Narratives of Creating Placement Plans among Formerly Pregnant Inmates." *Women & Criminal Justice* 29(6):385–407.

Romagnoli, Amy, and Glenda Wall. 2012. "'I Know I'm a Good Mom': Young, Low-Income Mothers' Experiences with Risk Perception, Intensive Parenting Ideology, and Parenting Education Programmes." *Health, Risk & Society* 14(3):273–89.

Rosenstein, Melissa G., Laura Norrell, Anna Altshuler, William Grobman, Anjali Kaimal, and Miriam Kuppermann. 2019. "Hospital Bans on Trial of Labor after Cesarean and Antepartum Transfer of Care." *Birth* 46(4):574–82.

Sandberg, Sveinung, and Thomas Ugelvik. 2016. "The Past, Present, and Future of Narrative Criminology: A Review and an Invitation." *Crime, Media, Culture: An International Journal* 12(2):129–36.

Sawyer, Wendy. 2017. "How Much Do Incarcerated People Earn in Each State?" Prison Policy Initiative, April 10. www.prisonpolicy.org.

Saxena, Preeta, and Nena Messina. 2021. "Trajectories of Victimization to Violence among Incarcerated Women." *Health and Justice* 9(1):1–12.

Schochet, Leila. 2019. "The Child Care Crisis Is Keeping Women out of the Workforce." Center for American Progress, March 28. www.americanprogress.org.

Schoneich, Sebastian, Melissa Plegue, Victoria Waidley, Katharine McCabe, Justine Wu, P. Paul Chandanabhumma, Carol Shetty, Christopher J. Frank, and Lauren Oshman. 2023. "Incidence of Newborn Drug Testing and Variations by Birthing Parent Race and Ethnicity before and after Recreational Cannabis Legalization." *Journal of the American Medical Association Network Open* 6(3):1–38.

Schroeder, Carole, and Janice Bell. 2005. "Doula Birth Support for Incarcerated Pregnant Women." *Public Health Nursing* 22(1):53–58.
Scott, Marvin B., and Stanford M. Lyman. 1968. "Accounts." *American Sociological Review* 33(1):46–62.
Sesame Workshop. N.d. "Incarceration." Sesame Workshop, accessed July 31, 2024. https://sesameworkshop.org.
Sharpe, Gilly. 2015. "Precarious Identities: 'Young' Motherhood, Desistance, and Stigma." *Criminology & Criminal Justice* 15(4):407–22.
Shelburne, Beth. 2018. "Alabama Women's Prison Opens First of Its Kind Lactation Room." *WAFB*, November 16. www.wbrc.com.
Shlafer, Rebecca J., Laurel Davis, Lauren A. Hindt, Lorie S. Goshin, and Erica Gerrity. 2018. "Intention and Initiation of Breastfeeding among Women Who Are Incarcerated." *Nursing for Women's Health* 22(1):64–78.
Shlafer, Rebecca J., Rachel R. Hardeman, and Elizabeth A. Carlson. 2019. "Reproductive Justice for Incarcerated Mothers and Advocacy for Their Infants and Young Children." *Infant Mental Health Journal* 40(5):725–41.
Shlafer, Rebecca J., Wendy Hellerstedt, Molly Secor-Turner, Erica Gerrity, and Rae Baker. 2015. "Doulas' Perspectives about Providing Support to Incarcerated Women: A Feasibility Study." *Public Health Nursing* 32(4):316–26.
Shlafer, Rebecca J., Jamie Stang, Danielle Dallaire, Catherine A. Forestell, and Wendy Hellerstedt. 2019. "Best Practices for Nutrition Care of Pregnant Women in Prison." *Journal of Correctional Health Care* 23(3):297–304.
Sichel, Dana L. 2008. "Giving Birth in Shackles: A Constitutional and Human Rights Violation." *Journal of Gender, Social Policy & the Law* 16(2):223–55.
Siegel, Jane A. 2011. *Disrupted Childhoods: Children of Women in Prison*. New Brunswick, NJ: Rutgers University Press.
Simon, Jonathan. 2007. "Rise of the Carceral State." *Social Research* 74(2):471–508.
Solinger, Rickie. 2005. *Pregnancy and Power: A Short History of Reproductive Politics in America*. New York: New York University Press.
Southall, Ashley. 2019. "She Was Forced to Give Birth in Handcuffs: Now Her Case Is Changing Police Rules." *New York Times*, July 3. www.nytimes.com.
State of Minnesota. 2021. "Governor Walz Signs Healthy Starts Act into Law to Support Health, Wellbeing of Incarcerated Mothers, Children." State of Minnesota, May 14. https://mn.gov.
Stemen, Don. 2017. "The Prison Paradox: More Incarceration Will Not Make Us Safer." Vera Institute of Justice, July. www.vera.org.
Stuebe, Alison. 2009. "The Risks of Not Breastfeeding for Mothers and Infants." *Reviews in Obstetrics & Gynecology* 2(4): 222–31.
Sufrin, Carolyn. 2017. *Jailcare: Finding the Safety Net for Women behind Bars*. Berkeley: University of California Press.
———. 2019. "When the Punishment Is Pregnancy: Carceral Restriction of Abortion in the United States." *Cultural Anthropology* 34(1):34–40.

Sufrin, Carolyn, Lauren Beal, Jennifer Clarke, Rachel Jones, and William D. Mosher. 2019. "Pregnancy Outcomes in US Prisons, 2016 to 2017." *American Journal of Public Health* 109(5):799–805.

Sufrin, Carolyn, Rachel K. Jones, Lauren Beal, William D. Mosher, and Suzanne Bell. 2021. "Abortion Access for Incarcerated People: Incidence of Abortion and Policies at U.S. Prisons and Jails." *Obstetrics & Gynecology* 138(3):330–37.

Sufrin, Carolyn, Lauren Sutherland, Lauren Beal, Mishka Terplan, Carl Latkin, and Jennifer G. Clarke. 2020. "Opioid Use Disorder Incidence and Treatment among Incarcerated Pregnant Women in the United States: Results from a National Surveillance Study." *Addiction* 115(11):2057–65.

Sutherland, Suzanne M. 1997. "Pregnancy: A Social Construction." MA thesis, Department of Sociology, Lakehead University, Thunder Bay, Canada, accessed July 31, 2024. www.collectionscanada.gc.ca.

Sutton, Caitlin Dooley, and Brendan Carvalho. 2017. "Optimal Pain Management after Cesarean Delivery." *Anesthesiology Clinics* 35(1):107–24.

Thomas, Karenna, Lynn Kao, Trisha Parayil, E. Sommers, B. Lulseged, A. Moss, Camille Kramer, Rebecca Shlafer, and Carolyn Sufrin. 2024. "Anti-Shackling Legislation and Resource Table." Advocacy and Research on Reproductive Wellness of Incarcerated People. Johns Hopkins University School of Medicine Department of Gynecology and Obstetrics. https://arrwip.org.

Thomas, Sarah Y., and Jennifer L. Lanterman. 2019. "A National Analysis of Shackling Laws and Policies as They Relate to Pregnant Incarcerated Women." *Feminist Criminology* 14(2):263–84.

Thompson, Christie. 2023. "Fighting the High Cost of Prison Phone Calls." The Marshall Project, February 25. www.themarshallproject.org.

Thulstrup, Stephanie Heinecke, and Leena Eklund Karlsson. 2017. "Children of Imprisoned Parents and Their Coping Strategies: A Systematic Review." *Societies* 7(2):15.

Timmermans, Sarah, Vincent W. V. Jaddoe, Albert Hofman, Régine P. M. Steegers-Theunissen, and Eric A. P. Steegers. 2009. "Periconception Folic Acid Supplementation, Fetal Growth, and the Risks of Low Birth Weight and Preterm Birth: The Generation R Study." *British Journal of Nutrition* 102(5):777–85.

Travis, Jeremy. 2005. *But They All Come Back: Facing the Challenges of Prisoner Reentry*. Washington, DC: Urban Institute Press.

Travis, Jeremy, Elizabeth Cincotta McBride, and Amy L. Solomon. 2005. "Families Left Behind: The Hidden Costs of Incarceration and Reentry." Urban Institute, June. www.urban.org.

Troutman, Michele, Saima Rafique, and Torie Comeaux Plowden. 2020. "Are Higher Unintended Pregnancy Rates among Minorities a Result of Disparate Access to Contraception?" *Contraception and Reproductive Medicine* 5(16):1–6.

Tully, Kristin P., Allison M. Stuebe, and Sarah B. Verbiest. 2017. "The Fourth Trimester: A Critical Transition Period with Unmet Maternal Health Needs." *American Journal of Obstetrics and Gynecology* 217(1):37–41.

US Department of Justice. 2016. "Review of the Federal Bureau of Prisons' Medical Staffing Challenges." US Department of Justice, March 28. https://oig.justice.gov.

Varghese, Charles, and Sheethal S. Kumar. 2022. "Marginality: A Critical Review of the Concept." *Review of Development and Change* 27(1):23–41.

Villarreal, Alexandra. 2020. "Pregnant Inmates Languish in US Prisons Despite Promises of Early Release." *The Guardian*, May 22. www.theguardian.com.

Wacquant, Loïc. 2010. "Class, Race, and Hyperincarceration in Revanchist America." *Daedalus* 140(3):74–90.

Wagner, Peter, and Alexi Jones. 2019. "The Biggest Priorities for Prison and Jail Phone Justice in 40 States." Prison Policy Initiative, September 11. www.prisonpolicy.org.

Wagner, Peter, and Bernadette Rabuy. 2017. "Following the Money of Mass Incarceration." Prison Policy Initiative, January 25. www.prisonpolicy.org.

Walmsley, Roy. 2018. "World Prison Population List." Institute for Criminal Policy Research, accessed July 31, 2024. www.prisonstudies.org.

Walsh, Alison. 2016. "States Help Families Stay Together by Correcting a Consequence of the Adoption and Safe Families Act." Prison Policy Initiative, May 24. www.prisonpolicy.org.

Walters, Alicia M. 2012. "Victory: No More Shackles on Pregnant Prisoners." American Civil Liberties Union, October 5. www.aclu.org.

Wang, Jian, and Liuna Geng. 2019. "Effects of Socioeconomic Status on Physical and Psychological Health: Lifestyle as a Mediator." *International Journal of Environmental Research and Public Health* 16(2):281.

Wang, Leah. 2021. "Rise in Jail Deaths Is Especially Troubling as Jail Populations Become More Rural and More Female," Prison Policy Initiative, June 23. www.prisonpolicy.org.

———. 2022a. "Both Sides of the Bars: How Mass Incarceration Punishes Families." Prison Policy Initiative, August 11. www.prisonpolicy.org.

———. 2022b. "Chronic Punishment: The Unmet Health Needs of People in State Prisons." Prison Policy Initiative, June. www.prisonpolicy.org.

Wang, Leah, and Wanda Bertram. 2022. "New Data on Formerly Incarcerated People's Employment Reveal Labor Market Injustices." Prison Policy Initiative, February 8. www.prisonpolicy.org.

Wang, Leah, Wendy Sawyer, Tiana Herring, and Emily Widra. 2022. "Beyond the Count: A Deep Dive into State Prison Populations." Prison Policy Initiative, April. www.prisonpolicy.org.

Warner, Jennifer. 2015. "Infants in Orange: An International Model-Based Approach to Prison Nurseries." *Hastings Women Law Journal* 26(1):65–92.

Weill-Greenberg, Elizabeth, and Ethan Corey. 2024. "Locked In, Priced Out: How Prison Commissary Price-Gouging Preys on the Incarcerated." *The Appeal*, April 17. https://theappeal.org.

West, Heather C., and William J. Sabol. 2009. "Prisoners in 2007." Bureau of Justice Statistics, February 12. https://bjs.ojp.gov.

Widra, Emily. 2023. "Where People in Prison Come From: The Geography of Mass Incarceration." Prison Policy Initiative, January. www.prisonpolicy.org.

Wildeman, Christopher, and Emily A. Wang. 2017. "Mass Incarceration, Public Health, and Widening Inequality in the USA." *The Lancet* 389(10077):1464–74.

Wodahl, Eric J. 2006. "The Challenges of Prisoner Reentry from a Rural Perspective." *Western Criminology Review* 7(2):32–47.

World Health Organization. 2023. "More Than a Third of Women Experience Lasting Health Problems after Childbirth, New Research Shows." World Health Organization, December 7. www.who.int.

———. 2024. "HIV and AIDS." World Health Organization, July 27. www.who.int.

World Medical Association. 2023. "WMA Statement on Body Searches of Prisoners." World Medical Association, January 17. www.wma.net.

Zinn, Howard. 1994. *You Can't Be Neutral on a Moving Train: A Personal History of Our Times*. Boston: Beacon Press.

INDEX

AAP. *See* American Academy of Pediatrics
abortions, ix, 53, 108, 200, 223n1, 223n52; correctional facility regulations for, 41–43; criminalization of, 192; drugs and, 43–44; incarceration and, 41–43, 54; laws related to, 43
abuse: of birth father, 49, 109; family causing, 53; reproductive-justice, ix; sexual, 53, 124–25, 153, 200
accessibility: doulas, 149, 229n21; of information, 89, 91–92, 112; medical care, 74–75, 77, 121, 143; prison nursery program, 149
ACOG. *See* American College of Obstetricians and Gynecologists
addiction, 17, 35, 66, 161; methamphetamine, 2, 28, 135–36; pregnancy and, 45
Adoption and Safe Families Act (ASFA), 65, 180
adoption plans, 100–101, 107
Advocacy and Research on Reproductive Wellness of Incarcerated People, 201, 217n12
aftermath: birthing, 149, 150, 151, 152, 188; childbirth, 132, 139, 145, 149; imprisonment, 160, 209, 231n25
agents of control, 39–40, 51; carceral regime and, 4; caregivers as, 167; families as, 99
American Academy of Pediatrics (AAP), 152, 225n45
American College of Obstetricians and Gynecologists (ACOG), 31, 60, 120, 141, 143, 225n45
Arrested Justice (Richie), 10
ASFA. *See* Adoption and Safe Families Act
Atwood, Margaret, ix, 217n4
autonomy, 11, 14, 21–22; during birthing, 113; bodily, 30, 88, 116; consent during incarceration and, 118; control and, 30; food related, 68

availability: of food, 68; of prenatal care, 73, 202; of resources, 25, 30, 91, 93, 96

barriers to motherhood, 168–70
basic needs, motherhood and, 182–85, 189
Bedford Hills Correctional Facility, 97–98
birth fathers, 48–50, 51–52, 101, 102–3, 203; abuse caused by, 109
birthing, 116–17, 217n12; aftermath of, 149, 150, 151, 152, 188; autonomy related to, 113; of Black women, 119–20; control related to, 112, 125, 133–34; disparities in, 119; freedom while, 121; interventions while, 95, 114, 118, 119; maternal web of control and, 112, 114; pregnancy and, xi, 9, 10; preparation for, 79, 82, 83, 88, 96, 106; relationship with baby after, 41; shackles while, 120–23; support companions for, 125–28
birth spaces, xiii, 12, 25, 198
Black women, x, 14, 37–38; birthing and, 119–20; discrimination of, 10, 184–85; drug testing and, 65–66; imprisonment of, 17; low-income of, 7, 36; maternal mortality rates in, 109–10; medical care systems and, 75–76; *No Mercy Here* depicting, 6; poverty of, 62, 104, 105, 110; reentry for, 184; reintegration for, 184; visitations, 165–66
Black Women's Caucus (1994), 8
bodily autonomy, 32, 43, 88, 116; control and, 8; incarcerated women and, x; maternal web of control and, 21–22; pregnancy and, xi, 3, 30, 110
body, maternal, 6, 54, 88, 111
breastfeeding, during incarceration, 152–53, 154, 156–57, 158, 160. *See also* lactation
breastmilk, 152, 153, 154, 155–57, 158, 160
Bureau of Justice Statistics, US, 73, 201

255

carceral control, 11, 64, 116, 151; babies and, 25; incarceration and, 196–97; reproduction and, 4
carceral environment, 15, 36, 105–6, 157, 169, 181, 211
carceral forces, xii, 13, 25, 41, 172, 195; health improvements and, 58; incarceration influenced by, 201; maternal web of control and, 168
carcerality, 8–9, 30, 50, 57; hospitals and, 116, 130; maternal web of control and, 193–94; in prison systems, 133–34; relationship with baby and, 85. *See also specific topics*
carceral regime, x, xi, 197; agents of control in, 4
carceral state, 15, 83, 86, 167; "free world" and, 210–11; lactation and, 152; motherhood and, 179, 185–87; power of, 125, 193, 210–11; surveillance of, 96, 189
Carceral State Project, 8–9, 219n40
carceral systems, xii, 11; child welfare system and, 9–10; fears of, 39–40; medical system as, 78, 116–17, 133–34; motherhood denied by, 89; power of, xii; punishment of, 111; racism and, 13–14; reproduction control of, 191–92
care, 88, 144, 149; custodial, 175, 176–77, 181, 182, 189; maternity, 78, 115, 119, 124, 139, 202; medical, 6, 31, 73, 74–77, 115; models of, 111, 113; postpartum, 137, 139, 140–43, 145–46, 159; prenatal, 31, 59–60; technocratic, 116, 118, 140
caregivers, 45, 97–99, 102, 150, 165, 203; agents of control as, 167; babies and, 146, 157, 168–69, 170, 176–77, 180; communities and, 98; family as, 44, 81, 100, 103, 127; "ghosting" of, 230n6; plans for, 25, 82, 84, 101, 105, 106–7, 162; power of, 188
cavity searches, 77–78, 225n70
CDC. *See* Centers for Disease Control and Prevention
cellmates, xiii, 72, 143–44, 151
Center for American Progress, 231n41
Center for Reproductive Rights, 223n54
centers: community transition, 27, 162–63, 174, 205, 206; reentry, 27, 174–75, 189

Centers for Disease Control and Prevention (CDC), 225n45
cervical examinations, 117–18
cesarean section (C-section), 2, 95, 114, 118, 119, 145; correctional officers during, 124–25, 141, 143–44
childbirth, 25, 82, 133; aftermath, 139, 145, 149; correctional officers during, 111, 123, 130, 131, 137; education about, 88, 89, 92–93; inductions during, 112–14; pregnancy and, 68–69, 90, 92; in prison system, 109; release from prison and, 5; shackles during, 122, 123; surveillance during, 110, 112; trauma about, 111
childcare, 127, 231n41; in communities, 183
child protective services (CPS), 57, 61, 224n9
children, 2, 8, 9, 99, 102; health of women in prison and, 110, 157, 202; legal guardianship of, 180; reintegration and, 183
child welfare system, xii, 4, 99, 104–6; carceral systems and, 9–10; medical system and, 10, 11, 192, 195; power of, 127; surveillance by, 9, 39–40, 49–50, 179
CO. *See* correctional officers
cocaine, 28, 53, 61, 66, 94, 161
collateral consequences, 15, 18, 19
Collins, Patricia Hill, 14
communities, xii–xiii, 32, 63, 165; caregiver appointments in, 98; childcare in, 183; health and, 75, 79, 204; implications of incarceration in, 197; mass incarceration in, 197; postpartum in, 137, 140–41, 149; poverty in, 47, 105; regulation in, 42; release from prison and, 25, 163–64; reproductive care in, 207–8; rural, 27, 36, 55, 109, 172, 174, 180, 184, 195, 198; transition centers in, 27, 162–63, 174, 205, 206
concealment of incarceration, 20
consent during incarceration, 6, 9, 119, 132, 202; autonomy and, 118; formal written, 114; induction and, 113
Constitution, US, 35, 121
contraband, 63, 77, 129, 147, 224n27
control, 6, 117; agents of, 4, 39–40, 51; autonomy and, 30; birthing and, 112, 125, 133–34; bodily autonomy and, 8; carceral, 11, 64, 116, 124, 151; forces of, 37, 46; of

maternal body, 91, 191; maternal web of, xiii, 4, 5, 8–9, 10–11, 15, 38–39; postpartum and, 25; pregnancy as a means for, 3–4, 24, 83, 194–95; regulation and, 7, 15, 83; routinization and, 138, 148; surveillance and, 9
coparenting, 48
correctional administrators, 37, 112, 113, 147, 148, 154
correctional facilities, 18, 23, 31, 93, 159, 226n19; abortions in, 41–43; administrators, 37, 112, 113, 147, 148; Bedford Hills Correctional Facility, 97–98; doulas and, 131; food in, 60; Hutchinson Correctional Facility, xi; maternal web of control and, 55; South Carolina, 68; treatment in, 63
correctional officers (CO), 2, 121, 228n53; cesarean section and, 124–25, 141, 143–44; during childbirth, 111, 123, 130, 131, 137; healthcare providers and, 110, 122; postpartum care administered by, 143–44; surveillance of, 110, 120, 124–25, 154, 204; trauma caused by, 124
correctional population of women, 16, 194
counseling, 42, 148, 149; grief, 132, 148; postpartum, 148, 150, 158–59
COVID-19 pandemic, 59, 142, 198
CPS. *See* child protective services
Crenshaw, Kimberlé, 12–13, 16, 184
crimes: of birth father, 49; deliberate commitment of, 34–35; nonviolent, 15, 22, 27, 38, 121, 221n104; violent, 22, 109, 221n104
criminalization, 8; of abortion, 192; incarceration and, 33; punishment and, 7, 10; surveillance and, 83
criminal legal reform, 16, 20, 197, 199, 208, 210; data for, 220n64; mass incarceration and, 233n1
criminal legal system, 4–5, 6, 9, 14, 17, 23, 36, 98; mass incarceration and, 172; racism in, 37–38; trauma and, 28
criminal record, 61, 163, 183–84
criminology, 4; feminist, 5; narrative, 18–19, 29
C-section. *See* cesarean section
custodial care, 22, 43, 175, 176–77, 181, 182, 189; postpartum depression related to, 179–80; reunification and, 165

Davis, Angela, 197
Davis-Floyd, Robbie, 117, 121
DCF. *See* Department of Children and Families
degradation ceremony (Garfinkel), 84
Department of Children and Families (DCF), 49
depression: birth trauma and, 139; postpartum, 125, 138, 147–49, 159, 160, 179–80
detection of pregnancy, 30, 32
discrimination, 10, 183, 184–85
disparities: birthing, 119; economic, 168; healthcare, 73, 79, 142, 146; of racism, 17, 37, 65, 66, 76, 110, 122, 142
documentation of pregnancy, 84–85
domination: matrix of, 14–15, 29, 38; pregnancy subjected to, 24; surveillance and, 10
doulas, xiii, 130, 141, 145, 204, 226n21, 228n65; accessibility to, 149, 229n21; correctional facility and, 131; educators as, 94–95; fetal health related to, 131
drugs, 171–72, 186–87, 209, 231n33; abortion and, 43–44; babies on, 65; birth father and, 49; cocaine, 28, 53, 61, 66, 94, 161; methamphetamine, 2, 28, 66, 135–36; opioid epidemic, 30; during pregnancy, 7, 28, 53–54; screening for, 65; stigmas about, 62–64; testing for, 64–66, 202; treatment programs, 62–64, 79, 195, 205; war on, 16
duration of imprisonment, 96, 140, 164, 175, 188
dynamics: family, 24, 106, 163; power, x, 7, 57, 73, 111, 118, 133, 155

economic conditions of pregnant women, 33, 35; disparities of, 168; incarceration related to, 39, 164; methamphetamines influencing, 135–36. *See also* low-income; middle-class
Edin, Kathryn, 56, 57
education for incarcerated women, 87, 95, 106; about childbirth, 88, 89, 92–93; maternal web of control and, 90–92
educators: doulas as, 94–95; families as, 95–96; peers as, 92–94
Eighth Amendment, US Constitution, 35, 121

emergency room (ER), 74
empowerment, 95, 111, 206
enslavement of women, x, 6
environments: carceral, 15, 36, 105–6, 157, 169, 181, 211; hostility of, 42–43, 82; mass incarceration related to, 196; punitive, 107, 169, 197; reentry of, 171–72; reintegration and, 186
ER. *See* emergency room
examinations: cervical, 117–18; postpartum, 141–42
expectations of motherhood, 60, 90; pregnancy and, 3, 6, 56
experience of pregnancy, 51, 81–82, 83–87

Fair Labor Standards Act, US, 230n38
families, 125, 199–200; abuse in, 53; as agents of control, 99; caregivers in, 44, 81, 100, 103, 127; dynamics of, 24, 106, 163; educators as, 95–96; foster care, 104, 163, 171; incarceration impacting, 18, 21, 44–45, 46, 128; low-income, 33, 36, 126; mass incarceration altering, 17, 208; maternal web of control in, 45; nuclear, 48, 109; preservation of, 198, 203, 204–5; pseudo-, 230n35; regulation of, 9; reunification of, 172, 175–77, 178, 180, 204
fears of carceral systems, 39–40
Federal Bureau of Prisons, 75, 121
feminist criminology, 5
fetal health, 24, 54, 61, 65, 78, 87–88; doulas contributing to, 131; healthcare and, 58, 202; incarceration and, 75; shackling and, 120. *See also* prenatal care
fetal-protection laws, 7, 55, 56, 58, 64, 67, 123
First Step Act (2018), 201
first-time offender, 38, 108
fitness and motherhood, 47, 114, 165, 166–67, 181, 189
food, 13, 35, 56, 60, 67; autonomy and, 68; miscarriages related to, 69–70; networks for, 71–72; scarcity of, 68, 70–72, 78, 80, 99; social positioning related to food, 70
forced induction during childbirth, 112–14
forces: carceral, xii, 13, 25, 41, 172, 195; of control, 37, 46; of oppression, 58, 164, 196; punitive, 38, 198, 200; social, xi, 14, 30,

50, 51, 146, 160; structural, 19, 164, 194; of surveillance, 15, 35, 165, 170, 179, 180
foster care: babies placement in, 81, 99, 105, 162, 187; families, 104, 163, 171; systems, 28, 99, 101, 105, 127, 162
fourth trimester, 134, 139, 150, 160
framework, 25; incarceration stories, 193–95; intersectional, 12–13, 29, 32; reproductive justice, xii, 5, 26
freedom: "free world," xii, 17, 21, 27, 163, 182, 220n73; reproductive, ix; reproductive justice and, 3; while birthing, 121
"free world," xii, 17, 21, 27, 163, 182, 220n73; carceral state and, 210–11; incarceration compared to, 182, 195–96; motherhood and, 177–78; White women and, 76
Frye, Marilyn, 10–11
funeral for stillborn, 132

Garfinkel, Harold, 84
gate fare, 162, 230n1
"ghosting" of caregivers, 230n6
grief of incarcerated women, 3, 131, 150, 152, 158–59; counseling, 132, 148; trauma and, 132, 134

Haley, Sarah, 6
handcuffs, 112, 116, 122, 123, 128
Handmaid's Tale (Atwood), ix, 217n4
HCF. *See* Hutchinson Correctional Facility
healthcare, 11, 30, 31–32, 201–3; disparities in, 73, 79, 142, 146; fetal health and, 58, 202; incarceration and, 60–61; maternal web of control role in, 73–74; postpartum, 137, 140, 144–46, 160, 172; poverty and, 145–46; prenatal, 72–74; as privileges, 59; provider for, 60, 74, 138, 142, 143, 145; socioeconomic status and, 55, 77; White women and, 76–77
health of incarcerated women, 60, 87, 203; children and, 110, 157, 202; communities and, 75, 79, 204; complications, 144–46; disparities in, 73, 79, 142, 146; exercise regimes, 56, 60; improvements in, 54–55, 58–62, 63, 66, 68, 72; incarceration as risk to, 59; incarceration impacting, 33–34; maternal body and, 58, 66, 73, 144, 201;

maternal web of control related to, 55; mental, 55, 73, 138, 148, 159, 202; nutrition and, 66; pregnancy and, 54–55, 56, 78; pregnancy tests, 30–32, 50, 136; prenatal care, 24

Hispanic women, 76

HIV. *See* human immunodeficiency virus

homelessness, 22, 27, 61, 186, 200

hospitals: carcerality in, 116, 130; prison systems and, 125; separation of mother and babies at, 97–98, 128–29, 134; staff at, 130, 141; transportation to, 113, 114–16, 119, 203; trauma at, 132; VBAC and, 119; visitation at, 126, 127

hostility of environments, 42–43, 82

human immunodeficiency virus (HIV), 17, 28, 200, 222n3

humanization of the incarcerated, 82, 210, 233n1

Hutchinson, Kansas, xi

Hutchinson Correctional Facility (HCF), xi

hypersurveillance, 57

identity markers, 12, 58; biracial, 22, 35, 53, 62, 221n99; intersectionality and, 34

imprisonment, 19, 36, 50, 88, 184, 198; aftermath of, 160, 209, 231n25; of Black women, 17; duration of, 96, 140, 167, 175, 188; lessons as result of, 195–97; punishment and, 193

improvements, in women's health, 54–55, 58–62, 63, 66, 68, 72

incarceration during pregnancy. *See specific topics*

inclusion, social equity and, 199–201

Indigenous women, 76, 142

induction, 112–14, 118, 126

industry of prison systems, 172, 173, 197, 231n22

information, accessibility of, 89, 91–92, 112

institutionalized racism, 8, 120, 146, 168, 193; poverty and, 110, 142, 165, 168, 199, 207

intake procedures, prison system, 31, 40, 136

intensive-mothering paradigm, 47, 88, 164, 165, 170, 223n64; expectations of, 90

intergenerational poverty, 169

intersectional framework, 12–13, 29, 32

intersectionality (Crenshaw), 12–13, 33, 34; health improvements in, 58–62; nutrition and, 70

interventions, birthing: cesarean section, 2, 95, 114, 118, 119; surveillance and, 65

jobs, incarceration impacting, 30, 175, 183, 185–86, 212; in prison, 72

Kefalas, Maria, 56, 57

Kolb, Abigail, 230n35

labor, 111–13; correctional officers during, 124; delay of, 114–16; positions during, 117; shackles during, 2, 3, 11, 116, 120–23

lactation, 139, 155, 156, 160; carceral state and, 152; regulation of, 153; rooms for, 73, 157–58, 205; support for, 154

Lamaze course, 91, 94

law enforcement, 35, 49; probation and parole, 39

laws: abortion, 43; fetal-protection, 7, 55, 56, 58, 64, 67, 123

lessons as result of imprisonment, 195–97, 231n25

low-income, 51, 87, 106; Black women, 7, 36; of color, 7, 50, 104, 189; families, 33, 36, 126; White women, 14, 33. *See also* poverty

marginalization, 13, 35, 219n53; of White women, 77; women and, 29, 32, 33, 56, 70

mass incarceration, x, 3, 8, 16, 194; in communities, 197; criminal legal reform and, 233n1; criminal legal system and, 172; environments allowing, 196; families altered by, 17, 208; maternal web of control and, 173

maternal body, 6, 54, 88, 111; control of, 91, 191; health of, 58, 67, 73, 144, 146, 201, 204

maternal incarceration, 19, 65, 204; stigmas of, 46–47, 51, 90, 180, 181, 210, 223n65

maternal-infant bond, 149, 157, 168–70, 188, 205; preservation of, 158, 166; trauma and, 83

maternal mortality rates, x, 76, 89, 95, 203; Black women, 109–10 maternal web of control, xiii, 4, 5, 8–9, 15, 38–39; birthing and, 112, 114; bodily autonomy and, 21–22; carceral forces and, 168; carcerality and, 193–94; correctional facility and, 55; disguises of, 195; drug screening and, 65; education and, 90–92; families contribution to, 45; Frye on, 10–11; health related to, 55; incarceration and, 24, 29; mass incarceration and, 173; motherhood and, xii, 40, 163–64, 192–93; postpartum and, 139; power and, 12; pregnancy and, 30, 192–93; resistance to, 129–31; role of healthcare in, 73–74; systemic poverty and, 199; vulnerability to, 14; women resisting, 72

maternal web of support, 197–99, 207

maternity care, 78, 115, 119, 124, 139, 202

matrices of oppression, 7, 38, 112, 148, 186

matrix of domination (Collins), 14–15, 29, 38

medical attention during incarceration, 60, 73, 74–77, 115

medical care systems, 6, 31, 73, 74–77, 115; accessibility to, 74–75, 77, 143; Black women and, 75–76, 137–38; health complications due to, 144–46; labor and, 114–16

medical instruments, 75, 111

medical models of care, 111, 113

medical systems, xi, xii, 25, 57, 65; breastfeeding hindered by, 154; as carceral system, 78, 116–17, 133, 134; child welfare, 10, 11, 192, 195; induction practices in, 112–14; prison system and, 12, 25, 133, 142, 145, 153, 154, 156

mental health, 17, 55, 73, 138, 148, 159, 202

methamphetamines: addiction to, 2, 28, 66, 135–36; economic conditions of pregnant women and, 135–36

middle-class: pregnancy rituals and, 82; women in, 22, 35–36, 37, 47, 48

Midwest, 2, 27; incarcerations of women in, 23, 42; prisons in, 19, 206; reproductive justices, 44

miscarriage, 74, 76, 225n63, 228n67; food related, 69–70; stillbirth and, 58, 75, 131–32, 147, 148, 149

Morgan, Lynn M., 5

mortality, maternal, x, 76, 89, 95, 110, 118, 203

motherhood: barriers to, 168–70; basic needs and, 182–85, 189; carceral state and, 179, 185–87; carceral systems denying, 89; challenges of, 178–80; education and, 89; expectations of, 60, 90; fitness and, 47, 114, 165, 166–67, 181, 189; "free world" and, 177–78; maternal web of control and, xii, 40, 163–64, 192–93; policing of, 56; postpartum depression and, 147; pregnancy and, xi, 40–41; preparation for, 24–25, 82, 85, 87, 93–94, 95; preservation of, 187–88; surveillance of, 165–67

narrative criminology, 18–19, 29

National Commission on Correctional Health Care (NCCHC), 31, 66, 73

National Commission on Correctional Health Care Guidelines, 31

national data on prison systems, 201, 232n8; criminal legal reform and, 220n64

NCCHC. *See* National Commission on Correctional Health Care

news: of incarceration, 37; of pregnancy, 28, 34, 39, 40, 44–46, 51, 55, 83

Nixon, Richard, 16

No Mercy Here (Haley), 6

nonviolent crimes, 15, 22, 27, 38, 121, 221n104

nuclear family, 48, 109

nutrition during pregnancy, 60, 66–70, 71; in breastmilk, 155, 156, 157

obstetricians (OB), 74; American College of Obstetricians and Gynecologists, 60

obstetric violence, xi, xii, 117–20, 129, 203, 217n15

opioid epidemic, 30; use disorder, 62

oppression, 14, 112, 199; forces of, 58, 164, 196; privilege and, 13; reproductive, 8, 24, 26, 61; systems of, 8, 29, 142, 192

pain medication during incarceration, 144–45, 148–49

Palys, Ted, 230n35

panopticon, 7, 57, 194

parole officers, 28, 39, 198, 206; supervision of, 22, 174, 176, 189, 217n10, 231n33

peers: as educators, 92–94; support of, 47, 63, 71, 92–93, 95, 104, 150–52, 204; White women as, 37. *See also* cellmates
phone calls, visitations and, 87, 97, 165, 170, 175, 203
plans, 98; adoption, 100–101, 107; caregiver, 25, 82, 84, 101, 105, 106–7, 162; reunification, 49
policing systems, 9, 29–30, 57, 104, 193, 196; of motherhood, 56
The Politics of Reality (Frye), 10–11
postpartum period, 10, 21, 217n13, 229n21; care during, 137, 139, 140–43, 145–46, 159; checkup, 138; in communities, 137, 140–41, 149; control and, 25; correctional officers administering, 143–44; counseling for, 148, 150, 158–59; depression, 125, 138, 146–49, 159, 160, 179–80; examinations, 141–42; fourth trimester, 134, 139, 150, 160; healthcare, 137, 140, 144–46, 160, 172; maternal web of control and, 139; prenatal care and, 73; punishment during, 139, 141; screenings, 142
poverty, 34, 39, 51, 185, 222n27; Black women in, 104, 105, 110; of color, 58, 59, 189; communities in, 47, 105; healthcare and, 145–46; institutionalized racism and, 110, 142, 165, 168, 199, 207; intergenerational, 169; White women in, 79, 119. *See also* systemic poverty
power, 117; carceral state, 125, 193, 210–11; carceral systems in, xii; of caregivers, 188; of child welfare system, 127; dynamics of, x, 7, 57, 73, 111, 118, 133, 155; knowledge as, 88, 91–92; maternal web of control and, 12
pregnancy: addiction and, 45; birthing, xi, 9, 10; bodily autonomy during, xi, 3, 30, 110; breastfeeding and, 152–53, 154, 156–57, 158, 160; childbirth and, 68–69, 90, 92; control and, 3–4, 24, 83, 194–95; detection of, 30, 32; documentation of, 84–85; domination over, 24; drug use during, 7, 28, 53–54; education about, 87–89; experience of, 51, 81–82, 83–87; fourth trimester, 134, 139, 150, 160; health, 54–55, 56, 78; Lamaze course for, 91, 94; maternal web of control and, 30, 40–41; news of, 28, 34, 39, 40, 44–46, 51, 55, 83; nutrition during, 60, 66–70, 71; preparation for, 83, 85, 90, 93; prison system, 4, 23; punishment, 5–8, 67; reframing of, 43–44; regulation of, 8, 83; rituals of, 82, 85, 107; shackling during, 120–22; stories of, xii–xiii, 19–23; surveillance of, 56–58; tests for, 30–32, 50, 136; as turning point, 55–56, 62, 78, 83, 87. *See also specific topics*
prenatal care, 31, 59–60; availability of, 73, 202; health, 24; healthcare for, 72–74; postpartum and, 73; punishment related to, 57–58; social positioning and, 60; White women and, 77. *See also* fetal health
preparation: birthing, 79, 82, 83, 88, 96, 106; motherhood, 24–25, 82, 85, 87, 93–94, 95; pregnancy, 83, 85, 90, 93
preservation: of families, 198, 203, 204–5; of maternal-infant bond, 158, 166; of motherhood, 187–88; of reproductive rights, 8
Presser, Lois, 18
primary custodial parent, 17
prison nursery program, 93, 96, 97–98, 103–4, 167, 200, 205; accessibility to, 149; benefits of, 157–58
Prison Rape Elimination Act, 78
prison system, US, x–xii, 9, 17, 37–38; carcerality in, 133–34; cavity searches in, 77–78, 225n70; cellmates in, xiii, 72, 143–44, 151; childbirth in, 109; data collection on, 201, 232n8; Federal Bureau of Prisons, 75, 121; food in, 67–70; food networks in, 71–72; history of, 15–16; hospitals and, 125; industry of, 172, 173, 197, 231n22; intake procedures, 31, 40, 136; interviews of women in, 22–23; medical systems and, 12, 25, 133, 142, 145, 153, 154, 156; Midwest, 19, 206; pregnancy in, 1–2, 4, 23, 178; prison nursery program, 93, 96, 97–98, 103–4, 167, 200, 205; Prison Rape Elimination Act, 78; profit of, 172–73; pseudo-families in, 230n35; refuge and safety in, 34–36, 162; release from, 2, 19, 22, 27, 171; reproduction and, 19; in rural areas, 115–16; safety net and, 14–15, 34, 62, 69, 167, 171; searches conducted in, 77–78, 225n70;

prison system (*cont.*)
   security counts in, 115; sentence length in, 22, 188–89, 230n14; sleeping arrangements in, 229n23; subculture within, 19, 34, 64, 71–72, 152, 221n93, 226n19; transportation to, 102, 140; as turning point, 55–56, 62, 78, 83, 87
privileges, 21, 46, 93, 203; healthcare as, 59; oppression and, 13; visitation, 44, 165, 166; White women having, 28, 184, 231n50
probation, 28, 38, 53–54, 217n10, 220n65, 221n2; law enforcement and, 39
programs, 90, 150; drug treatment, 63, 79; education, 95, 106; reentry, 171, 172–73
Promises I Can Keep (Edin and Kefalas), 56
prostitution, 28, 80, 161, 171, 222n26
pseudo-families in prison systems, 230n35
pumping for breastmilk, 152, 153, 154, 157, 158
punishment: carcerality and, 9; carceral systems and, 111; criminalization and, 7, 10; imprisonment and, 193; during postpartum, 139, 141; pregnancy and, 5–8, 67; prenatal care and, 57–58; reproduction and, 124, 129, 191–92, 193
punitive, environment, 107, 169, 197
punitive forces, 38, 198, 200
punitive policies, 9, 14, 16, 194
punitive system, 36, 51, 97

Rabuy, Bernadette, 217n10, 231n22
racism, 167; carceral systems and, 13–14; in criminal legal systems, 37–38; disparities related to, 17, 37, 65, 66, 76, 110, 122, 142; gendered racism, 6, 14, 38, 66, 76, 194; institutionalized, 8, 120, 146, 168, 193; systemic poverty and, 14, 110, 142, 199; visitation and, 165–66
Reagan, Ronald, 16
recidivism, 172, 200, 205, 206, 209, 231n19
reentry, 171–73, 177, 182, 186, 187–88, 206; Black women and, 184; centers for, 27, 174–75, 189; period of, 175, 176, 185. *See also* release from prison
reform: correctional, xiii, 23, 98, 201; criminal legal, 16, 20, 197, 199, 208, 210; reentry, 173, 206; rehabilitation and, 172

refuge and safety, prison system as, 34–36, 162
regimes: carceral, x, xi, 4, 197; pregnancy belonging to, 6
regulations: in communities, 42; control and, 7, 15, 42, 83; families and, 9; lactation, 153; pregnancy, 8, 83; reproduction, 15
rehabilitation, reform and, 172. *See also* reentry
reintegration, 173, 179, 189, 206–8, 218n3; with babies, 139; of Black women, 184; childcare and, 183; environments contributing to, 186; incarceration and, 182; support for, 163, 172, 176
relationship with baby: birthing and, 41; carcerality and, 85; incarceration impacting, 21
release from prison, 2, 19, 22, 27, 171; childbirth and, 5; community after, 25, 163–64; interviews after, 21
reproduction, 8, 57; carceral control and, 4; carcerality and, 50; carceral systems and, 191–92; Center for Reproductive Rights, 223n54; prison systems and, 19; punishment and, 124, 129, 191–92, 193; regulation of, 15; *Roe v. Wade* and, ix, x, 7, 41, 43, 191–92; surveillance of, 5
reproductive care, 8; in communities, 207–8
reproductive freedom, ix
reproductive governance, 5
reproductive justice, 8, 164; abuse, ix; framework for, xii, 5, 26; freedom and, 3; Midwest and, 44
reproductive oppression, 8, 24, 26, 61
reproductive rights, ix, x, xii, 8
resistance to maternal web of control, 129–31
resources: availability of, 25, 30, 47, 91, 93, 96; lactation, 153
reunification, 25, 99, 170, 189; custodial care and, 165; families, 172, 175–77, 178, 180, 204; plans for, 49
reverence of pregnancy and motherhood, 40–41
Richie, Beth, 10
rights: abortion, ix; reproductive, ix
rituals of pregnancy, 82, 85, 107

Roberts, Dorothy, 9, 101–2
Roberts, Elizabeth, 5
Roe v. Wade, ix, x, 7, 41, 43, 191–92
rooms for lactation, 157–58, 205
routinization, control and, 138, 148
rural areas: communities in, 27, 34, 36, 55, 109, 174, 180, 183, 195, 198; Midwest, 19; prison systems in, 70, 78, 115–16; spiritual undertones in, 61; stigmas in, 20, 62

safety net, prison systems as, 14–15, 34, 62, 69, 167, 171
Sandberg, Sveinung, 18
searches in prison systems: cavity, 77–78, 225n70; strip, 77–78, 114, 225n70
sentence length, 22, 188–89, 230n14
separation of mothers and babies, 97–98, 128–29, 134, 164; carceral consequences of, 146–47
Sesame Street, 207
sexual abuse, 53, 124–25, 153, 200
sex work, 7, 48, 69, 80, 161–62
shackles, 128, 130, 133, 202–3; birthing with, 120–23; laboring with, 2, 3, 11, 116, 120–23; during transportation, 120
Shattered Bonds (Roberts), 9
slavery, x, 6, 15, 191, 193, 194
social equity, inclusion and, 199–201
social forces, xi, 14, 30, 50, 51, 146, 160
social positioning, 12, 21, 45, 46; food related to, 70; prenatal care and, 60
social safety net, 30, 34, 35, 167
social service agency, 1, 20, 197, 206
social worker, 101, 127, 151, 162
socioeconomic status, 21, 87, 106, 119, 221n102; healthcare and, 55, 77
solitary confinement, 19–20, 72, 93, 152, 203–4, 225n69
South Carolina, correctional facility in, 68
stigmas, 48, 103, 104, 123, 178, 219n27; drug, 62–64; incarceration, 20, 33, 46–47, 180–81, 231n51; maternal incarceration, 46, 51, 89–90, 180, 181, 210, 223n65; in rural areas, 20
stillbirth, 218n2; miscarriage and, 58, 75, 131–32, 147, 148, 149

stillborn baby, 2–3, 74–75, 132, 148
storytelling: art of, 21; narrative criminology and, 18–19
stress related to incarceration, 59, 60–61, 124, 169
strip searches, 77–78, 114, 225n70
structural forces, 19, 164, 194
subculture within prison systems, 19, 34, 64, 71–72, 152, 221n93, 226n19
Sufrin, Carolyn, 4, 35, 201, 217n12, 218n2, 223n52, 228n67
suicide, 136–37, 161
support, 203–4; companions for birthing, 125–28; lactation, 154; maternal web of, 197–99, 207; peers as, 47, 63, 71, 92–93, 95, 104, 150–52, 204; for reintegration, 163, 172, 176; transitional, 173; women as systems of, 149, 150–52
Supreme Court, US, ix
surveillance: carceral state, 96, 189; childbirth and, 110, 112; child welfare system and, 9, 39–40, 49–50, 179; control and, 9; of correctional officers, 110, 120, 124–25, 154, 204; criminalization and, 83; domination and, 10; forces of, 15, 35, 165, 170, 179, 180; hypersurveillance, 57; interventions and, 65; of motherhood, 165–67; pregnancy under, 56–58; of reproduction, 5
Sutherland, Suzanne, 6
systemic poverty, 14, 36, 40, 172; maternal web of control and, 199; racism and, 14, 110, 142, 199
systems: carceral, xii, 11; child welfare, xii, 4, 9–10, 39–40, 104–6, 127; criminal legal, 4–5, 6, 9, 14, 17, 23; foster care, 28, 99, 101, 105, 127, 161, 162, 187; medical, xi, xii, 25, 57, 65, 78, 133–34; oppression, 8, 29, 142, 192; policing, 9, 29–30, 57, 104, 193, 196; prison, x–xi, xi–xiii; punitive, 36, 51, 97; women as support, 149, 150–52

tests: drug, 64–66, 202; pregnancy, 30–32, 50, 136
TOLAC. *See* trial of labor after cesarean
Torn Apart (Roberts), 9
transitional support, 173

transition centers, 162–63, 206; community, 27, 174, 205. *See also* reentry
transportation, 18, 102, 150, 168, 205, 223n1; to hospitals, 113, 114–15, 119, 203; to prison systems, 102, 140; shackles during, 120
trauma, 34, 158; childbirth and, 111; correctional officers causing, 124; criminal legal systems and, 28; education inhibited by, 89; grief and, 132, 134; at hospitals, 132; hospitals causing, 132; maternal-infant bond and, 83; postpartum depression and, 139
treatment programs, drug, 62–64, 79, 195, 205
trial of labor after cesarean (TOLAC), 119
turning point, xiii, 54; pregnancy in prison as, 55–56, 62, 78, 83, 87

Ugelvik, Thomas, 18
"the underground economy," 222n26
United States (US): Adoption and Safe Families Act, 65, 180; Bureau of Justice Statistics, US, 73, 201; Constitution, 35, 121; criminal legal systems, 4, 5, 6, 9, 14, 17; Fair Labor Standards Act, 230n38; First Step Act (2018), 201; mass incarceration in, x; Prison Rape Elimination Act, 78; prison system in, x–xi, xi–xiii, 17; Supreme Court, ix
unplanned pregnancies, 31, 33
US. *See* United States

vaginal birth after cesarean (VBAC), 119
vaginal tearing, 137, 138, 144
VBAC. *See* vaginal birth after cesarean
violence, obstetric, xi, xii, 117–20, 129, 203, 217n15
violent crimes, 22, 109, 221n104
visitations, 18, 102, 128, 158; babies and, 168–70; Black women and, 165–66; caregivers and, 98; hospital, 126, 127; phone calls and, 97, 170, 203; privileges for, 44, 165; racism and, 165–66

Wagner, Peter, 217n10, 231n22
War on Drugs, 16
White women, 12, 15, 38, 70, 175, 185; "free world" and, 76; healthcare and, 76–77; low-income, 33; marginalized, 77; peers, 14, 37, 184; poverty of, 79, 119; pregnancy of, 76; prenatal care and, 77; privilege of, 184, 231n50
Wichita, Kansas, 42
women: Black, x, 14, 37–38; bodily autonomy and, x; of color, 13, 14, 17, 33, 38, 59, 65, 120, 142, 166; correctional population of, 16, 194; enslavement of, x, 6; grief and, 3, 131, 132, 134, 148, 150, 152, 158–59; health of, 55; Hispanic, 76; Indigenous, 76, 142; marginalized, 29, 32, 33, 56, 70; middle-class, 22, 36, 37, 47, 48; relationship with baby, 21; sex work of, 7, 69, 80, 161–62; support systems of, 149, 150–52; White, 12, 15, 38, 70, 175, 185. *See also specific topics*

ABOUT THE AUTHOR

REBECCA M. RODRIGUEZ CAREY is Associate Professor of Sociology and Criminology at Emporia State University. Her work has appeared in *Women & Criminal Justice*, *Feminist Pedagogy*, and *Caged Women: Incarceration, Representation, & Media*. She is a recipient of the Ruth Schillinger Award.

www.ingramcontent.com/pod-product-compliance
Lightning Source LLC
Chambersburg PA
CBHW031144020426
42333CB00013B/504